Praise for *Mindfulne*…
A Practice Gu…

In this book Bhikkhu Anāla … f *ānāpānasati* with characteris… skilful reference to the textu… Through linking the central … walking meditation and the aggregates, he broadens its relevance to a wide range of Dhamma cultivation. Here then is a valuable resource for us to dip into, or to steadily work through, to gain access to this liberating practice.

– Ajahn Sucitto

Bhikkhu Anālayo's genius is, in part, to analyse the terse, sometimes obscure language of the Buddha's discourses and reveal them as fresh, practical guidance for contemporary meditators. Here the author takes up the discourse on mindfulness of breathing to lead us phrase by phrase into clear, precise instructions to calm the mind and realize the Buddha's deepest insights. The most complete and in-depth guide available for this classic meditation.

– Guy Armstrong, author of *Emptiness: A Practical Guide for Meditators*

Practical, inspiring, thought-provoking! This book achieves two great aims. First it offers meditators a clear practice sequence that is easy to apply. And second, it presents new translations and thoughtful analysis based on a comparative study of early Buddhist texts. This practical and thoughtful interpretation of the Buddha's sixteen steps will surely inspire readers to rediscover the joyful and liberating potential of mindfulness with breathing.

– Shaila Catherine, author of *Focused and Fearless: A Meditator's Guide to States of Deep Joy, Calm, and Clarity*

Also by Bhikkhu Anālayo:

Satipaṭṭhāna, The Direct Path to Realization

The Genesis of the Bodhisattva Ideal

A Comparative Study of the Majjhima-nikāya

Excursions into the Thought-world of the Pāli Discourses

Madhyama-āgama Studies

Perspectives on Satipaṭṭhāna

The Dawn of Abhidharma

Compassion and Emptiness in Early Buddhist Meditation

Saṃyukta-āgama Studies

Ekottarika-āgama Studies

The Foundation History of the Nuns' Order

Mindfully Facing Disease and Death

Buddhapada and the Bodhisattva Path

Early Buddhist Meditation Studies

Dīrgha-āgama Studies

Vinaya Studies

A Meditator's Life of the Buddha

Rebirth in Early Buddhism and Current Research

Satipaṭṭhāna Meditation: A Practice Guide

Bhikkhunī Ordination from Ancient India to Contemporary Sri Lanka

Mindfulness of Breathing: A Practice Guide and Translations

Bhikkhu Anālayo

Windhorse Publications

Windhorse Publications
17e Sturton Street
Cambridge
CB1 2SN
UK

info@windhorsepublications.com
windhorsepublications.com

As an act of Dhammadāna, Bhikkhu Anālayo has waived royalty payments for this book.

The index was not compiled by the author.

Drawings by Dido Dolmen (www.didodolmen.it)
Cover design by Dhammarati

Typesetting and layout by Ruth Rudd
Printed by Bell & Bain Ltd, Glasgow

British Library Cataloguing in Publication Data:
A catalogue record for this book is available from the British Library.

ISBN: 978-1-911407-44-7

CONTENTS

ABOUT THE AUTHOR

Born in 1962 in Germany, Bhikkhu Anālayo was ordained in 1995 in Sri Lanka, and completed a PhD on the *Satipaṭṭhāna-sutta* at the University of Peradeniya, Sri Lanka, in 2000 – published in 2003 by Windhorse Publications under the title *Satipaṭṭhāna, The Direct Path to Realization.*

Anālayo is a professor of Buddhist Studies; his main research area is early Buddhism and in particular the topics of the Chinese *Āgama*s, meditation, and women in Buddhism. Besides his academic pursuits, he regularly teaches meditation. He presently resides at the Barre Center for Buddhist Studies in Massachusetts, where he spends most of his time in silent retreat.

ACKNOWLEDGEMENT

I am indebted to Guy Armstrong, Bhikkhu Bodhi, Chris Burke, Bhikkhunī Dhammadinnā, Ann Dillon, Linda Grace, Bhikkhu U Jāgara, Jñānasiddhi, Dhivan Thomas Jones, and Yuka Nakamura for commenting on a draft version of this book and to the staff, board members, and supporters of the Barre Center for Buddhist Studies for providing me with the facilities needed to do my practice and writing.

PUBLISHER'S ACKNOWLEDGEMENTS

Windhorse Publications wishes to gratefully acknowledge a grant from the Triratna European Chairs' Assembly Fund and the Future Dharma Fund towards the production of this book.

We also wish to acknowledge and thank the individual donors who gave to the book's production via our "Sponsor-a-book" campaign.

FOREWORD BY JON KABAT-ZINN

The breath. So basic to life. So fundamental. So ever-present. And so easily ignored or taken for granted—that is, until you can't draw a breath easily, for whatever reason. In such a moment, we realize instantly how vital the breath is to our well-being, to our very life in this moment. We realize immediately how dependent we are on it, how important *this* breath is, this in-breath, this out-breath! And in that realization, we become more appreciative, and even more important than appreciative, more aware. So this realization, whether incremental or full-blown, is non-trivial, being about wakefulness itself, embodied wakefulness. It is also outside of time in the sense of being inseparable from the present moment we call now, the only moment we ever have in which to realize anything. And, seemingly paradoxically, but only seemingly, realization is also very much continually under development and therefore very much in time. If you devote yourself to its cultivation, breath awareness can be a process of developing insight and wisdom that can unfold, deepen, and ripen across one's entire lifespan.

The *Ānāpānasati-sutta*, upon which this book is based, is an ancient and highly revered training manual and guide to the human mind and heart and body in development, under meditative cultivation so to speak—yet also, realizable to one degree or another in any and every instant, if you are paying attention.

All meditative traditions feature the breath as a primary object of attention. The breath has many virtues. For one, you can't leave home without it. It is portable. Where you go, it goes. So it can remind you of the present moment. No one cares about the next breath, or the last breath. We only care about this one. This reminding is a key function of mindfulness, and a key element in the meaning of the word itself, *sati* (in Pāli, the language in which the Buddha's teachings were written down in Sri Lanka), as Anālayo points out in his translation, namely "what we need to remember to keep in mind." And the intersection of this *keeping in mind* and of *apprehending experience* arises and is held and known both conceptually and non-conceptually no place other than in awareness itself.

A second virtue of breathing as an object of attention is that the breath can function as a bridge of sorts between what we call *body* and what we call *mind*. When we get agitated, the breath is rough and irregular, and fast. When we are calm, the breath is smooth, and tends to slow down. When we feel threatened or thwarted, we might unwittingly hold our breath.

So breathing reveals the most basic interplay of mind and body. This interplay is a source of vital information for our ongoing growth and development and the deepening of mindfulness as a formal practice and as a way of being. We all know that what we call "mind" and what we call "body" are not two different domains but one seamless whole—giving rise to sentience, and the possibility of embodied wakefulness.

Virtue three: the breath pulsates with rhythmicity, like the heart itself. Both functions are impersonal. It would be a mistake even to call it "my breath," as if we were in any way ultimately responsible for it. Frankly, if it were up to "us," whoever we think we are, to keep the breath going (never mind the heart), we would have died long ago. A moment of distraction—whoops, dead! So it brings to the fore, with even a little investigation, the question of *who* is actually breathing? Whose breath is it? And who wants to know? Are we breathing or being breathed? And how might we make use of the experience of *intimacy* with our own breathing? Can we *befriend* our own breathing? Can we use it in the service of awakening to the actuality of things, to who we are, and to the true nature of what we call the world? All of these investigations, and this impulse to question the basics of our human experience, are pointers to the mystery of who we are underneath the personal pronouns we deploy so habitually and so unconsciously. And in that sense, they point to the empty quality of whatever we mean by the word "self," its essential insubstantiality and ever-changing patterning of energies and emergence, like whirlpools in a stream, insubstantial, and yet extant for a time—a brief moment, memorable perhaps—yet ultimately leaving no trace.

Four, it is equally apparent in our paying attention to the breath that no in-breath lasts, and no out-breath lasts. Here, we have a direct experience of the law of impermanence (*anicca*) built right into any open meditative investigation of breathing and its relationship to awareness itself. Moreover, *dukkha*, the intrinsic unsatisfactoriness of any identification, grasping, or clinging, is also built into breath awareness. We are only one in-breath away from being dead. And in some sense, when we give ourselves over to paying attention to the breath, we know that more vividly, not merely in thought, but more viscerally, in a more embodied way. And that knowing enlivens this moment, and makes it worth not missing. It makes it worth inhabiting completely.

As noted, this book is based on the exquisitely detailed, high-resolution yet easily engaged teachings of the Buddha about mindfulness of breathing as articulated in the *Ānāpānasati-sutta*. When it comes to breathing, and to awareness for that matter, and to liberation from suffering and the immanence of wisdom and awakening, what better instructor to have than the Buddha himself? His instructions here are incredibly succinct, clear, organized, and profound, freighted with transformative potential, which Anālayo skillfully reveals and guides us in throughout the book.

First, we are presented with a range of foundational preliminaries. These are followed by the sixteen basic practices of *ānāpānasati*. Each step makes use of the breath as the carrier of a specific instantiated potential insight, the sum total amounting to a glidepath to awakening to things as they are. Following the text of the *sutta* itself, the sixteen practices are presented stepwise, in four tetrads.

The individual steps are then linked to the teachings of the seven factors of awakening and their co-development in tandem with the tetrads. For those who want ever more subtle yet revealing distinctions or differences among other canonical texts, particularly from the Chinese *Āgamas*, Anālayo offers us a profoundly rich exegesis building on everything that has come before.

Most readers, aside from scholars, might do well to focus in on the practices unfolded in the sixteen steps and their relationship to the factors of awakening. After all, the ultimate purpose here is to live the practice of mindfulness of breathing to the full extent possible across the lifespan, while keeping in mind that there is only one moment any of us ever has. Our motivation to practice, coupled with the ongoing momentum and continuity of practice, once established, is paramount here.

Part of Anālayo's skill as a teacher, which I witnessed firsthand during a ten-day retreat we led together at the Insight Meditation Society on this very *sutta*,[1] is his emphasis on gentleness and non-striving and openness, rather than contracting around any one view or teaching. Rather than striving to "attain" what is being pointed to and invited in a particular practice, his emphasis is always on recognizing that quality's inherent presence. Whether it is breathing in or breathing out experiencing joy, or happiness, or impermanence, dispassion, cessation, or letting go, we simply invite that quality to manifest on its own as we attend to the in-breath and to the out-breath, and to the pauses between them.

This is not only a gentle, kind, and practical approach. It is also wise, inclusive, and non-dual. Each of the sixteen steps isolates and features a particular aspect of the one reality of being alive, of sentience, and of the possibility of waking up in any and every moment to the primacy of these completely inter-embedded dimensions of body (the first tetrad), feelings (the second tetrad), mind (the third tetrad), and reality/wisdom (fourth tetrad). The invitation is always the same: to just be with the experience of what is being attended to, coupled with awareness of breathing, which itself is of necessity co-extensive with pure awareness, beyond any object of attention.

1 Mindfully facing disease, death, stress, pain, and illness: Insight meditation retreat for experienced students on the confluence of classical and modern approaches to healing. March 25–April 1, 2018.

Many scholars and practitioners over the years have had a hand at exegesis of this profound "laboratory manual" that is the *Ānāpānasati-sutta*. Each has its particular virtues. This most recent one you have in your hands is a masterful evocation of nuance and subtlety, richness and profundity, anchored in the depths of Anālayo's scholarship, fluency with ancient languages and texts, and lived practice. And all this unfolds out of the life of a venerable monastic abiding by the precepts of his order. We are privileged to have such a voice on the planet at a time like this, a voice that is both precise and compassionate.

In fact, I would say that Anālayo's precision is itself a form of compassion, as are his flexibility and fluidity in inviting an easy approach to these instructions. It is more an exploration of wisdom within the timeless present moment than it is a narrow, inflexible prescription for enlightenment, even as it points precisely to that extinguishing in the last tetrad. Perhaps the E-word is fatally problematic within our modern context and our fixations with performance, perfection, and attainment. If so, it might make more sense for us to speak of enlightening moments rather than enlightened people. The former have no exclusion criteria. Everybody is equally welcome to recognize such moments in one's own life. And to benefit from them, which itself becomes a benefit to the wider world.

Anālayo not only shows us the way, bringing the Buddha's teachings to life out of all the texts he draws from here. His entire approach radiates a gentle and easy-going confidence in us as human beings, a sense that we can interface with these teachings in a variety of ways, and that we can find our own way in, in tandem with his multifaceted guidance. Following that thread, the thread of the breath, the thread of these step-by-step teachings, can be profoundly healing and illuminating, and above all, liberating.

Welcome then, to this priceless teaching, and to the discerning of what is always right beneath our noses, if we are only willing to attend to it.

Jon Kabat-Zinn
Northampton, MA
February 21, 2019

Being cultivated and made much of, meditation on mindfulness of breathing is peaceful, sublime, and immaculate, it is a happy abiding that allays and quells bad and unwholesome mental states as soon as they arise (SN 54.9).

INTRODUCTION

In this book I explore mindfulness of breathing from a predominantly practice-oriented perspective. My main source text is the *Ānāpānasati-sutta*, the "Discourse on Mindfulness of Breathing In and Breathing Out", which offers instructions on mindfulness of breathing in sixteen steps. The same discourse groups these sixteen steps into four tetrads of four steps, indicating that each corresponds to one of the four *satipaṭṭhāna*s. The entire meditative progression in the *Ānāpānasati-sutta* serves to stimulate a cultivation of the seven factors of awakening and has as its overarching purpose the gaining of knowledge and liberation.

The Buddha appears to have had a personal predilection for meditation on the breath. This is already evident during the time of his asceticism, before he reached awakening. The *Mahāsaccaka-sutta* reports three types of ascetic practices he engaged in, which are forceful mind control, breath retention, and fasting. The Pāli discourse describes only a single form of the other two practices, but in the case of breath retention it presents five different modalities in total (MN 36, see below p. 239 and Anālayo 2017e: 60–68). This conveys the impression that the future Buddha had a particular interest in the breath already at that time. Moreover, after his awakening he is on record for spending an entire retreat dedicated to mindfulness of breathing in sixteen steps (SN 54.11; see below p. 192, Anālayo 2016b: 245–247, and 2017e: 63–67).

In this way, a personal interest in the breath as a meditation object, already evident at the time of his quest for awakening, might have motivated the Buddha to develop a mode of cultivating breath meditation in such a way that it combines essential aspects of the path to liberation he had discovered. This involves, first of all, a shift from retention of the breath to its mere observation. It also entails integrating the four *satipaṭṭhāna*s and the seven awakening factors in an approach to meditating on the breath that at the same time gives sufficient room for the flourishing of both tranquillity and insight. This is precisely what informs the sixteen steps, a mode of practice that aptly reflects the Buddha's superb wisdom and skill as a teacher.

In other monograph publications on *satipaṭṭhāna* meditation, I have already had the opportunity to study aspects of mindfulness of breathing (Anālayo 2003b: 125–136, 2013b: 227–237, 2016b: 242–249, 2017e: 63–66, and 2018d: 90–95). Nevertheless, the practice of mindfulness of breathing in sixteen steps is of such importance that it deserves a study of its own.

The first six chapters in this book present practical instructions comparable to my practice guide on *satipaṭṭhāna* (Anālayo 2018d). As was the case with that practice guide, here as well my presentation is not meant to imply that mindfulness of breathing in ancient India was undertaken exactly in the way I describe in the following pages. I also do not mean to present my approach as the only viable way of putting into practice the instructions found in the *Ānāpānasati-sutta*. My aim is decidedly not to compete with other teachers, but only to enrich. What I am putting out here is done in the spirit of open-source. I present my understanding of the discourse, as the result of my own practice and teaching experience, in the hope of inspiring others to use what they find helpful to build their own practice and become self-reliant.

The book comes with audio files that offer meditation instructions, which can be freely downloaded from the publisher's website at https://www.windhorsepublications.com/mindfulness-of-breathing-audio/. For each of the first six chapters in this book, there are audio recordings with guided meditation instructions that build on each other gradually.

In the first six chapters I dispense with footnotes, as well as with references to studies by others. I use in-line quotation to refer to relevant passages from the Pāli discourses and to provide cross-references to relevant material in the final four chapters, which provide a more scholarly perspective as a backup for the preceding six chapters. In these final four chapters I translate extracts from the Chinese *Āgama*s that in one way or another appear to me to be of relevance for appreciating the early Buddhist perspective on the breath and the practice of mindfulness of breathing. The translations come with selected comments from a comparative perspective and attempts to interpret the relevant passage from a practice-related angle. The final part of the book has my conclusions, a survey of the canonical passages quoted, and a continuous translation of the instructions on the sixteens steps, extracts of which I have been quoting in each chapter.

In 1990 I had the great fortune to meet Ajahn Buddhadāsa and sit a retreat on mindfulness of breathing at his monastery Suan Mokkh in Thailand. This has set a firm foundation for my explorations of this practice in the intervening years up to now. In the meantime, my approach to mindfulness of breathing has evolved considerably, so that I cannot claim the venerable Ajahn's authority for anything that I present here. However, if what I describe here should be of use to the reader, then this must be due to the foundation laid back in 1990.

I

MINDFULNESS AND THE BREATH

As part of an illustration of the practice of mindfulness of breathing with the example of a condor, the preliminaries discussed in this chapter correspond to the condor getting up high into the air.

In this chapter I discuss the introductory practice which in the *Ānāpānasati-sutta* (MN 118) precedes the actual instructions for mindfulness of breathing in sixteen steps. Besides trying to draw out implications of this description by reference to other discourse passages and pertinent later works, my intention in what follows is also to present a practice-oriented approach to this introductory passage.

The progression through the sixteen steps is a rather profound and sophisticated form of practice. By way of preparation for that, I take up the preliminaries to these sixteen steps in considerable detail and endeavour to bring in additional perspectives that go beyond what is implied in the actual instructions. In this way I hope to make sure that the needed foundation for proceeding smoothly through the sixteen steps of mindfulness of breathing is in place.

The description of the preliminaries in the *Ānāpānasati-sutta* proceeds as follows:

> Here gone to a forest or to the root of a tree or to an empty hut, one sits down; having folded the legs crosswise, keeping the body erect, and having established mindfulness to the fore, mindful one breathes in and mindful one breathes out.

The above instruction gradually proceeds from the external to the internal. First comes withdrawal to a place that affords *seclusion*, next a description of the *posture* of sitting down with folded legs, combined with the need to keep the seated body erect, and then the *establishing of mindfulness*. Central topics in this instruction are thus "seclusion" as the appropriate external setting for cultivating mindfulness of breathing, "the posture" to be adopted for such practice, and the need to "establish mindfulness" to the fore. In what follows I examine each of these topics in turn.

SECLUSION

The first part of the above description mentions a forest, the root of a tree, and an empty hut as commendable places for the practice of mindfulness of breathing. Other discourses relate the three places of a forest, the root of a tree, and an empty hut to different meditation practices, making it clear that this description is not confined to mindfulness of breathing (Anālayo 2003b: 127n39).

In the ancient Indian setting, meditation would have regularly been done out in nature. Hence a forest or the root of a tree naturally commend themselves. They provide some degree of shelter from the sun as well as from rain, and at the same time afford seclusion from the hustle and bustle of villages or towns. With an empty hut situated in a secluded environment such protection becomes more thorough. In addition to coverage from sun or rain provided by the leaves of a single tree or a forest, such an empty hut also affords protection from being disturbed by various other living beings.

MORALITY

The *Bhayabherava-sutta* clarifies that the ability to retire into seclusion depends on having established a firm foundation in moral conduct (MN 4; Anālayo 2017e: 15). The discourse points to the relationship between lack of ethical restraint and the arising of unwholesome mental states once one retires to a secluded spot to meditate. This in turn reflects a prerequisite that holds for early Buddhist meditation practices in general, in that they build on a foundation in morality (see below p. 177).

In fact the instructions for mindfulness of breathing are explicitly addressed to a *bhikkhu*. In the translated extracts given at the outset of each chapter, I have chosen to translate *bhikkhu* as "one", in order to avoid giving the impression that the instructions are only meant for fully ordained male monastics. At the same time, however, these instructions are clearly intended for someone with a strong dedication to adopting ethical conduct and to living a life of renunciation of sensual indulgence.

This does not mean that our morality needs to be absolutely perfect before even beginning to meditate. Taking such a position would be losing sight of the interrelation between these two and the substantial contribution that meditative development of the mind offers to improving ethical conduct. An increase of mindfulness naturally fosters a clear recognition of what is wholesome and unwholesome, thereby informing our behaviour. Nevertheless, some degree of moral restraint has to be established first, in terms of avoiding major breaches of the basic precepts, in order to be able to go deeper in the practice of meditation.

In addition to establishing a foundation in moral conduct, daily life can become an opportunity to confront gross manifestations of the five hindrances (sensual desire, anger, sloth-and-torpor, restlessness-and-worry, and doubt). To the extent to which we approach situations outside of formal meditation as opportunities to work with the hindrances, to that same extent the hindrances will not show up, or at least be substantially weakened, when we sit down to meditate. Conversely, if we find that we are being overwhelmed by hindrances and defilements during formal meditation, it may be commendable to try to work on inner seclusion during daily life and see if there is scope to strengthen it in a meaningful manner.

DISTURBANCES

According to the *Visuddhimagga* (Vism 269), a central meditation manual in the Theravāda tradition, a prominent purpose of going to secluded places is to avoid being disturbed by noise. Hearing sound can become an obstruction in particular to cultivating absorption (AN 10.72; Anālayo 2017b: 137–146). Concern with avoiding noisy environments is regularly reflected in the early discourses. The Buddha and his disciples were apparently well known among contemporaries for their preference for silence and quietude (e.g. MN 77). In a discourse in the *Dīgha-nikāya*, the leader of a group of wanderers even goes so far as to scoff at the Buddha's secluded lifestyle (DN 25). When searching for a place to build a monastery for the Buddha and his disciples, Anāthapiṇḍika is on record for reflecting that such a place should better not be noisy, a consideration that eventually led him to choose Jeta's Grove (Vin II 158).

These passages imply that it is indeed meaningful to try to find a secluded and quiet place for our regular practice of mindfulness of breathing. From this viewpoint, a busy and noisy environment is not an ideal setting for deeply engaging in the practice.

By contrast, however, it is perhaps even more important to learn to handle whatever noise still manifests during actual practice. It will hardly do to make our meditation dependent on the maintenance of silence by others. What emerges in this way is the need to combine a proper choice of the location in preparation for meditation practice with the proper attitude once that choice has been made. In other words, ahead of engaging in formal sitting we try to find a secluded environment. Having done that much, we let go of any further concerns and let any sound that still arises be part of our practice.

Making sound and other disturbances part of the practice can be related to the theme of sense restraint (*indriya-saṃvara*). According to the standard description in the discourses, sense restraint requires that we do not grasp either the "sign" (*nimitta*) or the "secondary characteristics" (*anuvyañjana*) of what has been perceived (Anālayo 2003b: 225f; for more on the "sign" in relation to the cultivation of deeper concentration see also below p. 88). Here the "sign" stands for our first forming of an assessment (often already biased) and the "secondary characteristics" for further associations related to that first idea. The task is to steer clear of proliferating and reacting in ways that are unwholesome.

The point at issue is not just avoidance. This much can be seen from the *Indriyabhāvanā-sutta*, in which a brahmin student proposes that to avoid seeing and hearing is the proper way of cultivating the sense faculties (MN 152). The discourse continues by clarifying that, on adopting such a reasoning, the blind and deaf should be reckoned accomplished practitioners.

With proper cultivation of the sense faculties, we stay within the domain of experience but step out of reactivity to it. In the case of sound, a simple tool to accomplish this can be dropping any appropriation of silence as "mine", something that I own and am entitled to. Such appropriation naturally leads to negativity as soon as my privately owned property of silence is invaded by noisy others. Contemplation of the empty nature of whatever manifests at the sense-door of the ear can go a long way in countering this tendency.

In this way, the *sign* of "disturbance" need not be grasped at all, let alone the *secondary characteristics* of irritation and annoyance resulting in the reactivity that usually follows. Any noise becomes just sound, hearing which can remind us of the empty nature of experience. Moreover, what we hear is sound arisen right now, which can even serve as a reminder of the present moment. In this way, sound need not be perceived as a "disturbance" and can instead become an integral part of our practice, as we become better and better at not getting caught up in reactivity.

According to a discourse in the *Saṃyutta-nikāya*, sense restraint leads to delight (*pāmojja*) and joy (*pīti*), which in turn are conducive to concentration (SN 35.97). It follows that sound handled properly can become the starting point for a form of cultivation of the mind that eventually leads to gaining concentration, rather than invariably obstructing it.

DAILY LIFE

Nevertheless, the recommendation to retire to a forest, the root of a tree, or an empty place clearly presents secluded places as the appropriate setting for mindfulness of breathing. This description does not convey the impression that awareness of the breath was considered a form of practice to be undertaken in daily-life situations (see below p. 181 n. 20). In fact in the preliminary instructions from the *Ānāpānasati-sutta*, quoted above, mindfulness is directed to the breath only after one has reached a secluded place and sat down.

For continuity of mindfulness in daily life, a preferable approach would be to direct awareness to the whole body rather than to the breath only (Anālayo 2017b: 36–42). The whole body provides an easily accessible support for establishing mindfulness and encourages a broad form of awareness instead of an exclusive focus of attention, a topic to which I will return in the next chapter. Daily life requires a flexible and open mode of awareness for us to be able to act and react appropriately in different situations.

Cultivating such an open attitude, based on awareness of the whole body, can help in remaining centred when having to face different input through the senses. It can function similar to a strong post to which six different animals have been tied in such a way that they are unable to run away (SN 35.206; Anālayo 2003b: 123, 2013b: 55f, and 2018d: 19f). Due to the post of mindfulness of the body being firmly established, the animals of the six senses no longer wander far away.

The same mode of establishing mindfulness can come to our support even in the most challenging situation. The discourses illustrate this with the example of having to carry a bowl full of oil through a crowd at a dancing performance and being followed by someone ready to cut off the head of the carrier if even a drop of oil is spilled (SN 47.20; Anālayo 2003b: 122, 2013b: 56f, and 2018d: 20f). The carrier of the oil needs well-established mindfulness of the body to be able to execute this task successfully.

INNER SECLUSION

In terms of actual practice and going to some extent beyond what is implicit in the above passage from the *Ānāpānasati-sutta*, the instruction on seclusion could additionally be employed as a reminder to let go of our worries, concerns, responsibilities, and tasks when approaching the location which we have chosen for engaging in mindfulness of breathing. The idea is to tell ourselves that all such issues can be set aside for the time being, to be taken up again once the meditation period is over. Telling ourselves that now is not the time to be planning or making decisions can strengthen our ability to remain in the present moment instead of getting carried away into past or future.

This mode of reflection can take inspiration from a passage in the *Dīgha-nikāya* that describes a king who retires from his duties to engage in meditation (DN 17). Standing at the door to his meditation chamber, the king tells himself that thoughts of sensuality, ill-will, and harming should stay right here and not come along inside. In a similar way, we might tell all the various things that could agitate the mind to stay at the entrance to our meditation space, not allowing them to come inside. Setting up such a no-entry permit can be aimed in particular at the hindrances.

Parallel versions to the description of the preliminaries in the *Ānāpānasati-sutta* explicitly mention the need to overcome the hindrances before engaging in the sixteen steps of mindfulness of breathing (see below p. 181). The same perspective also appears to be implicit in the fact that the sixteen steps themselves do not show any concern with the removal of the hindrances but appear to set in at a stage when these are temporarily absent, a topic to which I will return in the next chapter (see below p. 43 and also p. 196). Understood in this sense, the topic of seclusion can be invested with both a bodily and a mental dimension. In addition to bodily withdrawal to a forest, the root of a tree, or an empty hut, seclusion of the mind from the hindrances can similarly serve as a foundation for the cultivation of mindfulness of breathing in sixteen steps.

In order to establish the mental dimension of seclusion fully, after letting go of our worries and concerns we can check in on the mind to see if any of the hindrances is present. If this should be the case, we set up a clear intention in relation to the hindrance, similar to the king in the passage mentioned above: "it would be better if you stayed outside and did not come inside!" If we find that the hindrance nevertheless barges in and tries to disturb the condition of our mind, gently but firmly we send it back outside, employing whatever antidote we are accustomed to and have found helpful on past occasions.

THE POSTURE

Besides specifying the locations suitable for the practice of mindfulness of breathing, the introductory passage also describes the proper posture. This requires "having folded the legs crosswise". The depiction of the sitting posture shows that, at least from the viewpoint of the canonical instructions, mindfulness of breathing was considered a form of sitting meditation. This does not mean that there is something wrong with becoming aware of the breath in another posture or in an everyday situation. But such awareness could perhaps best lead over to, and become integrated into, whole-body awareness, rather than being the starting point for proceeding through the sixteen steps of mindfulness of breathing.

The reference in the introductory passage to folding the legs crosswise reflects the typical way of sitting down on the floor in the ancient Indian context. From a practical perspective, the main issue is to establish a firm foundation for meditation with only a minimal need to change the posture. Instead of sitting on the ground, the same can also be achieved with the help of a bench or a chair.

Regarding sitting on the ground, the early texts do not refer to sitting cushions, but only to sitting mats. These appear to have been simply a piece of cloth or a padding made of grass, leaves, or straw, spread on the ground to provide protection and insulation. Sitting without a cushion to some extent enhances the stability of the sitting posture, as the area of bodily contact with the ground increases. Nevertheless, it is important to avoid associating spiritual progress with a particular sitting posture. What counts, in the end, is the condition of the mind.

MOTIVATION

Going beyond what is implicit in the actual instruction, the need to establish a firm foundation for sitting meditation through an appropriate posture can also be related to the mental domain. This can take the form of establishing a firm foundation for our meditation practice through an appropriate motivation. It can be very helpful to formulate such a motivation in the mind before beginning actual practice (Anālayo 2018d: 140f), perhaps right after having sat down. This could be an aspiration like: "May I progress on the path to liberation, for my own benefit and for the benefit of others." Setting up such a motivation provides a sense of overall direction as an orientation point. At the same time, it also arouses joyful inspiration, whose importance for continuity of practice can hardly be overestimated.

As regards the actual formulation employed for such an aspiration, it is particularly commendable to bring in an altruistic dimension. This fortifies us for times of difficulty, as we are practising for the sake of benefitting others and not just ourselves. It can also help to situate our meditation practice within the framework of the noble eightfold path. The cultivation of the four *satipaṭṭhāna*s (here in the form of proceeding through the four tetrads of mindfulness of breathing) is the seventh factor of this path. The second factor of the path is right intention, which has three dimensions. One of these is the intention for non-harm, which is an expression of compassion (Anālayo 2017c). Just as right intentions (based on right view) set the proper direction for a cultivation of the noble eightfold path, so the compassionate intention to benefit others can set the proper direction for the flourishing of our practice of mindfulness of breathing.

Yet another benefit of setting up our intention relates to the hindrances. Should a hindrance be present when we start with our practice, the formulating of our aspiration at this juncture can have the same function as the first in a set of five methods for overcoming unwholesome thoughts, mentioned in the *Vitakkasaṇṭhāna-sutta* (MN 20; Anālayo 2013b: 149). This function is to replace an unwholesome thought with a wholesome thought, similar to a carpenter who replaces a gross peg with a finer one. In this way, any gross unwholesome thought that might have been popping up in our mind can be replaced by the finer wholesome thought of formulating our motivation. If there are no hindrances manifesting right now, the joyful inspiration that has arisen from articulating our intention will make it considerably less probable that a hindrance will arise subsequently. The need to arouse joy right at the outset of the practice is also recognized in the *Visuddhimagga*, which recommends recollecting the qualities of the three jewels, that is, the Buddha, his teaching, and the community of those on the path to, or having attained, one of the levels of awakening (Vism 278).

BODILY POSTURE

Based on having established a firm foundation for sitting meditation in the bodily (and mental) domain, the next aspect described in the passage above is "keeping the body erect". The sitting posture needs to be such that the spine is kept straight. Here some degree of continuity of attention to the posture is required to avoid any slumping of the body.

The *Visuddhimagga* comments that the spine should be kept straight with vertebrae resting end to end to avoid the type of feeling tones that arise when the body is twisted in any way, which in turn would obstruct gaining unification of the mind (Vism 271). Keeping the body erect could be achieved by slowly passing our attention through the spine from bottom to top, relaxing each vertebra. Such relaxing enables a natural alignment of the spine, by just letting gravity pull downwards. The overall sense is as if the body were suspended from above, at the top of the head, and the rest of it relaxes downwards. The resulting erectness of the body is not something to be held in a fixed manner. Instead, the body remains flexible, comparable to a slender tree in the wind. Such flexibility allows for minor adjustments to occur whenever we notice that the body is not fully in balance. Needless to say, this does not mean we keep shifting around all the time, but just that we avoid holding the posture rigidly and with tension, be it when sitting on the ground, a cushion, a bench, or a chair.

In order to be able to keep the body erect, we of course need to be aware of it. Thus the present part of the instruction requires establishing awareness of the body as a whole in the sitting posture and to some degree also monitoring it throughout the meditation session, at least until such a deep level of concentration is reached that the posture of the body naturally remains firm. During stages preceding such deep concentration, cultivating whole-body awareness ensures that the body is kept erect and provides a grounding for the practice of mindfulness of breathing.

MENTAL POSTURE

Going beyond what the actual instructions say, the need for the posture of the body to be realigned whenever it is lost can be complemented by the need for the posture of the mind to be realigned whenever it is lost. Here the task is to stay in the present moment and avoid the mind succumbing to distractions. These two alignments could be combined in the sense that, after having aligned the spine by relaxing each vertebra, we can set up the firm intention to align the mind to the present moment by relaxing any tendency to distraction. Setting up such an intention at the outset can serve as a way of telling the mind to keep a lookout for whenever the present moment is about to get lost. Just as we realign the body whenever its straightness has been lost, so we keep realigning the mind whenever it has succumbed to distraction and become overpowered by one of the hindrances. Due to the direction set by our firm intention and the previous groundwork, a mere reminder of our overall aim can often suffice to ensure that any hindrance goes quickly into abeyance.

MINDFULNESS ESTABLISHED

The passage translated at the outset of this chapter continues after the description of the appropriate posture with the expression "having established mindfulness to the fore". The *Vibhaṅga*, an early Abhidharma text of the Theravāda tradition, relates the expression "to the fore", *parimukha*, to the nose tip or the upper lip (Vibh 252; see also below p. 236). A more general sense emerges in one of the explanations of this expression provided in the *Visuddhimagga* (Vism 271), according to which mindfulness should be set up in such a way that it faces (*abhimukha*) the meditation object (*kammaṭṭhāna*). References to mindfulness that is established "to the fore" occur in other Pāli discourses to introduce meditation practices that do not involve the breath (Anālayo 2003b: 128f). In such contexts an understanding of the phrase as referring to the nose tip or the upper lip makes less sense. In the case of one such occurrence, where mindfulness established to the fore leads to overcoming the five hindrances (MN 107), the Chinese parallel speaks instead of mindfulness that is "undivided" (MĀ 144; Anālayo 2020b).

In view of these indications, it seems fair to leave it open to individual practitioners at which particular physical location they observe the breath. This concords with a general attitude of flexibility in the early discourses. One discourse reports the Buddha approving of a monastic's own mode of practice of mindfulness of breathing (SN 54.6; see below p. 187). Only after such approval did the Buddha explain how mindfulness of breathing can be undertaken in an even better way, namely by proceeding through the sixteen steps. This shows that in ancient times mindfulness of breathing was taught in a flexible manner without the expectation that everyone had to practise in the exact same way.

Although the nostril area is a natural choice for becoming aware of the process of breathing, the same can also be achieved by attending to the back of the throat, to the chest, to the abdomen area, or else even without relying on a particular circumscribed physical location. For those who prefer to work with a single spot, it can still be helpful to broaden awareness beyond that spot to the whole of the breath. The suggestion is not to follow the breath in and out, but to broaden our perspective and arrive at a more complete apperception of the phenomenon under contemplation. This phenomenon is the breath as a whole and not only the sensation caused by the breath at a particular spot of the body. Encouraging a broader form of awareness in this way is helpful for the progression through the sixteen steps.

MINDFULNESS

The instructions for the ensuing four tetrads of mindfulness of breathing do not explicitly refer to mindfulness, *sati*. The term only comes up in relation to the preliminary practice of establishing *mindfulness* to the fore and then being *mindful* when breathing in and out. This requires simply turning attention to the natural flow of breathing as it manifests in the here and now. Such a simple form of attending to the breaths brings out essential qualities of mindfulness as a receptive and non-intrusive form of mental presence with what is.

In the *Ānāpānasati-sutta*, the meditative activities mentioned during the sixteen steps are that one "knows", "experiences", "calms", and "contemplates". All of these activities take place in the receptive mental space that has been created through establishing mindfulness on the process of breathing. Their execution in turn supports continuity of mindfulness.

In the *Satipaṭṭhāna-sutta* mindfulness is also not mentioned in the actual contemplations (MN 10; Anālayo 2013b: 36f). An explicit reference to *sati* occurs in the part that I have dubbed the "refrain", which comes after the description of each individual contemplation. In the *Ānāpānasati-sutta*, however, the reference to *sati* comes in the preliminaries, before the individual steps of practice are described. This puts an even stronger spotlight onto the need to establish mindfulness right from the outset.

Once mindfulness has been established to the fore, experience at any sense-door is met first of all by the gatekeeper of mindfulness. This relates to the topic of sense restraint already broached above, in that it is precisely the presence of mindfulness that facilitates not grasping either the sign or the secondary characteristics of whatever manifests at any sense-door.

Yet another dimension that could be related to the idea of establishing mindfulness to the fore is a first checking, by way of mindfulness, of the condition of our mind right now. Previous practice of *satipaṭṭhāna* meditation would have helped us become familiar with the texture of our mind when mindfulness is present. A brief checking in for that texture will enable us to recognize in what way practice is best adjusted in order to meet the mind where it actually is.

Such checking in would also enable us to discern if the mind is sufficiently balanced to engage in mindfulness of breathing at all. At times the mind might not be in a condition for this particular meditation, instead requiring other types of practices. It is also possible that some problem has manifested on the bodily level that interferes with natural relaxed breathing, or else due to some mental reason the body is in a cramped condition. Such a situation would make it advisable to opt for a different meditative exercise. In line with mindfulness as a way of tuning in to the present moment, it is important to allow space for such information to emerge and then adjust our practice accordingly.

Once the gatekeeper of mindfulness comes to be fully at the forefront of experience, it can furnish the appropriate input that enables guiding the mind from its present inner condition through the progressive cultivation of the sixteen steps of mindfulness of breathing or any other practice. The monitoring function of mindfulness as a form of meta-awareness is set up right at the outset of the practice, so as to serve as its foundation and continuous accompaniment.

By way of preparation, it can be helpful to remain for a moment just with mindfulness established "to the fore" in this way, becoming fully aware of the quality of the mind when it is being supervised by mindfulness, before turning to the breath. This would be similar to meeting a good old friend whom we are going to be working with on some project. We would naturally take some time first to say hello and catch up with each other before getting into the work before us.

The effect of similarly taking a moment to be with mindfulness is somewhat like switching on a head torch before going for a walk at night. In this way we have switched on the light of mindfulness to shine on our meditative progression through the sixteen steps of mindfulness of breathing.

THE BREATH

The instruction for turning to the breath enjoins that "mindful one breathes in and mindful one breathes out." This brief instruction delineates the main practice of which the sixteen steps are a more detailed elaboration. The task here is to discern with mindfulness the difference between inhalations and exhalations, which will be a continuous reference point throughout the ensuing meditative programme. Such basic discerning is comparable to the instruction in the *Satipaṭṭhāna-sutta* to be just mindful that there is a body, etc., for the sake of clear knowing and mindfulness.

In the *Ānāpānasati-sutta* the object of practice is the breath itself first of all and not only the sensations caused by the breath. The form of meditation we are practising here is called "mindfulness of inhalations and exhalations" (*ānāpānasati*) and not "perception of physical touch" (*phoṭṭhabbasaññā*). Although physical sensations related to the touch of the breath are of course what helps us be aware of it, mindfulness of breathing is concerned with the breath itself.

The present exercise requires giving attention to the breath itself, in particular to the distinction between inhalations and exhalations. This is the object of the meditation practice. For the purpose of such practice, bodily sensations related to the breath are only a means to an end. They serve this end to the degree to which they help us to be aware of the breath and in particular to discern if the flow of breathing moves inwards or outwards.

In a cold climate, the inhalation tends to be cooler than the exhalation, so that sensing the temperature of the breath can also offer support for cultivating the basic distinction between these two (see below p. 230). Whether attention is given to sensations of the direction of the flow of breathing or its temperature, however, the relationship of such sensations to the breath is similar to a finger pointing at the moon. The purpose of the finger is to encourage looking at the moon, rather than at the finger itself.

The distinction between the touch sensation of the breath and the breath itself is of additional relevance for cases when meditators are no longer able to experience the breath. This could in principle be due to two reasons. One is that the mind has become deeply concentrated, which usually occurs after considerable refinement of the practice. I will come back to this case in a subsequent chapter (see below p. 116).

The other reason is when certain physical sensations caused by the breath diminish to the extent of being hardly noticeable. This can already occur during early stages of practice and need not be related to a particularly deep level of concentration. When the breath is no longer distinctly felt, the *Visuddhimagga* recommends that one should not just get up, thinking the practice is over, but instead investigate in the understanding that the breath cannot have disappeared completely (Vism 283). From the viewpoint of the approach to the practice presented here, it can be helpful to keep in mind that the object of the practice is the breath itself and not just particular physical sensations caused by the breath. Close investigation of what is taking place can lead to finding a way of observing the inhalations and exhalations that does not rely on the particular physical sensation that has become too subtle for being distinctly perceived. In this way, continuity of practice can be achieved.

Later tradition distinguishes between knowing the felt sensation of the breath, considered to be pertinent for the practice of insight, and knowing the breath as a mental concept, this being appropriate for the cultivation of tranquillity. Such a distinction is not required for meditation undertaken from an early Buddhist perspective. When we are practising in a teaching lineage based on Theravāda exegetical texts, this type of distinction needs to be followed to benefit fully from the instructions given. But in relation to the mode of practice presented here, this distinction could be set aside for the time being.

The experience of sensations can help us recognize the difference between inhalation and exhalation and to that degree we rely on it, knowing that our main object is the breath itself. We learn to use conceptual input judiciously, only to the degree necessary to foster clarity of understanding, in the clear recognition that our main task is to experience the breath rather than imagine it or think about it. By finding a middle path in this way, the same basic mode of breathing in and out mindfully can be used to cultivate both tranquillity and insight (see also below p. 179).

Undertaken in this way, mindfulness of breathing can become a way of putting into practice the early Buddhist perspective on tranquillity and insight as distinct but closely interrelated qualities (Anālayo 2017b: 88–100 and 173f). This perspective could be illustrated by comparing tranquillity and insight to our two hands. These are distinct, yet they belong to the same body. Although at times we might use one hand for a particular task, often we employ both in conjunction. Some of us prefer to use the right hand for writing, but others rather employ the left hand. Trying to force a child to conform to the notion that one should write with the right hand can be detrimental to the child's growth. It is better to allow the child to grow up naturally and let it employ whichever hand it wishes to use for writing.

Similarly, trying to impose conformity with the notion that tranquillity has to be developed first, and then only insight, can become detrimental to our meditative growth. It is preferable to allow for emphasis on the one or the other of these two qualities (or even both in conjunction) to result from a natural unfolding of the practice.

INSIGHT

The insight perspective that emerges even with the simple practice of just being mindful of inhalations and exhalations is the direct experience of the constantly changing nature of the breath, a topic I will explore in more detail in relation to the fourth tetrad, corresponding to contemplation of dharmas (see below p. 100). Such direct experience clarifies impermanence in a very palpable way. As a manifestation of the wind element (see below p. 163), the breath is probably the most easily discerned token of constant change taking place in the body. Besides being easily noticed, the breath also conveniently reflects the early Buddhist notion of impermanence, according to which things arise, keep changing for some time, and then disappear (AN 3.47). This differs from the notion of momentariness prominent in later tradition, according to which phenomena disappear as soon as they have arisen (Anālayo 2013b: 105–108).

Rather than appearing and then disappearing on the spot, the motion of an incoming breath begins, continues for some time as a constantly changing phenomenon, and eventually the inhalation ceases completely. This is followed by a small gap and then an exhalation begins, continues for some time as a changing flow of breath, and then ceases completely. After another small gap, another inhalation starts, and so on.

TRANQUILLITY

In conjunction with this insight perspective, tranquillity can be cultivated already with this preliminary practice of mindfully breathing in and out. The breath as such usually causes neutral sensations. When attention is directed to the breath, the mind easily wanders off, simply because the experience of the breath as such is not interesting enough to attract attention. The underlying tendency of neutral feeling tones is towards ignorance (MN 44; Anālayo 2017h). In other words, we tend to ignore neutral feeling tones, as the mind looks out for some more entertaining alternative. Turning the hedonic dimension of mindfulness of breathing from neutral into a pleasant one, by cultivating the subtle pleasant feeling tone of being in the present moment, can go a long way in helping us to stay with the breath. I will return to explore this topic in more detail in the chapter on the second tetrad, corresponding to contemplation of feeling tones (see below p. 56).

Undertaken in this way, just mindfully breathing in and out can become a way of cultivating both tranquillity and insight, inculcating a basic collaboration of these two dimensions of meditative practice. Such collaboration can be pursued throughout the sixteen steps. In this way, the question becomes less which tetrad should be put into one of two boxes, either tranquillity or insight, but more how each step can offer its own unique blend of these two interrelated qualities.

BASIC PRACTICE

The basic mode of practice, where "mindful one breathes in and mindful one breathes out", is the one to come back to whenever we get distracted. On realizing that the mind has wandered, we smilingly come back to noticing with mindfulness whether the breath goes in or out.

As briefly mentioned above, a discourse in the *Saṃyutta-nikāya* reports a monastic describing his own approach to mindfulness of breathing, which the Buddha approved of, after which he proceeded to expound the sixteen steps (SN 54.6). In the Pāli version, this monastic's actual practice, based on having cultivated a mental attitude aloof from desire and aversion, is as follows: "mindful I breathe in and mindful I breathe out." The Chinese parallel has only the description of his attitude without mentioning the breath at all, perhaps the result of a textual loss (see below p. 187).

Be that as it may, the Pāli version clearly points to the need for some groundwork in order to emerge from defiled states of mind before embarking on the simple practice of being aware of inhalations and exhalations. Although the corresponding description in the extract translated at the outset of this chapter just enjoins "mindful one breathes in and mindful one breathes out", without mentioning the need to emerge from desire and aversion, this can be assumed to be implicit.

Just being mindful of inhalations and exhalations can become a summary of the whole trajectory of meditation practice to be explored in the next chapters. This practice requires maintaining awareness of the alternation between inhalations and exhalations without succumbing to any distraction or hindrance.

All of the sixteen steps of mindfulness of breathing feature as a single perception in a list of altogether ten perceptions given in another discourse, the *Girimānanda-sutta* (AN 10.60; Anālayo 2016b: 229). Being mindful of the inhalations and exhalations is indeed the one perception that continues throughout the entire scheme of sixteen steps. This is what they are all related to and this is what we always come back to: being mindful of the changing nature of the breath.

WALKING MEDITATION

The perception of change is a topic that can conveniently be carried over into walking meditation. In this posture, awareness of the breath, cultivated during sitting, can lead over to an encompassing awareness of the whole body as manifesting constant change. This is particularly evident when we walk, simply because the body is in motion. The resultant shift to a more general apperception of impermanence in this meditation posture goes beyond a narrow focus on the breath alone. Instead, the object of attention during walking meditation can become the whole body in that posture.

Practice in the walking posture could serve as yet another approach to cultivating the conjunction of tranquillity and insight, described above. On adopting this approach, the task would be to note the impermanent nature of anything experienced during walking meditation (including the breath whenever opportune) and at the same time cultivate the pleasant feeling tone of being in the present moment.

SUMMARY

On approaching our meditation seat, representative of whatever degree of seclusion is possible in our present living situation, we can consciously let go of our worries and concerns, setting them aside for the time being, and then check in briefly for the presence of any hindrance.

Placing our legs in such a way that they provide a firm foundation for the body in the sitting posture, we could also set up a firm motivation that informs our practice, to establish clarity about the direction in which this practice is to take us and to arouse joyful inspiration.

We briefly move our attention through the spine from bottom to top to allow a natural alignment of the body. At the same time, we could also set up the intention to remain in the present moment, thereby in a way telling our own mind to keep an eye on the tendency to distraction. Keeping the body erect and the mind in the present moment needs to be continued throughout the sitting, as both can easily be lost.

Next we give prominence to bringing mindfulness "to the fore". As a modality of sense restraint, we meet whatever manifests at any sense-door with the gatekeeper of mindfulness, without succumbing to mental reactivity. Such a mode of practice naturally leads to the experience of the pleasant feeling tone of being in the present moment.

Conjoining the pleasant feeling tone of being in the present moment to awareness of the flow of the breath exemplifies a conjunction of tranquillity and insight, the latter taking the form of noticing the arising of each inhalation or exhalation, their changing nature while they persist, and their eventual disappearance.

In this way the preliminaries could be made use of in a way that already touches on topics related to the four *satipaṭṭhāna*s. This is precisely the purpose of the whole sixteen steps of mindfulness of breathing, namely to fulfil the four *satipaṭṭhāna*s so as to lead, via a cultivation of the awakening factors, to knowledge and liberation.

In the case of the approach to the preliminaries presented here, we have established *bodily* seclusion and cultivated awareness of the whole *body* in the sitting posture, thereby touching on the main theme of the first *satipaṭṭhāna*. Having aroused joyful inspiration through formulating our motivation, we experience the pleasant *feeling tone* of being in the present moment, *feeling tones* being the object of the second *satipaṭṭhāna*. This enables keeping the *mind* in the present moment and being aware of the actual condition of the *mind*, which is a central task in the third *satipaṭṭhāna*. Mindfulness brought "to the fore" then arouses the first of the seven awakening factors, which are a central topic in the fourth *satipaṭṭhāna*, contemplation of *dharma*s. Once aroused, such mindfulness attends to the inhalations and exhalations as an exemplification of impermanence. This lays the foundation for the arising of liberating insight, which is the overarching concern of any *satipaṭṭhāna* meditation.

II

CONTEMPLATION OF THE BODY

With the completion of the present tetrad the condor has reached sufficient height and no longer needs to move its wings, but is able to glide along, flying effortlessly over mountaintop after mountaintop. The bodily stillness of the condor illustrates the bodily tranquillity achieved with the last step of the first tetrad. The continuously changing scenery through which the condor flies stands for the continuous awareness of impermanence that pervades the whole practice of mindfulness of breathing in and breathing out.

After mentioning the preliminaries, the *Ānāpānasati-sutta* (MN 118) continues by describing the first four steps of practice. The resultant tetrad corresponds to the first *satipaṭṭhāna*, contemplation of the body. The instructions are:

> Breathing in long, one understands: 'I breathe in long'; breathing out long, one understands: 'I breathe out long.' Breathing in short, one understands: 'I breathe in short'; breathing out short, one understands: 'I breathe out short.' One trains: 'experiencing the whole body I shall breathe in'; one trains: 'experiencing the whole body I shall breathe out.' One trains: 'calming bodily activity I shall breathe in'; one trains: 'calming bodily activity I shall breathe out.'

The topics to be discussed in relation to this instruction are the distinction between "long" and "short" breaths, the significance of the reference to "the whole body", and the injunction to train in "calming bodily activity". By way of preparation for these topics, I briefly look at the entire scheme from the viewpoint of the time it would take to proceed through the sixteen steps.

For progression from one step to the next in this and the ensuing tetrads, the *Girimānanda-sutta* offers implicit indications that help to gauge the time it would take to complete the entire progression of sixteen steps (AN 10.60; Anālayo 2016b: 213). The narrative setting of this discourse gives the impression that meditation on a series of perceptions, culminating in the sixteen steps of mindfulness of breathing, took place concomitantly with the recital of the discourse. This in turn makes it quite reasonable to proceed through the sixteen steps in a single session, rather than dedicating an entire sitting just to one or even a few steps only. In fact the power and profundity of the instructions offered in the *Ānāpānasati-sutta* emerge fully when one proceeds in a continuous manner through the entire scheme. Therefore my recommendation is to consider the sixteen steps as a continuous form of practice such that we might even proceed through the entire set repeatedly, at whatever speed seems suitable, during a single meditation session.

LONG AND SHORT BREATHS

The Pāli formulation for the first two steps involves the use of the disjunctive particle *vā*, which means "or". A peculiarity of its grammatical position is that it stands after each word concerned. If in English we would say "x or y", in Pāli the same would become "x *vā* y *vā*".

In the above passage the *vā* occurs four times, so that we get:

- breathing in long *vā*,
- breathing out long *vā*,
- breathing in short *vā*,
- breathing out short *vā*.

This could be interpreted in two different ways, which is why I prefer not to translate *vā* explicitly, so as to avoid taking a definite stance on one of these two alternatives. One interpretation would be to take the *vā* to refer only to the difference between inhalations and exhalations. This would then be: breathing in or out long *and* breathing in or out short. The other would be to take it as expressing that long and short breaths are also alternatives. This would then be: breathing in or out long *or else* breathing in or out short.

The first interpretation would imply that we should proceed from first being aware of long breaths to subsequently turning to short breaths. This could be achieved by taking an intentional long breath at the outset and then watching how this naturally becomes shorter. On adopting the other interpretation, however, we should just be aware of the length of the breath as it is, noting whether it manifests as a long or as a short breath.

The *Satipaṭṭhāna-sutta* (MN 10) has a simile, not found in its parallels, that illustrates the practice of the first two steps of mindfulness of breathing with an example that could be taken to convey some degree of intentional influence. The simile reads as follows:

> It is just as a skilled turner or a turner's apprentice who understands, when making a long turn: 'I make a long turn'; understands, when making a short turn: 'I make a short turn.'

Making a turn on a lathe is something done intentionally by the turner. On this understanding, the simile conveys a nuance of intentional influence, which in turn would support the suggestion of taking a long breath (or even several, if that seems opportune) intentionally and then observing how breathing gradually becomes shorter. I will come back to the turner simile below.

The structure of the remaining steps provides further support for the interpretation that we should proceed from first experiencing long to subsequently having short breaths. The whole scheme of sixteen steps clearly involves tetrads of practice and the *Ānāpānasati-sutta* identifies each set of four steps with one *satipaṭṭhāna*. The case of contemplation of the body corresponds to the four steps of long breath, short breath, experiencing the whole body, and calming bodily activity. If the *vā* is taken to imply that either long or else short breaths should be contemplated, contemplation of the body would only involve three steps and not a tetrad, namely:

- understand long or short,
- experience the whole body,
- calm bodily activity.

The situation changes, however, in discourses in the *Saṃyukta-āgama* (see below p. 203) that also provide the same basic correlation between the sixteen steps and the four *satipaṭṭhāna*s. Here the instruction in the preliminaries (discussed in the previous chapter), which just requires one to be aware of the breath going in and going out, is included under the heading of contemplation of the body. On following this description and taking the distinction between long and short as referring to alternatives, the resultant tetrad would be:

- breathe in and out mindfully,
- understand long or short,
- experience the whole body,
- calm bodily activity.

It follows that the task after breathing in and out mindfully would be to discern the length of breath. It would require simply turning attention to the length of the breath and then determining if this is comparatively long or relatively short, without any need to take an intentional long breath in order to ensure that breathing is first long and then becomes shorter.

Now the idea that practice invariably proceeds from long to shorter breaths does in fact not necessarily reflect the subjective experience of meditators. Some find that the breath seems to become longer with increasing calmness of body and mind. To some degree this involves the question of whether the gauging of the length of the breath should include the gap that occurs after an inhalation or an exhalation. If this gap is considered to be part of the length of the breath, it might indeed appear that the breath becomes longer with increasing tranquillity, even though in actual fact the gap has become longer, as the body requires less oxygen. Given that the inhalations and exhalations are considered a manifestation of the wind element, representative of the principle of motion, the reference to long and short breaths in the instruction would probably refer just to the actual flow of the breath in and out, without taking into account the gaps. This would make it meaningful to depict a progression from longer to shorter breaths.

Nevertheless, the interpretation according to which the *vā* only serves to set apart inhalations from exhalations, leading to the conclusion that we should first understand long and then short breaths, becomes less convincing when the remaining steps are taken into consideration. The same particle *vā* is not used for any of the remaining fourteen steps, even though these still involve an alternation between breathing in and out. Had the function of the *vā* been to drive home the fact that the same type of contemplation should be done with either the inhalation or the exhalation, it would have been more natural for it to be used throughout. From this perspective, it would seem that the particle *vā* in the case of the first two steps just conveys the idea of knowing if the breath is either long or else short (although to convey that idea it would have been more straightforward if the *vā* had been used only twice, once after breathing in and out long and again after breathing in and out short).

The main form of practice in the remainder of the scheme is clearly about simply observing the breath, rather than trying to change it in any way. Before his awakening, the Buddha had experimented with breath control and found it not conducive to awakening (MN 36; Anālayo 2017e: 60–63). Instead of attempting to control the breath, the mode of meditation related to the breath he recommended to his disciples involves the cultivation of mindful observation. This appears to be the main thrust that informs the exposition given in the *Ānāpānasati-sutta*, which makes it less probable that to get started requires an intentionally long breath.

According to the formulation employed, the long and short breaths are matters that we should "understand", a terminology that points to a sense of observation rather than intentional influence. Only in relation to the remaining fourteen steps does the Pāli discourse enjoin that we should "train" ourselves, which expresses a more active nuance. However, *Saṃyukta-āgama* discourses appear to speak of training even for the first two steps (see below p. 182) and other parallel versions do not speak of training at all (Anālayo 2013b: 231). Nevertheless, at least the Pāli version's description of the actual steps conveys the impression that the first two steps should involve less intentional effort than the remaining steps. From this viewpoint, the turner simile could also be interpreted differently. After all, the comparison is between the turner's understanding of the length of the turn and the meditator's understanding of the length of the breath. This need not be taken to imply that the breath should now be cultivated in a way similar to the piece on the lathe.

On evaluating the different perspectives that have emerged in this way, it seems to me best to approach this part of the instructions in a flexible manner, without making a definite decision as to which interpretation is the more appropriate one. In practical terms, my recommendation would be to begin by first taking a long and deep breath intentionally and then observe how the breath naturally becomes shorter and softer. Once we have moved through the sixteen steps, however, on repeating the sequence it might be preferable to follow the alternative interpretation and thereby avoid any intentional long breath. Taking such an intentional long breath can be quite helpful when we have become distracted and need to put in extra effort to regain our grounding in the present moment's experience of the breath and thereby set a clear contrast to whatever mental distraction had been present. But when practice is progressing smoothly, taking an intentional breath can be too coarse. In such a case we might just be mindful of the inhalations and exhalations as a first step and then proceed from that to discerning if these are long or short as a second step.

In this way, both interpretations can be put to use alternatively. The interpretation that supports proceeding from long to short would be particularly relevant when a substantial distraction has occurred. When only minor distractions occur or when we just wish to repeat the first tetrad of body contemplation, it can be preferable to proceed from noticing the distinction between inhalation and exhalation to discerning the length of the breath as long or short, and then continue with the remaining steps. What really counts, in the end, is to employ the first two steps to arouse a keen sense of interest in order to sustain attention on the length of the breaths.

INVESTIGATION AND CONCEPTS

The categories "long" and "short" themselves are open to subjective assessment. Here we need to investigate and discern clearly at what point exactly it seems right for us to shift from the notion "long" to the notion "short". The purpose is not to find the only correct mode of using the respective label, but to arouse a sense of enquiry during this part of the practice, in order to keep the mind interested in what is going on. The appropriate attitude would be a sense of curiosity, as if asking ourselves: "is this breath really still long or is it already short?"

What emerges from considering the first two steps is of relevance throughout for the scheme of sixteen steps. The instructions given should not be turned into something that limits and restricts the natural unfolding of our meditation. Keeping in mind the overall purpose of a particular sequence of steps, we remain open to adjusting our personal practice to what the present moment requires. The task is not to execute with total precision one step after the other, but much rather to allow a flexible evolution of our meditation practice, informed by an understanding of the rationale behind the sequence of steps delineated in the discourse.

Employing the distinction between long and short breaths, as well as other aspects cultivated during the remaining steps, requires the judicious use of concepts. These are best relied on only to the degree to which they support clarity during actual practice. We might briefly formulate the relevant concept explicitly in our mind and then rest in the resulting experience without continuing to employ concepts. In the case of gauging the length of the breath, we might simply note "long" and then observe for a while until we feel time has come to note "short". In the case of other tasks to be performed with subsequent steps, we might arouse the relevant concept in relation to one cycle of inhalation and exhalation and then remain with the resultant experience for another two, three, or more cycles. In this way the benefit of the use of concepts can be reaped without risking that we end up just mentally fabricating experience.

The amount of time spent just observing, after the initial input made by the use of whatever concept is relevant to a particular step, can be adjusted according to the degree of collectedness of our mind. If the mind is rather scattered, it can be preferable to keep bringing in concepts at shorter intervals, in order to counter the tendency to distraction. Once the mind is more settled, however, progress through the sixteen steps can involve longer periods of just resting in the experience of each step, savouring the particular characteristic that has emerged fully due to the initial and brief conceptual input. With ongoing practice of the sixteen steps, the sequence will become ever more familiar until it eventually becomes so ingrained and natural that hardly any intentional conceptual input is needed for proceeding from one step to the next.

It is also useful to introduce some variation into the practice, rather than settling on a particular time duration per step and just keeping to that for any meditation session. We need to avoid the mind going into autopilot mode. At times it might be preferable to continue savouring a particular step for quite some time, either as long as it feels appropriate or else until we realize that the mind is about to drift off and only then proceed to the next step. At other times it might be best to move through the entire series of sixteen steps swiftly in order to get a clear appreciation of the inherent dynamics. The guideline overall is situational creativity, in the sense of practising creatively and adjusting to whatever the present moment appears to require.

In order to keep adjusting the practice moment by moment, the same quality of investigation, which at the outset served to discern the length of the breath, can be employed throughout the remainder of the practice of mindfulness of breathing. In this way, the scope of investigation broadens from the length of the breath to the overall condition of our body and mind, all the while performing the function of keeping the mind interested in, and attentive to, what is taking place.

THE WHOLE BODY

The Pāli expression used in this part of the instruction to refer to the body is *kāya*, which in principle can convey different nuances. Besides referring to the physical body, the same term can also carry a figurative meaning. Later exegesis has taken each of these two meanings and developed corresponding meditative approaches.

The *Visuddhimagga* follows a figurative sense when it understands the third step to refer to the whole body of the breath, in the sense of its entire length (Vism 273). In fact the *Ānāpānasati-sutta* reckons the breath to be a certain kind of body (see below p. 204 n. 74). From a practical perspective, however, such an understanding of the third step does not offer a distinctly new perspective, because knowing the entire length of the breath was already required for the previous two steps in order to be able to determine if the breath was long or short (see below p. 175 n. 6). Each step in the remainder of the scheme, although clearly building on the preceding one, introduces something new and distinctly different.

Several parallels to the instruction in the *Ānāpānasati-sutta* employ terms that support taking the instruction as referring to an experiencing of the whole physical body rather than just of the whole breath (Anālayo 2013b: 231). In some practice lineages, this understanding appears to have led to the idea that one is to experience the breath throughout the whole body (see below p. 237). Without intending to deny the practical benefits that can be derived from such an approach, the actual instruction for the third step in the present tetrad on body contemplation, found similarly in a range of canonical parallels, is just about "experiencing the whole body". It is not about experiencing the breath in the whole body.

Take the example of the corresponding third step in the next tetrad on contemplation of feeling tone. This requires "experiencing mental activity". Executing this step does not require experiencing the breath in mental activity. Similarly, the third step in the first tetrad does not require experiencing the breath in the whole body.

In other words, the third step of the present tetrad on body contemplation needs to be interpreted in such a way that the same type of instruction also works for the remainder of the scheme. The instructions for the remainder of the scheme, described in the discourse, are not about experiencing the breath in a special way, be it in the whole body or in mental activities, etc. Instead, the instructions are to train ourselves in combining various tasks with the same awareness of the distinction between breathing in and breathing out. In each case, the inhalations and exhalations are observed alongside various tasks, rather than being merged with them. The same holds for the present third step of experiencing the whole body.

In sum, the instructions for the third step of the present tetrad of body contemplation give the impression that the main meditative task is to experience the whole physical body, which takes place alongside a second task of remaining aware of the process of breathing. In the approach to mindfulness of breathing I am presenting here, such experiencing of the whole body then becomes a way of reconnecting to the main mode of practice established earlier when keeping the body straight in the sitting posture, namely mindfulness of the body as a whole.

At the same time, this reconnection involves a refinement of whole-body awareness. When sitting down and keeping the body erect, a more rudimentary awareness of the body had been cultivated. At the present juncture, attention paid to the process of breathing has attuned the mind to more subtle bodily experiences, related to the manifestation of the wind element. As a result, the type of whole-body awareness cultivated now can become a more in-depth sensing of the body at a much subtler level. It is a feeling into the body on a more refined and energetic level.

The shift that can emerge here is comparable to the progression in the *Satipaṭṭhāna-sutta* from contemplation of the anatomical parts to contemplation of the elements. Although both exercises are concerned with the constitution of the body, contemplation of the elements approaches this topic on a more refined level. Similarly, awareness of the whole body cultivated in the context of mindfulness of breathing can proceed from a basic mode, oriented on its anatomy, to a subtler mode, more attuned to the wind element as representative of bodily energies. Such subtler experience of the whole body naturally leads over to the next step of calming bodily activity. After all, any such bodily activity is a manifestation of the wind element.

MODES OF ATTENTION

On the interpretation proposed here, the first and second steps involve an exercise in a more focused type of attention. Although this takes place within a continuity of whole-body awareness, clearly the breath is at the forefront of attention. This is precisely what enables scrutinizing the breath closely enough to be able to determine its length. With the third step, however, whole-body awareness comes to the forefront of attention, and with ensuing steps other meditative themes. In short, the first two steps are about being aware of the breath alone, the remaining steps about combining awareness of the breath with some other meditative task.

The earlier focus on the length of the breath has the advantage of enabling a quick discerning of the mind's tendency to wander. As we follow the length of the breath closely, any tendency of the mind to move off target can swiftly be noticed. Therefore focus on the length of the breath can serve as a useful tool to counter distraction. However, this mode of paying attention can also generate mental tension and excessive striving. These can more easily be avoided with a broad form of attention that takes the whole of the body as its main object and in addition also remains aware of the inhalations and exhalations. Understood in this way, the amount of time dedicated to gauging the length of the breath and when to shift to whole-body awareness can be informed by our clear understanding of both the benefits and the potential disadvantages of focused attention.

The progression that unfolds during the first tetrad of body contemplation can then be understood to offer us an opportunity to experiment with the skilful use of the two basic modalities of a more open and encompassing awareness and a more focused and directed form of attention (that is nevertheless still situated within the basic modality of embodied mindfulness). As part of the preliminary practice, an embodied awareness has been established in particular when keeping the body erect in the sitting posture. This is to be maintained throughout, which requires at least a minimal degree of awareness of the bodily posture. Within that field of whole-body awareness, a stronger focus during the first two steps enables clearly discerning the length of the breath. Although the focus of attention becomes much stronger than it was before, it is still set against a background field of peripheral awareness that maintains the continuity of being mindful of the whole body.

Once such focus has fulfilled its purpose of providing some degree of absence of distraction, practice returns to giving full emphasis to an encompassing and broad type of awareness with the third step. Throughout the remainder of the sixteen steps, the breath is simply noted as going in or out, without any further concern about its length or any other of its qualities. For fulfilling this purpose of just noting inhalations and exhalations, peripheral awareness of the breath suffices.

Focused attention and peripheral awareness, considered on their own, make distinct contributions to our mental experience. Whereas focused attention picks out one aspect and thoroughly processes it, peripheral awareness involves a more receptive,

open, and inclusive perspective that enables seeing things from a distance, as it were, and in their relationship to each other. Due to its powerful thrust, focused attention can more easily fuel tendencies to fixate; at the same time, it also facilitates a more thorough analysis of the chosen object and provides more depth of information about it. Peripheral awareness is less prone to trigger fixation, at the price of potentially remaining more superficial and imprecise.

In the case of contemplating the breath, the ability to maintain a fairly stable awareness can be improved if the degree of focused attention we employ during the first two steps is combined with some degree of peripheral awareness. In other words, just focusing on the breath alone to the exclusion of everything else might at first allow us to dip in deep, but we also get more easily lost. This is because the tunnel view that results from such exclusive focus makes it difficult to notice when a diversion is about to lead to a displacement of attention. With some degree of peripheral awareness maintained, however, even though the initial plunge is less deep, the advantage is that potential diversions can be noticed when they enter the edges of our field of awareness and thus before they have successfully captivated our attention.

Imagine looking at something through binoculars. Although details that are far away can be discerned, others that are close by are outside the range of our vision. Now suppose we were to use a telescope instead and do so by keeping the other eye open. In this way, it would still be possible to view details far away without at the same time overlooking something that might be happening close by. This takes a bit of training, just as the maintenance of peripheral awareness while using focused attention takes a bit of training.

Applied to mindfulness of breathing, alongside a stable focus on the length of the breath we learn to allow the peripheral areas in the field of awareness to be also part of our experience. The result is somewhat as if we were to increase the bandwidth of our experience to include both what we are focusing on and its surroundings. In other words, the recommendation is to see if it is possible to keep attention focused while still allowing the mind to remain at least to some degree broad.

When we then proceed from the second to the third step, the attention that has enabled us to discern the length of the breath shifts to the whole body. It is as if breath and whole body have exchanged places in the field of our awareness. At first the breath was right in front and the whole body in the background. Now the breath steps back, as it were, and the whole body steps forward. As the focus on the breath becomes more relaxed, peripheral awareness of the breath steps into its place and ensures that the breath is not completely lost sight of. Since the whole body is a broader object than the breath, its coming to the forefront in the field of our attention naturally encourages a broader form of awareness.

The earlier shift towards increased focus with the first two steps and the present shift back to less focus could be illustrated with the example of contemplating a beautiful painting. In order to get a clearer appreciation of some details, we might at times step closer to examine these from nearby. Such stepping closer illustrates discerning the length of the breath as long or short. Having examined the details of the painting, we step back again to enjoy the whole picture. Such stepping back to take in the whole picture illustrates the shift towards letting awareness of the whole body be at the forefront of our awareness.

TRAINING

The injunction to "train", mentioned from the third to the last of the steps of mindfulness of breathing in the *Ānāpānasati-sutta*, can then be understood as pointing to the need to maintain the constant alternation between inhalations and exhalations in peripheral awareness while undertaking each of the meditative tasks described in the subsequent steps of practice. Once the bodily phenomenon of the breath recedes into the background, full importance can be given to the progressive themes of the ensuing steps as a way of cultivating all four *satipaṭṭhāna*s. To execute such training requires in particular keeping the five hindrances well at bay, as a surfacing of any hindrance would obstruct our ability to maintain peripheral awareness of the breath and at the same time cultivate the particular step we are practising.

A discourse in the *Saṃyutta-nikāya* implicitly indicates, in agreement with its Chinese parallel, that the reference to "training" is indeed related to the hindrances (SN 54.12; see below p. 196). According to its presentation, those who have forever eradicated the hindrances no longer require any training when proceeding through the sixteen steps of mindfulness of breathing.

For most of us, however, such training is still required. The task set by such training then also implies that, if a hindrance has overpowered the mind, it might be necessary to let go of whatever step of mindfulness of breathing we are engaged in and give full attention to emerging first of all from this detrimental mental condition.

Here previous experience with contemplation of the hindrances, as described in the *Satipaṭṭhāna-sutta*, comes in handy. During such contemplation, we learned to develop expertise in recognizing the conditions that lead to a hindrance as well as those that help us emerge from it (Anālayo 2018d: 151–169). Once the hindrance that had manifested strongly has been dealt with, ideally while keeping the breath in peripheral awareness, we could either continue with our practice at the point where we left off or else start the progression through the sixteen steps from the beginning in order to build up momentum gradually.

The shift to a form of training with the third step is also of interest in so far as the instructions express a sense of determination. The remaining steps are formulated with the expressions "I shall breathe in" and "I shall breathe out." The preliminary practice and the preceding two steps differ in this respect. The preliminary practice requires that mindfulness is established concomitantly with the experience of the breath: "mindful one breathes in and mindful one breathes out." For the first two steps, practice is at least somewhat retrospective, as understanding "I breathe in (or out) long" or else "I breathe in (or out) short" will usually occur at the completion of that breath. Of course, once the inhalation has been discerned as either long or short, when the corresponding exhalation begins, we might expect it to be of similar length. Yet, we will be fully certain of this only when that exhalation has come to its end, as at times inhalations and exhalations can differ in their respective lengths. Thus it is indeed only at the end of a breath that we can come to a decision about its length.

In this way, the meditative progression so far relates to the three periods of time (past, present, and future) in a way that allows them to be connected to the experience of the breath in the present moment. The preliminary practice has established mindfulness of the present moment. Based on the continuous establishment of such present-moment awareness, the first two steps are concerned with something slightly retrospective when we discern the length of the breath once it has come to an end. This in a way broadens the meditative vista to include the immediate past. With the remaining steps of the scheme the emphasis is on what is still to come and thus is more forward-looking. We set up beforehand the attitude of training to undertake a particular meditative task. This broadens the meditative perspective to include the immediate future. Taken together, the net result is a broadening of the meditative field of attention beyond a narrow focus on only what is present right now.

All of this does not conflict with the idea that mindfulness is to be established in the present moment. Due to the breadth of mind that can be cultivated with mindfulness, it is quite possible to be fully in the present moment and at the same time include what has just happened or what is just about to come in the broad scope of our field of attention. In fact knowing the length of the breath is not really concerned with something that is past. The actual task is to be mentally present continuously, throughout the entire duration of the breath, and at its end to draw the conclusion whether this breath should be reckoned long or short. Similarly, the training to be undertaken from the third to the last step is not about planning ahead for a distant future. Much rather, it is simply about inclining the mind in such a way that practice proceeds in accordance with the steps delineated in the instructions.

CALMING BODILY ACTIVITY

The fourth step is to calm bodily activity. The expression "bodily activity" translates *kāyasaṅkhāra*, where the term *saṅkhāra* occurs in the singular. The *Cūḷavedalla-sutta*, in the context of a discussion leading up to the topic of the cessation of perception and feeling tone, defines the term *kāyasaṅkhāra* as inhalations and exhalations (MN 44), a definition also found in a discourse in the *Saṃyutta-nikāya* (SN 41.6; see below p. 173).

The *Paṭisambhidāmagga*, an exegetical treatise found in the Theravāda canon, applies this definition of *kāyasaṅkhāra* to the present context and then expands it to include, besides the breath itself, motions of the body in general (Paṭis I 184). This offers a helpful perspective for actual practice, in that, after becoming aware of the whole body, the task is to calm the body in general and the breathing in particular. In fact, calming the body will calm the breath, and calming the breath will in turn lead to calmness of the body as a whole. Here the previous step of experiencing the whole body alongside noting inhalations and exhalations has prepared the ground for the present fourth step of calming both.

ABSORPTION

Strictly speaking a complete calming of the bodily activity of breathing takes place with entry into the fourth absorption (Anālayo 2003b: 132n64). A discourse in the *Aṅguttara-nikāya* explicitly states that bodily activity is calmed with the attainment of the fourth absorption (AN 4.38). This could not be the implication of the reference to calming bodily activity in the present passage, however, since the instruction is to "breathe in (or out) calming bodily activity", a formulation that clearly implies the continuity of the experience of the breath. The same holds for ensuing steps in the scheme, all of which take place against the background of continuous awareness of breathing in and out. Given that according to the discourses the breath ceases for one who dwells in the fourth absorption (see below p. 160), it would no longer be possible to be aware of any inhalations or exhalations during such attainment, be it in relation to the present step or to subsequent steps. Moreover, when progressing through the sixteen steps, "concentrating the mind" occurs only in the third tetrad, making it more probable that the same has not yet been fully achieved with the first tetrad.

Although the formulation of the fourth step would not be about entry into the fourth absorption, such a deep state of concentration is not without some practical significance to the present juncture of practice. Once the fourth absorption has been attained, body and mind reach a superb degree of mental imperturbability. The idea of imperturbability resonates with the practical flavour of the present step, even though this involves a level of imperturbability far below that reached with the fourth absorption.

The progression through the sixteen steps has a remarkable potential to bring about tranquillity of body and mind; in fact the attainment of the four absorptions features among a range of possible attainments to be gained through this practice (see below p. 216). At the same time, however, the overall purpose of mindfulness of breathing is not just to facilitate entry into absorption. Instead, as indicated explicitly in the *Ānāpānasati-sutta*, the chief purpose of the instructions is to lead via a cultivation of the four *satipaṭṭhāna*s and the seven awakening factors to the gaining of knowledge and liberation.

Had the point at issue been absorption, one might wonder why this is not more explicitly indicated. The benefits of absorption are such a recurrent topic elsewhere in the discourses that it would be difficult to understand why they should not be mentioned directly in the exposition of mindfulness of breathing in the *Ānāpānasati-sutta*, had this really been the main concern of the instructions.

This relates back to the collaborative perspective on tranquillity and insight mentioned in the previous chapter. Keeping this collaborative perspective in mind when progressing through the scheme of sixteen steps, including the preliminaries, can reveal the profundity of the instructions given in the *Ānāpānasati-sutta*.

Rather than requiring entry into the fourth absorption, the step of calming bodily activity, coming after awareness of the body as a whole has been established, appears to imply that a deep relaxation can be allowed to occur throughout the body.

If we are meditating after having had a particularly stressful day or encounter, it can be helpful to cultivate a more structured relaxation when coming to this step. A possible way of doing this would be to combine an inhalation with a brief scanning of the body for any possible tension and then relax any such tension with the ensuing exhalation. This can be done once for the whole body, or else during several breath cycles we might scan first the feet and legs, then the hips and torso, then the hands and arms, then the shoulders and neck, and finally the head (in particular relaxing the lower jaw and the facial muscles during the exhalation). Each time, a scan during an inhalation could be followed by relaxing during the exhalation.

With or without such additional aids, the deep relaxation that can eventually occur at this stage of practice results simply from a calming down of the breath and any other bodily activity or tension. The breath in a way breathes itself, and we do not feel any need to become active on the bodily level at all.

CALMNESS IN GENERAL

A counterpart to the present step of mindfulness of breathing in the Mahāsāṅghika *Vinaya* speaks of "letting go" rather than of "calming" bodily activity (Anālayo 2013b: 229 and 231). The Mahāsāṅghika *Vinaya* also employs the term "letting go" for the last step in the next tetrad about contemplation of feeling tone, which in the *Ānāpānasati-sutta* concerns "calming mental activity". In both contexts, this alternative expression in a way fleshes out the implications of "calming", which indeed requires letting go of anything that might prevent a deepening of calmness.

Although the resultant sense of calmness is experienced internally by the meditator, its results can also become externally visible. A case in point is the description of a monastic whose lack of bodily fidgeting, whether alone or seated with others, stood out to such a degree that it was noticed by the Buddha and by other monastics. According to the Buddha's explanation, the tranquil bodily behaviour of this monastic was the outcome of his practice of mindfulness of breathing (SN 54.7; see below p. 190).

This in turn suggests that the calming effect of mindfulness of breathing can continue beyond the practice of this particular step in the scheme. It would hardly do justice to the description in this discourse to assume that, whenever the Buddha or other monastics were looking, this monastic was right at that time engaged in the fourth step of mindfulness of breathing. Instead, the point at issue rather seems to be that the practice of mindfulness of breathing leads to a general degree of bodily calmness in one's behaviour, which comes to express a sense of ease and inner peace, whatever the external situation may be.

This bodily calmness is the result of the previous progression through the preliminaries and the first three steps of mindfulness of breathing, which in turn build on maintenance of moral conduct as the foundation for meditation practice. As the consummation of all this groundwork, bodily calmness and tranquillity express the fruition of morality and the meditative training undertaken up to this point, and continue to inform the ensuing steps and eventually our overall behaviour in any situation. Cultivated in this way, and perhaps inspired by the example of the monastic mentioned above, we can allow the sense of bodily tranquillity to accompany us during the day, even when we have to be active in one way or another.

WALKING MEDITATION

In addition to a general sense of bodily calmness during any activity, the third step from the present tetrad of body contemplation, "experiencing the whole body", would be particularly relevant to walking meditation. Experiencing the whole body would include the breath as part of the experience of the body, be it seated or walking, but without a specific focus on the breath alone to the exclusion of everything else. In this way, when shifting from sitting to walking meditation or any other activity, an element of continuity throughout the day (and night) could be whole-body awareness. Whatever we need to do, we can do it with our whole body, and ideally also with the natural dignity of bodily calmness.

Such a shifting to whole-body awareness during walking or any other activity can be accompanied by checking whether mindfulness is established in such a way that it does not get lost but equally that it does not have too strong an attentional focus. In this way, the basic experimenting with the modalities of focused attention and peripheral awareness, suggested in this approach to cultivating the first four steps of mindfulness of breathing, can continue with any other activity. Throughout, the one quality that provides feedback on what adjustment the present moment requires remains mindfulness itself.

THE MEDITATIVE PROGRESSION

Looking back at the progression through the present tetrad of four steps, which fulfils the first *satipaṭṭhāna* of contemplation of the body, a relationship to the preliminaries discussed in the previous chapter emerges. Taking a long breath intentionally as a starting point to observe the length of the breath offers a way of checking if we are really keeping the body erect, as otherwise such a long breath will meet with some degree of inner obstruction. For the breath to become gradually shorter and softer provides another checkpoint, since for that to occur the body has to be maintained straight in a relaxed manner, rather than being held stiffly. In this way, feedback regarding the appropriate posture, which should be straight and relaxed, is a side effect of the first two steps concerned with long and short breaths (if practised according to the interpretation of having first long and then short breaths).

The ability to shift from more focused attention on the length of the breath to becoming aware of the whole body provides a check on mindfulness. If we have really brought mindfulness "to the fore", made *sati* predominant, it will be easy to shift from maintaining a stronger focus on the length of the breath to awareness of the whole body without succumbing to distraction. Resting in whole-body awareness with the wide-angle lens of mindfulness established, we can allow body and mind to calm down until all bodily activity has become superbly still and a deep sense of relaxation occurs throughout body and mind. This confirms that we have indeed been able to establish the mental dimension of seclusion, mentioned at the outset of the preliminaries, without which some agitation or the other would interfere with the tranquillity experienced at this point.

As we cultivate this tetrad of body contemplation, a gradual refinement of the practice takes place in relation to modes of attention. The instructions begin by mentioning the long breath and the short breath, after which the focus on the breath leads over to a mode of contemplation that encompasses the whole body and at the same time maintains awareness of the inhalations and exhalations. Finally, both body and breath are allowed to become completely calm, thereby issuing in a deeply relaxed and subtle experience of contemplation of the body.

The present tetrad of body contemplation thereby offers a gradual transition from the basic establishing of mindfulness on the inhalations and exhalations as a preliminary practice to the progression through the remaining steps. A continuous keeping in mind of the alternation between breathing in and breathing out forms the backbone of practice throughout. This gradual transition takes place by first of all giving increased attention to the breath, in terms of its length, during the first two steps. Next the breath is allowed to move into the background of the field of awareness. From this point onwards, the continuous establishing of mindfulness on the breath finds explicit mention as a training. We train "I breathe in" doing such and such meditative activity and we train "I breathe out" doing that same meditative activity. The breath held in peripheral awareness provides an anchoring for each of the ensuing meditative tasks to be undertaken.

THE *SATIPAṬṬHĀNA-SUTTA*

In the *Satipaṭṭhāna-sutta* the present tetrad is one of its different contemplations of the body. A comparative study of the parallel versions makes it probable that the first tetrad of mindfulness of breathing was not from the outset an integral part of the *satipaṭṭhāna* of contemplating the body (see below pp. 165 and 167). The comparative perspective instead suggests contemplation of the anatomical parts, of the elements, and of a decaying corpse to be the common core of this *satipaṭṭhāna* (Anālayo 2013b: 52–54). This invests the first *satipaṭṭhāna* with a strong emphasis on cultivating insight into the nature of the body, in particular revealing its lack of inherent beauty, its empty nature, and its mortality.

With the first tetrad of mindfulness of breathing, the cultivation of such insights is not apparent in a way comparable to the *Satipaṭṭhāna-sutta*. The main thrust of the present tetrad of body contemplation appears to be one of calming the body (and by implication the mind). Nevertheless, the breath as such can in principle serve as a reminder of mortality. In addition, as a manifestation of the wind element the breath has a natural connection to contemplation of the elements. In this way, based on previous cultivation of *satipaṭṭhāna* as described in the *Satipaṭṭhāna-sutta*, it is quite possible that insight-related experiences unfold, bringing home the impermanent and empty nature of the body. The lessening of attachment to the body, as a result of such insight, will in turn strengthen the ability to calm the body. However, such cultivation of insight is not explicitly mentioned in the instructions for the present tetrad and thus would probably require previous practice of *satipaṭṭhāna* in order to emerge on its own when proceeding through the present set of steps.

In a way, the *Ānāpānasati-sutta* could be considered as taking off from where the contemplations common to the *Satipaṭṭhāna-sutta* and its parallels lead, namely a condition of diminishing attachment and obsession with the body that will facilitate a calming of bodily activities. As already mentioned in the previous chapter, the progression through the sixteen steps seems to take for granted the temporary absence of the hindrances and thus builds on freedom from sensual obsession and aversion in relation to the body. I will return to the relationship between the *Satipaṭṭhāna-sutta* and the *Ānāpānasati-sutta* in subsequent chapters.

SUMMARY

By way of beginning we might first take a deep and long breath intentionally and then observe mindfully how the breath naturally becomes shorter and softer. The same procedure of taking a deep and long breath on purpose also commends itself for occasions when a major distraction has occurred, in order to ground ourselves in the experience of the breath in the here and now, setting a clear contrast to the mental proliferation that has just been taking place. When the mind is not distracted, however, to bring in intentional breathing can become too gross an approach and could disturb the smooth flow of our practice. In such a situation, it would be preferable to direct awareness simply to the distinction between inhalations and exhalations, as described in the preliminaries to the practice, and then to discern the length of the breath as being either long or short.

Assessments like "long" and "short", as well as other concepts relevant to the remaining steps of mindfulness of breathing, could be applied explicitly for one breath cycle, followed by simply resting in the resultant experience for several breath cycles. Judicious use of concepts in this way leads to clarity during practice without resulting in mental proliferations and fabrications that divert us from the actual experience of the breath.

The more focused mode of attention used in the first and second steps, in order to distinguish clearly the length of the breath, leads to more emphasis on awareness of the whole body with the third step. This progression can be used to experiment with the modalities of focused attention and peripheral awareness.

With the fourth step of practice we can allow the breath and the body to become increasingly calm, such that a sense of deep relaxation pervades the whole of our bodily experience. The deep sense of tranquillity that informs meditative experience at this stage, being the fruition of the foundation in moral conduct built previously, forms the culmination point of the first tetrad of mindfulness of breathing.

III

CONTEMPLATION OF FEELING TONES

With the conclusion of the second tetrad, the head of the condor starts to become transparent. The transparency of the head symbolizes the clarity of the mind due to the absence of mental chatter, once thought activity has gone into abeyance. The changing scenery continues to represent awareness of impermanence that has become even more apparent due to the transparency of the head.

The second tetrad, corresponding to the *satipaṭṭhāna* of contemplating feeling tones, proceeds as follows in the *Ānāpānasati-sutta* (MN 118):

> One trains: 'experiencing joy I shall breathe in'; one trains: 'experiencing joy I shall breathe out.' One trains: 'experiencing happiness I shall breathe in'; one trains: 'experiencing happiness I shall breathe out.' One trains: 'experiencing mental activity I shall breathe in'; one trains: 'experiencing mental activity I shall breathe out.' One trains: 'calming mental activity I shall breathe in'; one trains: 'calming mental activity I shall breathe out.'

The topics to be discussed in relation to this instruction are "joy" and "happiness" and the significance of the reference to experiencing and calming "mental activity".

JOY AND HAPPINESS

The terms "joy" and "happiness" translate *pīti* and *sukha* in Pāli, both of which can carry a range of nuances in their usage in the discourses. One of these usages is as factors of absorption, and it would be this usage that inspired the *Visuddhimagga* to relate the present two steps to absorption attainment (Vism 287). This mode of explanation continues a tendency already mentioned in the previous chapter, where a later interpretation of the text proceeds based on identifying terminological similarities that do not necessarily fit the practical context within which these terms occur.

Now the presentation in the *Visuddhimagga* has a point in so far as the type of joy and happiness mentioned in this part of the instructions for mindfulness of breathing shares with entry into absorption the quality of being secluded from sensuality and unwholesome states. However, such joy and happiness can be experienced in a variety of ways that need not involve entry into absorption (Anālayo 2003b: 133f). Such a broader understanding would do better justice to the overall thrust of the instructions in the *Ānāpānasati-sutta*, whose concern is quite explicitly the gaining of knowledge and liberation. For this purpose, absorption attainment has of course a significant contribution to offer. Nevertheless, absorption is not explicitly mentioned anywhere in the actual instructions in the *Ānāpānasati-sutta*, leaving little room to consider the mode of mindfulness of breathing described in this discourse, or some specific steps, as being predominantly concerned with absorption attainment.

The *Kandaraka-sutta*, for example, depicts a gradual refinement of non-sensual types of happiness, experienced at various stages of the gradual path. According to its presentation, maintenance of moral behaviour results in the experience of the happiness of blamelessness, *anavajjasukha* (MN 51; Anālayo 2003b: 167 and 2012b: 161). This type of happiness does not require the ability to enter absorption.

As mentioned in the first chapter (see above p. 23), a source of subtle pleasant feeling tones can be tapped through the simple fact of establishing mindfulness "to the fore". With mindfulness at the forefront when encountering anything through the senses, sense restraint can be implemented by not grasping either the "sign" or the "secondary characteristic" of what has been perceived. Instead of proliferating and reacting in unwholesome ways, when mindfulness is established it becomes possible to remain just receptively aware of the experience of the present moment in whatever way it manifests. As also mentioned in the first chapter, a discourse in the *Saṃyutta-nikāya* explicitly indicates that sense restraint leads on to delight and joy, *pīti* (SN 35.97). Such joy also does not require the ability to enter absorption.

In sum, it seems fair to follow the presentation in the Theravāda exegetical tradition only to the extent that the joy and happiness relevant to the present steps of mindfulness of breathing should be aloof from sensuality and unwholesomeness, without going so far as to restrict the practice of these steps to absorption attainment. As in the case of the last step of the preceding body-contemplation tetrad, which requires calming bodily activity, so too the mere occurrence of certain terms in the present case does not really warrant an equation of these steps with absorption.

Another similarity with the bodily calmness experienced in the last step of the body-contemplation tetrad is that the arising of joy at the present juncture is the fruition of the preceding practices. Both calmness and joy share in particular the need for a firm foundation in ethical conduct. Building on this foundation and its resultant happiness of blamelessness, another source for the arising of joy can be the inspiration gained from our motivation for practice, which I recommend formulating mentally when sitting down. A type of motivation that has an altruistic dimension of practising not only for our own benefit, but also to benefit others, has an especially strong potential to arouse joy. Yet another source of joy can be the awareness that we are practising a type of meditation that was regularly undertaken by the Buddha himself, as mentioned in the introduction to this book (see above p. 1). The joyful inspiration that can arise when recollecting the Buddha and the fact that we are now closely following in his footsteps can substantially empower our cultivation of mindfulness of breathing.

THE POTENTIAL OF JOY

The breath itself is a bland object and for this reason the sensations it causes are usually neutral ones. Since neutral feeling tones tend to trigger the underlying tendency to ignorance, it is no surprise that attention is not easily sustained on the breath, as its very nature of having a neutral hedonic tone causes it to be easily ignored.

This basic predicament can be better appreciated with the help of the concept of reward-based learning from cognitive psychology. From primitive animals to human beings, habits and preferences are based on positive reinforcement. If a particular action has positive outcomes, it will be repeated in the future. If it has negative outcomes, it will be avoided. This basic principle helps to ensure the survival of species, which relies on increasing the likelihood of access to nutrition and successful reproduction, both fostered through the pleasure-seeking principle of reward-based learning.

Applied to the case of mindfulness of breathing, fostering the habit to stay with the breath instead of wandering off into some distraction or the other can be greatly enhanced through making intelligent use of this principle of reward-based learning. This can take place by joining the subtle pleasant feeling tone of being in the present moment to the experience of the breath. Such joining can take place already during the preliminary practice of just being mindful of inhalations and exhalations. Having cultivated the subtle pleasant feeling tone of being in the present moment from the outset of the practice, this can then conveniently serve as the foundation for the arising of joy with the present step. Such arising of joy in turn boosts our ability to stay with the breath.

THE FIRST TETRAD

The potential of joy to empower the practice of mindfulness of breathing appears to have been lost sight of, to some degree, in later traditions. One reason contributing to this state of affairs could well be that at some relatively early stage in the oral transmission of the discourses the first tetrad of mindfulness of breathing appears to have been extracted from its setting in the sixteen-step scheme and turned into a practice in its own right (see below pp. 165 and 228).

This can be seen, for example, in the *Kāyagatāsati-sutta* and the *Satipaṭṭhāna-sutta*, where the first tetrad of mindfulness of breathing stands at the outset of the list of contemplations of the body. In itself this is a natural move, since the *Ānāpānasati-sutta* identifies this tetrad as an implementation of contemplation of the body (see below p. 204). Therefore, as part of an apparent tendency to flesh out possible applications of mindfulness directed to the body by collecting various practices related to this topic, it is hardly surprising if the first tetrad ended up in this rubric. As a result, however, the impression easily arises that the first tetrad of mindfulness of breathing is a complete practice by itself.

Although the first tetrad can indeed be practised on its own, as a result the connection to the ensuing steps is lost. This holds in particular for the very next step: experiencing joy. Once the body-contemplation tetrad becomes a contemplation in its own right, the need to practise in such a way that joy and happiness arise is no longer self-evident. In such a situation, other tools have to be found in order to foster the ability to stay with the breath.

An example in point is the counting technique, according to which one should count each breath, such as counting from one to ten and then starting over again from one (see below p. 232). Such techniques are not found as part of the instructions on the sixteen steps in the early discourses, probably because of the ability of joy and happiness to counter distraction on their own, without a need for additional props like counting. Excessive counting can in fact at times stimulate conceptual activity in the mind, rather than quieting it.

JOY

The task of remaining anchored in the experience of the breath can conveniently be achieved by relating the subtle pleasant feeling tone of being in the present moment to the breath. The breath is what keeps us in the here and now, hence it is only natural that the resultant pleasantness should be related to its experience. This pleasant feeling tone is strengthened by the previous establishment of the happiness of blamelessness through moral conduct. The *Kandaraka-sutta*'s description of successive types of happiness, cultivated with different aspects of the gradual path, speaks of an immaculate happiness, *abyāsekasukha*, that arises as the outcome of sense restraint (MN 51; Anālayo 2003b: 167 and 2012b: 161). Such happiness can be tapped through simply being with mindfulness established in the here and now.

With the momentum of the previous practices and based on the deep relaxation brought about by the preceding step of calming bodily activity, at the present juncture joy can often arise quite spontaneously, at least in a subtle form. All that is required is to recognize even rather delicate manifestations of joy. Such recognition fulfils the present step and at the same time tends to strengthen the joy that has arisen.

If needed, at times a brief recollection of our wholesome moral conduct can be used as an aid to encourage joy.

Alternatively, as mentioned above, recollection of our motivation or of our practice as following in the Buddha's footsteps can serve the same purpose. Another possible tool is to formulate an aspiration of the type: "may joy arise", which is best done as if inviting joy into the mind in a reverential manner. Having formulated such an aspiration, we then simply remain receptively open to whatever happens, allowing sufficient room within the mind for joy to manifest in whatever form it may arise.

Tension or else becoming distracted will prevent joy from arising. This in turn means that, if we have difficulty arousing joy, we might need to go back to the previous steps leading up to calming bodily activity and make sure that any tension or mental agitation is really left behind. In addition, it would also be good to make sure that we are not generating tension anew by way of expectation, almost as if we are trying to force joy to arise. Just realizing that there is such tension and relaxing it will often suffice for joy to arise.

HAPPINESS

With increasing calmness of the mind, the experience of joy tends to turn into the more tranquil experience of happiness. The mind experiences inner contentment and is able to let go of the (at least at times) exhilarating experience of joy and settles on the peacefulness of happiness within.

If for some reason joy has not manifested at all, proceeding to experience at least happiness can simply take the form of cultivating contentment with the present situation just as it is. Arousing the happiness of contentment in this way can suffice for continuing with the practice of the ensuing steps. Sooner or later on subsequent occasions of proceeding through the sixteen steps, some degree of joy will manifest.

The cultivation of contentment is crucial for successful meditation practice. Much of mental restlessness that prevents the mind becoming calm is due to a lack of contentment with what is. Be it wanting more pleasant experiences or wanting to push away what is unpleasant, the resultant agitation and its unsettling repercussions on the condition of our mind can be countered by adopting an attitude of contentment. This does not mean giving up all aspirations and no longer putting in any effort. It only means that our wholehearted dedication to the practice comes in conjunction with an attitude of contentment that is independent of how quickly results of our practice manifest.

The steps of experiencing joy and happiness can at times be related more closely to the noting of inhalations and exhalations. This can take the form of giving more emphasis to what fuels and strengthens either joy or happiness during the inhalation, followed by more emphasis on just relaxing and dwelling in the condition of either joy or happiness during the exhalation.

The progression from joy to happiness as such reflects a gradual deepening of mental tranquillity. At the same time, in keeping with the basic notion of a conjunction of tranquillity and insight as relevant to the practice of mindfulness of breathing throughout, an insight-related dimension can also be discerned in this progression. It is precisely through diminishing our attachment to the more intense joy that happiness can manifest. In other words, the progression here requires at least some lessening of craving and some degree of dispassion.

THE FOUR NOBLE TRUTHS

Craving is of course a central aspect of the second noble truth. To some degree the meditative progression of mindfulness of breathing can in fact be related to the whole teaching on the four noble truths. Admittedly, a correlation between the four noble truths and the four *satipaṭṭhāna*s is more apparent with the contemplations described in the *Satipaṭṭhāna-sutta* (Anālayo 2018d: 206f). This is not surprising, since the instructions in the *Satipaṭṭhāna-sutta* reflect considerably more emphasis on the characteristic of *dukkha* compared to the instructions in the *Ānāpānasati-sutta*. Nevertheless, an application of the four noble truths to the sixteen steps of mindfulness of breathing is also possible. Such an application can help to bring out some aspects of the practice and its potential.

Insight into the first truth of *dukkha* could be related to the last step of the body-contemplation tetrad, calming bodily activity, which then leads over to the joy experienced at the outset of the present tetrad on contemplation of feeling tone. Leaving behind the common assumption that happiness requires sensual indulgence and bodily activity, insight into the ultimately unsatisfactory nature of such pursuits makes it clear that the stilling of the body leads to a more profound and peaceful experience of joy and happiness than the agitation of sensuality could ever yield. Taking the same reflection further, however subtle the breath might have become, if it were to become still more refined, we would be even more calm and at ease. This reveals that, in the final count, having to breathe, however subtly, is still within the realm of *dukkha*. Although this usually becomes evident only when we are sick or have respiratory problems, closer inspection exposes the fact that the same applies even to normal breathing when bodily activity has become calm.

As already mentioned, the second truth concerning the role of craving could then be related to the progression from joy to happiness. Unless we are willing to relinquish the more exhilarating and intense joy, it will not be possible to progress to the more peaceful and calm happiness. The same thrust of diminishing attachment continues with the next step of practice, which requires stepping back, as it were, from being immersed in joy and happiness, in order to be able to discern mental activity. Even attachment to wholesome types of happiness needs to be left behind at this point.

Before turning to the practical implications of this next step, however, the correlation with the four noble truths needs to be completed. In the case of the next tetrad on contemplation of the mind, this correlation can be understood in the same way as in the *Satipaṭṭhāna-sutta*, in that the temporary experience of the mind free from the hindrances and distracting thought activities can give us a foretaste of the final goal. This becomes particularly prominent with the last step in the third tetrad, when practice builds up to "liberating the mind".

The fourth truth of the path then correlates with a series of insight perspectives in the fourth tetrad on contemplation of dharmas, which proceed from impermanence to dispassion, cessation, and letting go. The last three closely mirror the insight themes required to bring the awakening factors to fruition, a topic to which I return in a subsequent chapter.

In sum, although clearly not as evident as in the case of the exercises found in the *Satipaṭṭhāna-sutta*, the progression through the four tetrads in the *Ānāpānasati-sutta* can also be related to the four noble truths.

MENTAL ACTIVITY

The reference to "mental activity" in the third step of the present tetrad on contemplation of feeling tone corresponds to the Pāli term *cittasaṅkhāra*. The term *saṅkhāra* can have a range of meanings (Anālayo 2006b). In its most general sense, it stands for anything that is conditioned. Alternatively it can carry a more specific meaning, standing in particular for intention or volition.

In the context of a discussion leading up to the topic of the cessation of perception and feeling tone, the *Cūḷavedalla-sutta* defines the term *cittasaṅkhāra* as comprising feeling tones and perceptions (MN 44; see also Paṭis I 188). On this reading, the manifestations of mental activity that need to be experienced (and then calmed with the next step) are feeling tones (*vedanā*) and perceptions (*saññā*). However, the parallels to the *Cūḷavedalla-sutta* differ in their definition (Anālayo 2011: 282). From their perspective, mental activity rather stands for perceptions and intentions (*cetanā*).

Combining the definitions of mental activity found in the *Cūḷavedalla-sutta* and its parallels respectively, the task could be considered as requiring us to keep an eye out for those feeling tones, perceptions, and intentions that stand a chance of triggering an increase of mental activity. Such feeling tones, perceptions, and intentions run counter to the general thrust towards gradually deepening mental tranquillity that is characteristic of the present tetrad on contemplation of feeling tone. For this reason, they need to be noticed (and then allowed to become calm).

STEPPING BACK

Actual practice of the third step of experiencing mental activity can begin by discerning that the shift from joy to happiness involved a shift from a comparatively more active mental condition to a less active one. As already mentioned above, this required a stepping back, as it were, from being immersed in the joy.

Such stepping back exemplifies a general characteristic of the early Buddhist attitude towards deeper levels of concentration. Instead of reifying these in one way or another, this attitude is concerned with non-attachment, viewing even intense bliss and deep concentration from the perspective of their conditionality. The understanding is that, on having aroused such and such factors, such and such a level of concentration can come to be.

Such a non-attached attitude can be trained with the present step. This requires moving from being fully immersed in the experience of whatever degree of joy and happiness has manifested to stepping back and discerning the type of mental activity whose calming will lead onwards to even deeper tranquillity of the mind.

In practical terms, the stepping back to be implemented here is comparable to shifting from seeing to being aware of seeing. We could even experiment with this right now, while reading these lines. We might just be reading along, taking in whatever information we find relevant, or else we might be reading (and taking in information) while being aware of the fact that we are reading. The perceptive activity continues as earlier, but it comes in the company of a form of meta-awareness that knows what is taking place rather than being just fully immersed in it.

Be it seeing or any other perceptual activity, a particularly helpful tool for shifting to such meta-awareness is mindfulness of the whole body. This provides stability and also fosters some degree of turning inwards as opposed to being concerned entirely with what happens outside, in the external world. Turning inwards or stepping back in this way, we bring the mind home, so to speak.

Having experimented with such stepping back, it becomes easier to proceed from experiencing happiness to being aware of the perception of happiness. From that we can then proceed to awareness of feeling tones, perceptions, and intentions in general, in whatever way these arise at this stage of practice, viewing them as mere manifestations of mental activity in which we do not need to get actively involved. Understood in this way, the present step offers a training ground in the ability to remain passively at ease in the midst of activity, in finding an observational vantage point of stillness that allows us to remain at peace and unshaken by whatever takes place in the mind.

FEELING TONE

The verb used for this step, as well as the preceding two steps, is the same term *paṭisaṃvedeti*, "to experience". Elsewhere in the sixteen-step scheme this verb occurs only for the third step in the previous body-contemplation tetrad, which requires us "to experience" the whole body, and in the first step in the next tetrad on contemplation of the mind, which instructs us "to experience" the mind. The verb itself combines the prefixes *paṭi-* and *saṃ-* with *vedeti*, of which the last is etymologically closely related to *vedanā*. It seems fair to take the use of the same verb for the present triad of steps, covering joy, happiness, and mental activity, to convey the same sense of a felt form of experiencing.

In fact the entire tetrad is concerned with contemplation of feeling tone. This in turn makes it commendable, from a practical viewpoint, to keep an eye in particular on the dimension of the feeling tone of whatever mental activity is experienced, on its affective tonality. In other words, from *feeling* joy and *feeling* happiness the progression to the present step can lead to a clear noting of the *feeling* tone of mental activity.

This perspective has an immediate practical advantage, since it offers a convenient access point for being aware of mental activity. The simplicity of feeling tone, compared to the complexity of other aspects of mental activities, makes it easier to observe without getting carried away. The affective dimension of mental activity can become an expedient handle for mindful investigation to get a secure hold on present-moment experience without becoming involved in it. A skilful way to go about this involves the subtle pleasant feeling tone of being in the present moment. This is something we have been cultivating from the outset of mindfulness of breathing and which now, due to the previous experience of joy and happiness, is naturally present as the tone of the present moment.

What can happen with the present third step in this tetrad on contemplation of feeling tones is somewhat comparable to what happened with the third step in the previous tetrad on body contemplation, which concerned experiencing the whole body. In our earlier practice we already attended to the breath during the preliminary practice, and with the first two steps of the body-contemplation tetrad the breath became the focus of our attention. From being at the centre of attention in the form of long and short breaths for the duration of these two steps, the breath then shifted to our peripheral awareness. This served as an aid and reference point to stabilize the mind and at the same time freed up mental space to allow other aspects of our meditative experience to become the main object of attention, namely the whole body with the third step.

Similarly, since the preliminary practice we have been giving attention to the subtle pleasant feeling tone of being in the present moment. With the first two steps of the present tetrad on contemplation of feeling tone, such pleasant feeling tone became the central object of our attention in the form of the experience of joy and happiness. Having explored these for the duration of these two steps, now pleasant feeling tone can also come to be more in our peripheral awareness. By joining the pleasant feeling tone of being in the present moment to the breath in this way, both can be together in peripheral awareness and serve in conjunction as aids and reference points to stabilize the mind.

The shift of pleasant feeling tone to our peripheral awareness in a way frees up mental space to allow mental activity in general to become the main object of our attention. With pleasant feeling tone remaining in the background of our experience, through being held in peripheral awareness, all we need to do while watching mental activity is to keep an eye on that pleasant feeling tone, that is, on the basic affective flavour of our experience. If the subtle pleasant feeling tone should get lost, we can be fairly sure that we are about to get carried away. Instead of just watching the game of the mind, we are about to join in and become active participants. Simply noting this can often suffice to help us regain the vantage point of uninvolved observation.

Practising in this way sooner or later leads to a crucial insight. This is the realization that meditation does not invariably require a thought-free mind. Instead, with the present step we can learn to be aware while thought activity continues. Once this has become a matter of personal experience, our meditation practice becomes relieved from the burden of trying to force the mind to be still so that we can finally become real meditators. Instead, almost like a mother who is watching her children play without sensing any need to become part of the game, we can be at ease watching the frolics of the mind without getting involved in them.

When we let go of the strain and tension created by (often vain) attempts to force the mind to be still and simply remain aware of mental activity, as a result the mind tends to become more and more calm on its own. This is precisely the topic of the next step, the calming of mental activity.

CALMING MENTAL ACTIVITY

The mental activity that has been discerned clearly with the previous step can now be allowed to settle down naturally. Here "calming mental activity" does not mean that all types of mental activities have to be entirely tranquillized. Without the presence of any feeling tones and perceptions it would not be possible to continue the practice any further. The distinction between inhalations and exhalations relies on being aware of feeling tones and perceptions, a distinction relevant throughout the remaining steps. The target of practice at the present juncture is only to calm down mental activity to such a degree that we are able to experience the mind itself, which is the first step in the ensuing tetrad on contemplation of the mind.

The present step could be illustrated with a description given in the *Vitakkasaṇṭhāna-sutta* (MN 20; Anālayo 2003b: 175f and 2013b:

152f). In its original context the description is concerned with unwholesome thought processes; in fact the discourse presents modalities of right effort rather than of the practice of *satipaṭṭhāna*. Nevertheless, the imagery used in the *Vitakkasaṇṭhāna-sutta* to explain one of its approaches for overcoming persistent unwholesome thoughts can be taken out of its original context and employed to illustrate the present step. The discourse describes a person engaged in walking who realizes that there is actually no need to continue walking and then decides to stand still, thereby adopting a more relaxed and comfortable posture. The same type of realization leads from standing to sitting and eventually to lying down. In this way more active and comparatively grosser bodily postures are replaced by progressively less active and more comfortable bodily postures.

The same takes place, in a way, when the experience of mental activity leads over to the less active and more comfortable mental posture, if it can be called such, of allowing a calming of whatever is happening in the mind. All it takes is being aware of mental activity without getting involved in it and things naturally tend to become more tranquil.

The ability to allow a calming of mental activity relies on the previous practices. In particular the blamelessness of ethical conduct makes a substantial contribution at this juncture. Another factor is the diminishing of attachment, which enables letting go of both the thinking process and our personal stake in being mentally active. By relating these to the continuous experience of the inhalations and exhalations as a reference point held in peripheral awareness and by making intelligent use of the potential of joy and happiness, the present tetrad builds up to a stage of practice where mental activity can become effortlessly still.

This exemplifies a potential regularly associated in the discourses with mindfulness of breathing, namely the stilling of thoughts (see below pp. 164 and 186). Such potential is hardly evident with practice of only the first tetrad on contemplation of the body. Although with the third and fourth step of this first tetrad the breath is kept in peripheral awareness, this mode of practice really acquires its full potential only when the bland experience of the breath has led via joy and happiness to experiencing and then calming mental activity. It is with the present tetrad that it indeed becomes readily apparent how mindfulness of breathing can offer substantial aid in overcoming distracting thoughts.

The calming of mental activity that can be achieved in this way could be illustrated with the example of coffee, which in some cultures is prepared in such a way that the ground coffee beans are just allowed to sink to the bottom (rather than being filtered out).

Similarly, whatever could trigger an increase of mental activity can just be allowed to sink to the ground and no longer disturb the clarity of the mind. In this way, the present step can either result in an experience of the still mind, or else, if for whatever reason the mind should not become completely calm, at least a reduction of mental activity will be possible.

Attention could then be directed to discerning the subtle pleasant feeling tone resulting from the stillness of the mind that has become fully settled in the present moment. In this way the emphasis on felt experience, evident in the previous three steps, can continue and serve as a practical expression of the correspondence of the present tetrad to contemplation of feeling tone.

Similarly to the experience of joy and happiness, the progression to calming mental activity comes with a strong flavour of tranquillity. Although entry into absorption is not mentioned explicitly in the *Ānāpānasati-sutta*, the present tetrad naturally prepares for and inclines towards deepening concentration. The same holds even more so for the next tetrad on contemplation of the mind, whose completion is perhaps the most natural entry-door into actual absorption attainment, from the viewpoint of the scheme of sixteen steps.

INSIGHT

At the same time, the present tetrad on contemplation of feeling tone can also make a contribution to the cultivation of insight into the three characteristics of impermanence, *dukkha*, and not-self. Awareness of impermanence is kept up throughout this (and any other) tetrad, as each step comes in combination with peripheral awareness of the constant alternation between inhalations and exhalations. The characteristic of *dukkha* is less prominent throughout, but insight into the lack of lasting satisfaction inherent in the joy experienced with the first step is what facilitates a smooth progression to the experience of happiness with the second step. The same lessening of attachment applied to happiness then helps us to step back and discern mental activity with the third step.

Such an ability to step back relates to some degree to growing insight into emptiness, inasmuch as a letting go of our identification with first joy and then happiness is required. The same diminishing of identification becomes even more prominent with the last step in the present tetrad, as the calming of mental activity requires us to let go of what we invest much of our sense of identity in: our thoughts, reflections, memories, intentions, and plans. In the ordinary world these make up much of who we think we are and how we present ourselves to others. Yet, at the present juncture we are to drop these like dregs or coffee grounds, considering them as something that, for the time being, is no longer of any real use for us and could best be allowed to sink down to the ground.

Understood in this way, the present tetrad of practice can be seen to combine a prominent concern with the cultivation of deepening mental tranquillity with an implicit pointer at some degree of insight.

The corresponding contemplation of feeling tones in the *Satipaṭṭhāna-sutta* requires recognizing the three feeling tones (pleasant, unpleasant, and neutral) as well as distinguishing these into worldly and unworldly occurrences. A central insight to be gained through such practice is the conditionality of feeling tones, the degree to which their affective input leads to subsequent reactions.

In the case of the present progression of practice, the *Ānāpānasati-sutta* again seems to build on what the *Satipaṭṭhāna-sutta* inculcates. From having learned to discern the conditionality of feeling tones through practice according to the *Satipaṭṭhāna-sutta*, with the present tetrad of mindfulness of breathing we are putting this conditionality to good use. This takes place through the intentional arousing of joy and happiness, which serve as conditions for calming mental activity.

WALKING MEDITATION

During walking meditation, we can implement the gist of the step of experiencing mental activity, in the sense of directing mindfulness to knowing what is going on in the mind while we are walking. The skilful use of the conditionality of pleasant feeling tones can also accompany us at such times. With an eventual calming of mental activity, we become able to walk with a still mind, with a mind that is free from the type of thought activity that would cause a loss of the happiness of remaining in the here and now.

The centring power of being mindful of the breaths, together with cultivating the natural rewards of joy and happiness that keep the mind interested in the meditation topic, can also be related to other meditation practices. Keeping the breath in peripheral awareness while engaging with some meditation topic or other, in conjunction with the wholesome joy of being in the present moment, can have a remarkable impact on our ability to prevent distraction and sustain continuity with a range of other meditation practices.

SUMMARY

Based on the previous practice up to calming bodily activity as the final step in the preceding body-contemplation tetrad, the arising of joy can be experienced as the first step in the present tetrad on contemplation of feeling tones. As the mind becomes increasingly calm, the experience of joy turns into the happiness of a mind inwardly contented and tranquil.

Just as we stepped back from being immersed in joy to experience happiness, so we step back further to become aware of mental activity in general, with a particular focus on noting what could lead to its increase and keeping an eye on the feeling tone of the present moment. Learning to maintain awareness of thought processes builds the foundation for mental activity to calm down on its own and the mind eventually becomes naturally tranquil and still.

IV

CONTEMPLATION OF THE MIND

With the conclusion of the third tetrad on contemplation of the mind, in the way described here, the torso of the condor becomes transparent. The transparency of the condor's torso signifies that the sense of an 'I' has gone into abeyance. Due to the increasing transparency of the condor, the changing scenery becomes still more visible, reflecting the increasingly comprehensive vision of impermanence due to relinquishing all self-notions.

The third tetrad of mindfulness of breathing, which corresponds to the *satipaṭṭhāna* of contemplating the mind, proceeds in the following manner in the *Ānāpānasati-sutta* (MN 118):

> One trains: 'experiencing the mind I shall breathe in'; one trains: 'experiencing the mind I shall breathe out.' One trains: 'gladdening the mind I shall breathe in'; one trains: 'gladdening the mind I shall breathe out.' One trains: 'concentrating the mind I shall breathe in'; one trains: 'concentrating the mind I shall breathe out.' One trains: 'liberating the mind I shall breathe in'; one trains: 'liberating the mind I shall breathe out.'

Topics to be discussed in relation to this instruction are "experiencing the mind", the arising of "gladness" and "concentration", and implications of the reference to "liberating" the mind.

THE MIND

In the instructions translated above, "mind" renders the Pāli term *citta*. In the early discourses, *citta* stands predominantly for our subjective mental state. The significance of *citta* is aptly conveyed by its translation into Chinese, which involves a character that represents the "heart". As evident from the listing of different types of *citta*s in the *Satipaṭṭhāna-sutta*, such mental states could be with or without a defilement (like anger), or else concentrated or not concentrated, for example.

Another Pāli term for the mind is *manas*, which stands more for the intellective dimension of subjective experience. As the sixth sense, *manas* stands on a par with the five physical senses (eyes, ears, nose, tongue, and body) as an avenue of experience. Alternatively, *manas* serves as the third door of action, where it comes together with bodily and verbal forms of activity.

Yet another relevant Pāli term is *viññāṇa*, usually translated as "consciousness". In its general usage, *viññāṇa* stands for the quality of knowing that takes in information through any of the six sense-doors (including *manas*). In addition, *viññāṇa* also has a central role in relation to continuity during life and from one life to another (Anālayo 2018c: 9–14). In this role, *viññāṇa* stands in a reciprocal conditioning relationship with name-and-form (Anālayo 2015a: 106–110).

Although the instructions in the *Ānāpānasati-sutta* employ only the term *citta*, in its explanation of the present step of practice the *Paṭisambhidāmagga* brings in a series of different terms for the mind, including *manas* and *viññāṇa* (as well as *hadaya*, the "heart"). In the case of *viññāṇa*, the *Paṭisambhidāmagga* mentions not only consciousness as such, but also the aggregate (*khandha*) of consciousness and the element (*dhātu*) of consciousness (Paṭis I 190). From the viewpoint of the *Paṭisambhidāmagga*, "experiencing the mind" as the first step in the present tetrad concerns a discernment of mind in its different modalities, including consciousness. Elsewhere in the discourses, *citta* and *viññāṇa* can indeed at times function as near synonyms (Anālayo 2011: 791n166).

THE NATURE OF THE MIND

From a practical perspective, with the successful calming of mental activity in the previous step it becomes now possible to have a direct experience of mind as such, when it is in an unperturbed condition, resting in itself and aware of the breath. In this way, the present step of mindfulness of breathing can be related to a concern with the experience of the "nature" of the mind, prevalent in a range of practice traditions (Anālayo 2017d).

These practice traditions tend to employ a variety of methods and approaches in order to stimulate a recognition of the nature of the mind. In the tradition of the "Great Perfection" (*rdzogs chen*), this can take the form of "pointing out" instructions given by an accomplished master to students. Among Chán traditions there is an approach nowadays best known by the Japanese term *kōan*. This approach employs somewhat cryptic sayings or enigmatic statements that are to be contemplated in such a way that eventually, with the suspension of thought activity, a realization of the nature of the mind takes place. Alternatively, stilling of mental activity through silent sitting is also promoted in some Chán traditions as capable of leading to such an experience.

In the present context of mindfulness of breathing, as described in the early Buddhist discourses, a suspension of thought activity has been brought about through the previous steps of practice. This holds in particular for the last two steps of the second tetrad on contemplation of feeling tones. With thoughts and mental activity stilled, mind as such can be experienced.

Such experiencing of the mind could be illustrated with the example of reading, already employed in the previous chapter. A first step in such experimenting requires that we just stay with awareness at the sense-door (in this case the eye) and become aware of the fact that we are reading. Based on this first step of staying at the sense-door of the eye, a further step can be taken to arrive at the mind itself. Instead of staying at the eye, awareness now follows the information that is read inside, as it were, where it is being known by the mind. In the present case this is eye-consciousness.

In this way it becomes possible to pay attention to each of the three dimensions of sense experience described regularly in the discourses: the sense, its object, and the corresponding consciousness. In the case of seeing, the standard description points out that eye-consciousness arises in dependence on the eye and visual objects. By countering the usual tendency to be just absorbed in what is being seen, awareness stays first with the eye itself, and next turns to eye-consciousness. Turning inside in this way can lead to a direct experience of consciousness.

The task here is not to find a specific location where consciousness manifests, as we might physically locate the visual object (or the eye that sees the object). Instead, the point is to allow the movement inwards to lead to an encounter with the mind as such, that which knows what is being read.

A comparable experience can take place with the first step of the present tetrad on mind contemplation, when we train ourselves to experience the mind that knows the breaths. Having previously experimented with turning inwards in such a way will make it easier to become aware of that which knows inhalations and exhalations, a bare knowing which, due to the calming of mental activity, has become more easily discernible.

Turning to the knowing of the alternation between inhalations and exhalations is particularly apt for discerning the nature of the mind, as it directly relates the experience of the mind to the fact of impermanence. The breath being impermanent, the mind that knows the breath must also be impermanent. If the knowing mind were permanent, it could not be cognizing changes in an object like the breath. The very fact that it is possible for us to follow continually the alternations between inhalations and exhalations, and even discern changes occurring within an inhalation or an exhalation, makes it clear that our knowing faculty must also be changing and cannot be some sort of a permanent entity. In spite of the tranquil nature of the mind as such that manifests at this juncture of practice, and in spite of the fact that the ability to know is continuously present in all our experiences, in the end it is nevertheless just a flow, a process of knowing.

This sets the appropriate context for the experience of the mind as the first step in the present tetrad of mindfulness of breathing. The very approach used for its recognition is directly conjoined to impermanence. Such conjoining marks a significant contrast to some later practice traditions concerned with recognition of the nature of the mind, where at times a tendency to reification manifests, even to the extent of positing the mind as an unchanging and permanent agent in experience. Such a position is not compatible with early Buddhist thought, where mind or consciousness is seen as a changing process, subject to causes and conditions. In this way, the present step enables placing the powerful experience of the mind as such within its proper context by ensuring that its impermanent nature is not lost sight of.

TURNING INWARDS

The experience of the mind as such with the present step of practice relies in particular on the two preceding steps of experiencing mental activity and calming it. As mentioned in the previous chapter, experiencing mental activity requires taking a step back, as it were, in order to shift from the experience of happiness to discerning mental activity. The present step requires a further stepping back of the same type, as from discerning and calming mental activity we move even further inwards towards discerning the mind itself.

The progression through these three steps could be illustrated with the example of being in the ocean (and having some type of equipment that enables us to continue breathing even when under water). Experiencing mental activity is similar to floating on the surface of the ocean, experiencing its waves without struggling against them. Calming mental activity corresponds to allowing ourselves to sink down deep into the water, where no more waves are felt. Experiencing the mind in turn finds illustration in eventually reaching the bottom of the ocean.

With the degree of inner tranquillity established by calming mental activity, mind as such can be directly apprehended. Once it is no longer covered by its usual overlay of thoughts and associations (let alone coloured and clouded by the hindrances or other defilements), with the present step mind can be apperceived in a condition of bareness, perhaps even nakedness. At times, a sense of awe can accompany such a direct encounter with the mind. As long as this does not lead to any reification of the mind, such a sense of awe can serve as a skilful means to deepen the experience.

Turning to the mind itself concords with the general thrust of contemplation of the mind in the *Satipaṭṭhāna-sutta*, where recognizing the different mental states listed in the instructions requires an inward monitoring in order to check the current condition of the mind. Instead of the ingrained tendency to give all our attention to what is happening on the outside, the basic requirement for contemplation of the mind is to turn inwards and note how the mind reacts to whatever is happening (Anālayo 2018d: 127). The more this tendency is strengthened, the easier it will be to become aware of the condition of the mind in any situation, even in the most challenging circumstances.

For the different steps of the present tetrad on contemplation of the mind, this same turning inwards is a central element. This holds also if the present tetrad is used as a launching pad into absorption attainment, which can most conveniently be done with the last step of liberating the mind. I will explore the topic of entry into absorption below, when discussing this step.

From the viewpoint of the cultivation of insight, apperceiving the mind as such has considerable potential as a pointer to its empty nature. This is an approach that can easily be implemented during walking meditation and other daily activities, a topic to which I return in more detail at the end of this chapter. All that is required is to stay with the basic quality of knowing instead of allowing ourselves to be carried away by activity. The principal rule is to remain receptively aware instead of becoming mentally active. Keeping in mind that this quality of tranquil knowing is impermanent ensures that the mind as such will not be reified into being a permanent entity. Practising in this way can lead to a growing appreciation of the empty nature of subjective experience.

GLADNESS AND CONCENTRATION

Once the mind rests in itself, this naturally leads to the arising of gladness. In a way gladness (as well as becoming concentrated) is already a facet of the very experience of the mind as such, so that the two ensuing steps can be considered as fleshing out with additional detail what is already implicit in the first step. In this respect, the present tetrad differs from the preceding two tetrads on contemplation of body and feeling tones, which involve a pattern of one step (the first and the third) introducing a particular theme or practice, followed by its calming or relaxing in the ensuing step (the second and the fourth). This can be illustrated by relating the respective topics (on the left side) to the corresponding steps (on the right side) for each of the tetrads under discussion.

In this way, the topic of the length of the breath, introduced with long breaths (1), leads to the comparatively calmer short breaths (2). Similarly, introducing the whole body (3) leads to calming its activity (4). Again, pleasant mental states are introduced with joy (5), leading on to the comparatively calmer happiness (6). In the same vein, mental activity is first introduced (7) and then calmed (8).

First Tetrad (Contemplation of the Body):

Topics:	**Steps:**
length of breath:	1) understand it to be long → 2) understand it to be short
body:	3) experience whole of it → 4) calm its activity

Second Tetrad (Contemplation of Feeling Tones):

Topics:	**Steps:**
pleasant mental states:	5) experience joyful state → 6) experience happy state
mental activity:	7) experience it → 8) calm it

In the present tetrad on contemplation of the mind, however, the trajectory instead leads from the first to the fourth, via two steps that take up aspects of the first step (the same basic pattern continues with the next tetrad on contemplation of dharmas). In this way, in the present tetrad all four steps relate to a single topic only.

Third Tetrad (Contemplation of the Mind):

Topic:	**Steps:**
Mind:	9) experience it → 10) gladden it → 11) concentrate it → 12) liberate it

The reference to "gladdening" (10), found in the step under discussion of the mind-contemplation tetrad, employs the verb *abhippamodati*, which is closely related to *pāmojja/pāmujja*, "gladness". Gladness belongs to the same type of mental tonality as joy and happiness. In other passages, gladness often serves as the condition for joy to arise, which then leads on to happiness. In the present context, however, gladness occurs at a stage subsequent to the occurrence of joy and happiness, which already came up with the first and second steps of the preceding tetrad on contemplation of feeling tones. The decisive difference from the previously arisen joy and happiness appears to be that gladness arises at the present juncture of practice after mental activities have been calmed; it manifests based on the experience of the mind as such.

According to the *Paṭisambhidāmagga*, with this step of mindfulness of breathing gladness arises on seeing the unification of the mind that is free from distraction (Paṭis I 190). In this way, whereas joy (5) and happiness (6) functioned in the previous tetrad on contemplation of feeling tones as conditions for calming mental activity and thereby led to the absence of any distraction, the arising of gladness (10) is the fruition of the calmness brought about by precisely this meditative progression. This accords with the suggestion made above that the gladness manifesting now is in a way a dimension of the experience of the mind as such. In practical terms, the present step involves a shifting of attention to this aspect of gladness as a dimension already inherent in the previous step in a subtle form. Such a shift of attention will lead to an intensification of that gladness.

The gladness experienced in the present tetrad on contemplation of the mind is more profound and still than the joy and happiness of the previous tetrad concerned with feeling tones. In fact the term used is not just *pamodati*, but *abhippamodati*, with the addition of the prefix *abhi-* that in Pāli can convey a nuance of intensification or superiority. The use of *abhippamodati* appears to be quite specific to the present context and could thus be expressing the fact that the gladness arising at this juncture of mindfulness of breathing is different from gladness in other contexts, which do not employ the prefix *abhi-*. The "superior" gladness, if we may call it such, that manifests now is indeed more refined than the earlier joy and happiness. With mental activity gone into abeyance, the gladness experienced is quite profound; it in a way touches us deep within.

By way of illustration, we might imagine a swiftly flowing rivulet as an exemplification of the joy experienced with the first step of the previous tetrad on contemplation of feeling tones. Suppose at some point this rivulet enters a large lake. The flowing into the lake illustrates the happiness of the second step of the tetrad on contemplation of feeling tones. There is still some motion, but it is no longer as swift and lively as earlier. Once the water has settled in the midst of the lake and become quiet, this then represents the gladdening of the mind with the second step of the third tetrad on contemplation of the mind.

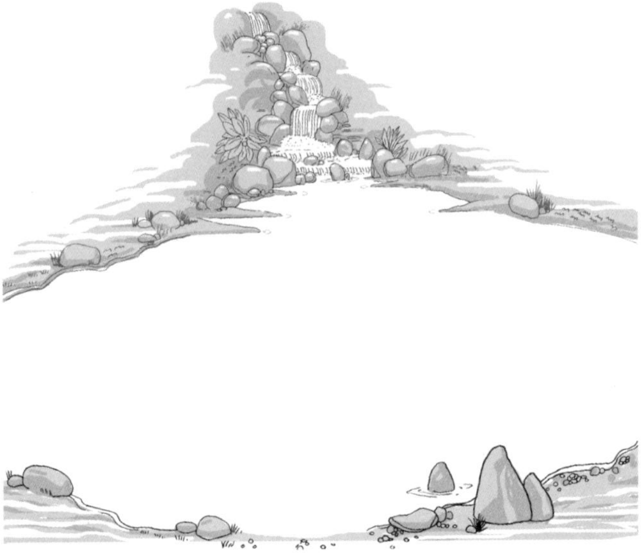

The image is not meant to convey the idea that these are static conditions that invariably manifest in the same manner. Progressing through the sixteen steps repeatedly will result in different experiences of joy, for example, or of happiness or gladness.

The water simile only aims to illustrate how these three states relate to each other. Joy, happiness, and gladness are just different modalities of a basically positive mental condition conjoined with pleasant feeling tones, all of which can be illustrated with the example of water. The joy is more active, the happiness is in comparison quieter, and the gladdening of the mind more profoundly still, in line with the general shift from mental activities in the previous tetrad to the mind as such in the present tetrad. Over the course of sustained meditative training, each of these three will mature and incline the mind ever more to a deep inner sense of mental composure.

CONCENTRATION

A mind that is glad and aware of itself will of its own accord become concentrated. The trajectory here reflects a natural progression described in the discourses in relation to the awakening factors, where tranquillity leads to happiness, which in turn results in concentration (see below p. 208 and Anālayo 2013b: 216). The basic dynamic underlying this progression finds application twice during progress through the steps of mindfulness of breathing. The fourth step of calming bodily activity (as one dimension of tranquillity) leads on to joy and happiness as the first two steps in the second tetrad on contemplation of feeling tones. This second tetrad ends with calming mental activity, which at the same time completes the cultivation of tranquillity (by complementing the bodily tranquillity achieved earlier). This then leads (via experiencing the mind) to gladness and concentration.

This doubling up strengthens the ability of the scheme of mindfulness of breathing to lead into deep concentration. It also explains why, once joy and happiness have already been aroused with the previous tetrad on contemplation of feeling tones, at the present juncture gladness is brought in, namely to lead over to concentration. This second application of the same basic dynamics takes place at a deeper level of the mind than earlier during the previous tetrad on contemplation of feeling tones. The two in combination can result in profound concentration indeed.

Here the term "concentration" does not refer to a narrow focus that excludes anything that does not fit into the circumscribed passageway of its restricted field of attention (see also below p. 191 n. 46). Instead, in the way of practice described here, the cultivation of "concentration" carries more a flavour of a natural converging, a coming together in an effortless unification of the mind that rests within itself, composed and at ease. It is as if the whole of subjective experience is held in a loving and caring embrace such that it becomes completely unified, with no trace of its usual fragmentation left. At this juncture, then, the whole-body awareness practised throughout becomes a whole-body-and-whole-mind experience.

The previous steps of the present tetrad on contemplation of the mind already involve a lessening of control, and this will become even more prominent with its last step, "liberating the mind". Keeping this basic dynamic in mind helps to steer clear of any attempt to force concentration, however subtly, by way of imposing control. Instead, at least at the present juncture of practice, concentration is very much the result of non-interference, of giving up the sense of being in control and thereby allowing the progression of practice to result in the mind becoming effortlessly composed and unified, settled within and at ease.

LIBERATING THE MIND

The reference to "liberating" the mind is based on the Pāli causative verb *vimoceti*, which conveys the sense of causing something/someone to become liberated or free. The noun *vimutti*, "liberation", holds different meanings in the Pāli discourses (Anālayo 2009a). The term "liberation of the mind", *cetovimutti*, used on its own, can refer to temporary freedom of the mind from the hindrances. Such liberation relates to the cultivation of tranquillity, in particular the attainment of absorption.

Liberation of the mind is also possible at levels of concentration falling short of absorption, such as when cultivating the *brahmavihāras*. Here liberation takes place by leaving behind any confines, resulting in the boundless experience of a *brahmavihāra* (Anālayo 2015a: 54–63). Such boundless experience is for the time being liberated from its respective opposite. In the case of *mettā*, for example, the mind is temporarily liberated from ill-will. Compassion becomes a liberation of the mind from harming, sympathetic joy from discontent, and equanimity from passion (and aversion). In all these cases, liberation is not a final and irreversible condition. The roots of unwholesomeness are still in the mind, yet for the time being these do not manifest and the mind is temporarily free from them.

"Liberation by wisdom", *paññāvimutti*, stands for the irreversible type of freedom reached by progressing through the four stages of awakening recognized in early Buddhist thought. This type of freedom is irreversible because certain fetters are abandoned for good and have no scope to manifest again. With such liberation by wisdom, the freed condition of the mind has in turn become unshakeable. Liberating the mind from defilements and fetters is the supreme and overarching goal in early Buddhist thought.

In this way, the interrelation between tranquillity and insight is evident even in the very concept of liberation. Liberations of the tranquillity type are not in themselves the final goal of practice, as they do not liberate the mind once and for all from defilements (Anālayo 2017b: 109–123 and 163–175). Nevertheless, they deserve to be reckoned as types of liberation. They do liberate, even if only temporarily, and are for this very reason an integral part of the path to final liberation.

The different nuances carried by the term *vimutti*, as used in the Pāli discourses, leave considerable room for interpreting the injunction to liberate the mind in the final step of the third tetrad on contemplation of the mind. As mentioned briefly in the previous chapter, when cultivating mindfulness of breathing the present step seems the most natural choice for entering into absorption, which requires that the mind be completely *liberated* from even the slightest trace of any hindrance.

Although the *Ānāpānasati-sutta* does not explicitly mention absorption in its actual instructions, the trajectory of deepening mental tranquillity that underlies the previous and the present tetrad naturally leads to a point where the mind can be allowed to enter absorption naturally. In what follows I will explore this option, on the understanding that, similar to my discussion of some of the preliminaries to mindfulness of breathing in the first chapter, what I present here goes to some extent beyond the actual instructions in the discourse.

Applied to actual practice, if the mind inclines towards deep concentration we might proceed swiftly through the first three tetrads and then allow it to enter absorption, simply by refraining from any further interference. During progression through the steps leading up to "liberating the mind", for some practitioners an inner experience of light manifests. This can already start quite early and emerge more fully with the first step of the present tetrad, experiencing the mind. The next step of gladdening the mind can then lead to an increase in brightness and the subsequent step of concentrating the mind can foster its stability. The way the light appears depends on the degree of inner collectedness the mind has acquired. By deepening and strengthening that collectedness, the light becomes stable.

In later practice traditions such inner light experiences are often referred to with the term *nimitta*, literally a "sign" or "mark" that is characteristic of something experienced and thereby enables us to recognize it (Anālayo 2003a). In the context of cultivating deeper stages of tranquillity, the *nimitta* then refers to the sign or mark of the concentrated mind. Although concern with the cultivation of such a *nimitta* is characteristic of later tradition, a precedent can be found in the *Upakkilesa-sutta*, which reports that the Buddha and some of his disciples encountered inner light experiences during their gradual cultivation of concentration (MN 128; Anālayo 2017e: 32–38).

In the *Upakkilesa-sutta* the experience of inner light (and forms) only serves to reflect whether the mind is becoming more concentrated or else has succumbed to some minor defilement that obstructs entry into absorption. The discourse does not give the impression that the light itself should become the object of meditation, in fact no object of meditation is described at all. This holds similarly for the standard account of absorption attainment in the discourses, which describes the condition of the mind by listing the mental factors characteristic of a particular level of absorption but without any additional reference to an object employed for entering absorption.

Now the experience of unification possible with absorption implies a merger of the subject and the object. Such an experience of merging could in principle be considered from the viewpoint of the subject experiencing the merger or from the viewpoint of the meditative object with which the subject has merged. Whereas in later exegetical tradition the emphasis appears to be more on the object, the standard account of absorption in the discourses instead places more emphasis on the subject. This need not imply that the experience of absorption itself must be substantially different for one following the discourses or else later exegesis. It would only imply a different perspective on how to enter and abide in absorption. From this viewpoint, the standard descriptions of the four absorptions do mention an object, in a way, namely the mind.

If I read the position taken by the discourses correctly here, the mind in absorption is aware of its own absorbed condition. Such emphasis on the subjective in the standard account of absorption in the discourses is the same for any meditation topic and therefore sufficient for any mode of practice. The perspective taken in this way throws into relief the main task: abiding in a condition of the mind in which the absorption factors are strongly present. Giving full importance to this main task would also facilitate discerning when the stability of the mind, required to remain in absorption, gets slightly weaker, evident in a subtle shakiness or feebleness of one of the absorption factors. On being noticed immediately, due to the overall emphasis on the mind itself, this can then quickly be remedied.

By pointing out that the description in the *Upakkilesa-sutta* does not present the experience of light as the object of the practice, I do not intend to imply that there is anything wrong in focusing on the light, once it has become naturally bright and stable. My point is only that this mode of practice is not evident in the *Upakkilesa-sutta* and, although for many meditators it can be a very powerful approach, it need not be considered the only possible route into absorption.

The light *nimitta* reflects the condition of our mind just as a mirror reflects the condition of our face. If we see some spot on the face, we will clean the face and not the mirror. Similarly, for the light *nimitta* to become stable, the mind needs to be cultivated accordingly. That is, the main concern can be throughout with the mind itself that has become already evident with the first step of the present tetrad. Such "experiencing the mind", in its condition of knowing the breath, can continue to inform the gradual progression towards entry into absorption, in line with what is the main theme of the present tetrad: the mind.

The instruction to liberate the mind can in turn be taken to refer to a stepping back from any interference. The last obstacle that could still be preventing absorption can indeed be the sense of being in control. Once this has been let go of, absorption takes over and we find ourselves immersed in deep bliss and peace. The mind has become so finely balanced that entry into absorption can occur as if of its own accord, in a seamless manner. The result is an experience of complete unification of the mind in which the subject–object duality vanishes.

Such unification is the fruition of the previous practices, where the contentment of having maintained basic moral conduct enabled experiencing the pleasant feeling tone of being in the present moment, which in turn facilitated the arising of joy and happiness and the eventual calming of mental activity, as a result of which the mind finally rested in itself with gladness and collectedness. With this whole trajectory in place, liberating the mind can simply take the form of relinquishing any attempt to exercise further control over it.

The idea of a simple act of relinquishment could be related to a definition of the faculty (*indriya*) of concentration, found in several discourses in the *Saṃyutta-nikāya* (SN 48.9, SN 48.10, SN 48.11, and SN 48.50). According to this definition, concentration and unification of the mind can be gained on "having made letting go the object", *vossaggārammaṇaṃ karitvā*. In addition to the supreme type of letting go when experiencing Nirvāṇa, this expression could also be taken to inspire an approach to deepening concentration by way of thoroughly letting go at a more ordinary level. Based on the previously established conditions, such letting go will indeed lead to an intensification of concentration.

In this way, taking the step of liberating the mind in the sense of thoroughly letting go can serve to tap the potential of mindfulness of breathing to lead into deep concentration (see below p. 170). Such letting go of the last vestige of control builds on the way in which the progression through the first three tetrads has enriched the condition of the mind, an enriching that implicitly covers not only the cultivation of *satipaṭṭhāna*, but also the awakening factors, a topic to which I will come back in Chapter 6 (see below p. 122).

Alternatively, a slightly more structured approach to absorption could be employed. This could be achieved by formulating an aspiration, a topic already broached in relation to joy in the previous chapter. Such an aspiration, made in the attitude of a reverential invitation, could in the present case be formulated for the five factors that are characteristic of the first absorption (MN 43). These are as follows in Pāli, followed by English renditions that express my personal understanding of their respective significance as factors of absorption:

- *vitakka*, "application of the mind",
- *vicāra*, "sustaining of the mind",
- *pīti*, "joy",
- *sukha*, "happiness",
- *ekaggatā*, "unification".

The aspiration could be made by employing just the Pāli terms; in fact the implications of the first two factors are debated and not everyone will necessarily be comfortable with the translations I have supplied. Much depends on whether we take *vitakka* in the present context as a reference to thought activity. A close examination of relevant passages and the perspective provided by translations into Chinese makes it in my view preferable to consider *vitakka*, in the context of absorption, as distinct from fully fledged conceptual thought activity (Anālayo 2017b: 123–128). Hence I prefer to understand *vitakka* as "application of the mind" when it serves as a factor of the first absorption. Be that as it may, by employing the Pāli term we can avoid taking a definite stance on one or the other interpretation of *vitakka* in relation to the first absorption.

Having formulated an aspiration or reverential invitation for the absorption factors to manifest with full strength, we then wait in a receptive manner for the invited factor to do so. Once all five factors are fully manifest in the mind, we could then formulate an aspiration for the first absorption to manifest, for example: *paṭhamaṃ jhānaṃ upasampajja vihareyyaṃ*, "may I dwell having attained the first absorption."

With each of these aspirations, the key point is not to issue commands to ourselves, but much rather to invite something to manifest on its own. We set up the conditions and invite, without any attempt to control. For those who are not comfortable with the idea of such an invitation, simply paying attention to the five factors of absorption can serve the same purpose.

The progression through the previous steps of mindfulness of breathing has in fact already laid the groundwork for these five factors of absorption to manifest fully (see also below p. 137). The focus developed with the first two steps of the body-contemplation tetrad (long and short breaths) can be seen as a precedent for the manifestation of *vitakka*, in the sense of an initial application of the mind. The shift with the ensuing steps to a broader mode of attention that continues on the trajectory of absence of distraction, by keeping the inhalations and exhalations in peripheral awareness, resembles the role of *vicāra* as a sustained application of the mind (which to some degree is in fact already required during the first two steps of body contemplation). Joy and happiness are explicitly mentioned in the first two steps of the tetrad on contemplation of feeling tones. Concentration as the third step in the present tetrad brings to fulfilment the quality of unification of the mind. Understood from this perspective, the progression through the first twelve steps of mindfulness of breathing has gradually put in place precisely those mental conditions that can ripen into absorption attainment.

The *Visuddhimagga* indeed understands the present step to imply liberating the mind so that absorption can take place (Vism 289). According to its presentation, this could be liberation from anything that might obstruct entry into the first absorption, or else liberation from those mental factors of a lower absorption that need to be left behind in order to dwell in a higher absorption.

INSIGHT

The *Visuddhimagga* also brings in the topic of insight, suggesting that on emerging from an absorption one should contemplate it with insight as impermanent, *dukkha*, and devoid of self. The *Paṭisambhidāmagga* lists various defilements from which the mind could be liberated with the present step, including conceit, *māna* (Paṭis I 191). Ajahn Buddhadāsa has made a related suggestion, associating the present step in particular to cultivating insight into the futility of clinging to anything as "I" or "mine" (see below p. 180 n. 14).

In practical terms, on adopting this perspective the experience of the breath can be divested altogether of self-reference, of all conceited notions of an "I" that breathes, and of any appropriation of the breath (or any other phenomena related to it) as "mine". Simply said, the task would be to "breathe without a breather". Once we learn to step out of selfing in relation to breathing, it becomes easier to do the same in relation to other aspects of our experience as well.

Practising in this way prepares the ground for an emphasis on the cultivation of insight in the next tetrad on contemplation of dharmas. Bringing in the characteristic of not-self also complements the continuous awareness of impermanence, evident in the alternations between inhalations and exhalations, that underlies the whole scheme of practice. On adopting this interpretation, the mind can come to be (at least temporarily) "liberated" from self-reference.

Training ourselves in associating the step of liberating the mind with emptiness can take on an intriguing dimension. This dimension emerges once the alternative route of entry into absorption is taken. Due to previous training in associating this step with emptiness, such entry into absorption can come together with a sense of non-identification: experiencing absorption without having any identification with it, without a sense of "I am" the one who attains it.

Such a lack of identification is reflected in a series of discourses in which Sāriputta reports his ability to enter any level of absorption without any sense of an "I" in relation to such attainment (SN 28.1–9). Ānanda relates this to the fact that Sāriputta had for a long time overcome all underlying tendency to conceit and to the construing of a sense of "I" and "mine".

Due to previously developed insight, an experience of deep concentrative states can take place entirely free from any tendency to selfing and appropriation. Following the example set by Sāriputta, a powerful utilization of the union of tranquillity and insight becomes possible, where the empty mind naturally rests in deep concentration and the very quality of being empty itself takes care of any possible distraction. Even the slightest tendency of the mind to depart from its absorbed condition can just be allowed to dissolve into emptiness by being discerned as void of "I" and "mine".

The suggestion of conjoining tranquillity and insight is not meant to imply that insight is to be cultivated while actually being absorbed. Descriptions of the experience of absorption in the early discourses point to a condition of deep mental tranquillity, such that it would not be possible to be immersed in absorption and at the same time be contemplating insight into impermanence, for example (Anālayo 2017b: 109–175). The point I am making here is only that previously cultivated insight, in particular an understanding of emptiness, can continue to inform the actual experience of meditative absorption and can serve as an aid when the mind is not yet (or no longer) fully in an absorbed condition, due to some minor distraction.

Comparing the present tetrad to the corresponding contemplation of the mind in the *Satipaṭṭhāna-sutta* shows again that the *Ānāpānasati-sutta* to some degree builds on what the former has established. Contemplation of the mind in the *Satipaṭṭhāna-sutta* requires a clear recognition of pairs of mental states, the last of which is the "liberated mind" in contrast to the "not liberated mind". Whereas in the *Satipaṭṭhāna-sutta* the task is recognition, the *Ānāpānasati-sutta* shows how to achieve a liberated mind, which forms the culmination point of the present tetrad.

Moreover, the trajectory that leads up to "liberating the mind" in the *Ānāpānasati-sutta* more explicitly reflects the important contribution that cultivation of tranquillity makes to progress towards liberation. It shows how with mindfulness of breathing the "not concentrated mind" can gradually evolve to becoming a "concentrated mind", two categories listed in the *Satipaṭṭhāna-sutta* under contemplation of the mind.

WALKING MEDITATION

For walking meditation, two steps from the present tetrad could be taken up for practice. The first step of experiencing the mind would naturally build on the type of walking meditation described in the previous chapter in relation to contemplation of feeling tone. There the calming of mental activity led to a thought-free experience of walking, which can easily be developed further by becoming aware of the mind as such. This mode of practice has a remarkable potential to bring inner balance and lack of attachment to any situation or activity. Such potential is based on reversing the natural tendency of the mind to reach out for whatever object presents itself and then to react to it. If instead the internal experience of our own mind is given prominence, this tendency is countered and we learn to recognize clearly what is taking place within, in our own mind. The question is no longer what others should or should not have done, but the question throughout is how our own mind handles that.

Building on the ability to stay attuned to what happens in the mind, the last step in the present tetrad on contemplation of the mind would fall into place in the way just described above, which is liberating the mind from selfing. In this way, walking meditation can become a walking in emptiness. The same holds for other activities. All of these can be voided of self-referencing, of I-making and my-making. This has the surprising result that whatever we have to do is performed with more ease and increased efficiency. In addition, it becomes an integral part of the path to the final goal of full liberation, whereby all tendency to selfing and ego-centredness will be left behind for good.

SUMMARY

Based on the calming of mental activity brought about with the previous tetrad on contemplation of feeling tones, mind as such can be experienced in its bare condition. As this experience results from turning inwards towards that which knows the alternation between inhalations and exhalations, the changing nature of this knowing quality is apparent throughout. This enables a profound experience of the mind as such without leaving room for reifying it as a permanent entity.

Gladness and concentration are to some extent already dimensions of the experience of the mind as such. Turning attention to them deepens their manifestation. The trajectory underlying the present tetrad on contemplation of the mind has a prominent flavour of tranquillity, which for some practitioners leads to the manifestation of an inner light. With the experiences of gladness and concentration, the light tends to become brighter and more stable.

Moving on to liberating the mind can then lead to entry into absorption which, although not explicitly mentioned in the *Ānāpānasati-sutta*, is a natural result of the trajectory of practice up to the present point. An entry point for absorption could simply be a thorough letting go, or else an aspiration for absorption to arise could be employed.

Opting instead for the cultivation of insight could find its expression in liberating the mind from all conceit and sense of self-reference, by "breathing without a breather". Such de-identification and de-appropriation of experience can carry over into daily-life activity and even inform entry into absorption, all of which can become integral dimensions of a gradual deepening of insight into emptiness.

V

CONTEMPLATION OF DHARMAS

With the practice progression in the present tetrad, the wings of the condor also disappear. The condor still keeps flying effortlessly over mountaintop after mountaintop, but it is no longer visible. Due to the condor having become completely transparent, the changing scenery is in turn completely visible, which reflects bringing impermanence right to the forefront of attention at the outset of this tetrad on contemplation of dharmas.

The last tetrad, corresponding to the *satipaṭṭhāna* of contemplating dharmas, takes the following form in the *Ānāpānasati-sutta* (MN 118):

> One trains: 'contemplating impermanence I shall breathe in'; one trains: 'contemplating impermanence I shall breathe out.' One trains: 'contemplating dispassion I shall breathe in'; one trains: 'contemplating dispassion I shall breathe out.' One trains: 'contemplating cessation I shall breathe in'; one trains: 'contemplating cessation I shall breathe out.' One trains: 'contemplating letting go I shall breathe in'; one trains: 'contemplating letting go I shall breathe out.'

In what follows I take up the topics of "impermanence" and "dispassion and cessation", followed by "letting go". Several parallel versions to this last tetrad follow a different pattern, where insight into impermanence instead leads to contemplating abandoning (or eradication) as the second step, followed by dispassion as the third and cessation as the fourth step. The sequence where abandoning (*pahāna*) is followed by dispassion (*virāga*) and then cessation (*nirodha*) occurs frequently in other Pāli discourses (Anālayo 2012b: 47–50), but not in relation to mindfulness of breathing.

For actual practice of the fourth tetrad, I prefer to follow the sequence found in the *Ānāpānasati-sutta* (as well as in the Sarvāstivāda *Vinaya*; see below p. 185 and Anālayo 2016b: 249), which matches more closely the way the awakening factors are to be cultivated. This cultivation takes place in dependence on seclusion, dispassion, and cessation, culminating in letting go. I will discuss this similarity in more detail in the next chapter.

IMPERMANENCE

Impermanence is a prominent theme continuously present as a backdrop throughout the entire practice of mindfulness of inhalations and exhalations. The same theme is important for *satipaṭṭhāna* meditation in general, inculcated in the *Satipaṭṭhāna-sutta* with the instruction that each of its respective exercises should lead on to contemplating the nature of arising, passing away, and both.

The emphasis given to insight into impermanence in this way reflects its central importance in the early Buddhist path to liberation. A discourse in the *Saṃyutta-nikāya* states that cultivating the perception of impermanence will eliminate all types of passion as well as ignorance and conceit (SN 22.102). A discourse in the *Aṅguttara-nikāya* adds that perception of impermanence establishes the perception of not-self and thereby leads to the destruction of conceit and the realization of Nirvāṇa here and now (AN 9.1).

The point made by these two passages provides a context for appreciating the role of contemplation of impermanence in the present tetrad on contemplation of dharmas. A relationship between the perception of impermanence and the undermining of passion, mentioned in the *Saṃyutta-nikāya* discourse, finds implementation right away with the next step in this tetrad, contemplation of dispassion. In this way, insight into impermanence serves to counter the tendency to sensual passion.

The other dimension of the perception of impermanence, evident from the *Aṅguttara-nikāya* discourse, is to lay the groundwork for insight into emptiness or not-self to thrive. Once it has become unmistakeably clear that all phenomena are impermanent, it follows that they are for this reason incapable of yielding lasting satisfaction: they are *dukkha*. What is *dukkha* is not fit for being taken as a self or being appropriated as pertaining to a self. In short, it is empty.

The importance of impermanence for the cultivation of liberating insight is also evident in the scheme of "insight knowledges", often employed in Theravāda meditation traditions as a framework for the meditative progression that leads up to stream-entry. A key stage in this scheme is the knowledge of the arising and passing away of phenomena and thus insight into impermanence. The continuation of the scheme, from the knowledge of arising and passing away onwards, can to some extent be seen as a more detailed elaboration of the basic progression mentioned above and found regularly in the early discourses, according to which insight into impermanence leads to a deepening appreciation of *dukkha*, which in turn issues in realization of not-self (Anālayo 2012a, 2013b: 233, and 2019c).

In this way, from the early discourses to later Theravāda tradition, insight into impermanence comes with a clear thrust towards renunciation of attachment regarding what is incapable of yielding satisfaction. The appropriate response to the realization of impermanence is thus not that we should just learn to enjoy fleeting pleasures as long as they last. Instead, genuine insight into impermanence serves to bring about disenchantment and the quest for liberation, rather than delighting in evanescence as productive of variety and enchantment. A growing disenchantment and inclination towards liberation indeed underlies the present tetrad, which has a strong drive towards the eradication of ignorance (*avijjā*) and the arousing of liberating knowledge (*vijjā*).

The fact that the breath is impermanent implies that the body must be impermanent; the body's very survival is in fact entirely dependent on a constant supply of oxygen (see below pp. 159 and 242). Moreover, as already mentioned in the previous chapter, since the mind is able to contemplate a changing phenomenon like the breath, this implies that the very faculty of knowing must also be subject to change. In this way, mindfulness of the changing nature of the breath can lead to a comprehensive insight into the impermanent nature of body and mind.

THE FIVE AGGREGATES

The *Paṭisambhidāmagga* understands the present step to imply contemplating the impermanent nature of the entire set of the five aggregates of clinging, namely form, feeling tone, perception, volitional formations, and consciousness (Paṭis I 191). Such contemplation is also the starting point of the instructions in the *Girimānanda-sutta* on a series of ten perceptions, which culminate in the sixteen steps of mindfulness of breathing (AN 10.60; Anālayo 2016b: 214–216). In the discourses in general, contemplation of the impermanent nature of the five aggregates of clinging stands out as a particularly powerful approach for gaining liberating insight.

In order to do justice to this potential, the scheme of the five aggregates can be employed to refine the present step of contemplation of impermanence. Although not explicitly mentioned in the actual instructions, for those who find it helpful to enrich the practice with additional details and perspectives, it would be possible to apply the scheme of the five aggregates to the present step of mindfulness of breathing. All it takes is to discern the five aggregates as components of the meditative experience of mindfulness of breathing. At times this can be done by progressing from one aggregate to the next, at times by giving particular importance to one aggregate that has become prominent in our experience for some reason or another, and at times by seeing all five aggregates collectively.

Awareness of the whole body as constantly changing due to the fact of breathing exemplifies the impermanent nature of the first aggregate of *form*. The changing sensations of the breath point to the impermanent nature of *feeling tones*. The ability to distinguish between inhalations and exhalations reflects the impermanent nature of *perceptions*. The intention to direct attention to the breath is either followed by another intention to the same effect, or else by an intention to attend to something else, leading the mind off into distraction. Both types of intention exemplify the impermanent nature of *volitional formations*. The process of knowing all these changing phenomena implies the impermanent nature of *consciousness*.

Attending to each of the five aggregates in this way builds on the groundwork laid with earlier steps, some of which already combined paying attention to each of the aggregates with peripheral awareness of the impermanent nature of the breath (see also below p. 137). The body became the main object of attention during the third step of the body-contemplation tetrad, which required experiencing the whole body. Feeling tones of the pleasant type were particularly prominent with the first two steps of the second tetrad on contemplation of feeling tones, experiencing joy and happiness. Right away the next step in the same tetrad, experiencing mental activities, is relevant to two aggregates, since (in addition to feeling tones) perceptions and intentions are mental activities (see above p. 64). The first step of the third tetrad on contemplation of the mind then led to an experience of mind as such, which can conveniently be related to the aggregate of consciousness.

In this way, the aggregates of body, feeling tone, and consciousness have already been objects of individual steps that combined their respective experience with an awareness of impermanence. Perceptions came up together with intentions (which correspond to the fourth aggregate of volitional formations) in a single step. This circumstance would make it advisable to dedicate some additional attention to their impermanence at the present juncture of practice, in order to ensure that their individual features and impermanent nature are appreciated with as much depth and clarity as the other three aggregates of body, feeling tone, and consciousness.

Based on discerning the five aggregates of clinging individually, in the way they manifest during the practice of mindfulness of breathing as being subject to the law of change, we will eventually be able to see all of them together as combined facets of our being mindful of the process of breathing. This process of breathing itself can make impermanence become very palpable, due to the clear manifestation of an arising, a change while persisting, and a complete ceasing. In particular noting change while persisting helps to establish the early Buddhist conception of impermanence as distinct from later notions of momentariness, which consider arising to be invariably followed by immediate cessation.

Besides so conveniently driving home the truth of impermanence, inhalations and exhalations also manifest due to causes and conditions, such as the appropriate bodily motions, the existence of the nostrils and so on. In this way, by cultivating a deepening appreciation of impermanence, insight into conditionality can also arise.

WALKING MEDITATION

The present step of "contemplating impermanence" is also particularly apt for shifting to walking meditation. The process of walking itself, as well as the changing scenery that results from our moving from one place to another, is an easily accessible pointer to impermanence. By paying attention to this, the practice of walking meditation can become an experience of constant flow. This can then be extended from walking to any other activity.

Needless to say, such experience of constant flow does not require foregoing the joy of being in the present moment. Although at times we might decide to give more importance to the flow dimension in order to deepen insight and at other times put more emphasis on the pleasant feeling tone of being in the present moment as a way of fostering tranquillity, the two can be combined with each other. This could lead to cultivating tranquillity and insight in conjunction in the same manner as when being mindful of the breath in the sitting posture.

DISPASSION AND CESSATION

The need to allow the implications of impermanence to sink into and transform the mind becomes evident with the next two steps. Similar to the preceding tetrad on contemplation of the mind, here, too, the second and third steps can be considered as fleshing out what is already to some degree implicit in the first step. Just as experiencing the mind led to liberating it via gladdening and concentrating it, in the same way impermanence leads to letting go via the two interim steps of dispassion and cessation. These two steps can be seen as drawing out implications of impermanence.

DISPASSION

The first of these two interim steps concerns "dispassion", corresponding to the Pāli term *virāga*, which at times can also convey a sense of "fading away" (Anālayo 2009b). Attending to the dimension of the fading away of phenomena is in fact particularly apt for arousing dispassion. Appreciation of their constant change and eventual disappearance will undermine whatever passion we have for them, revealing the ultimately unsatisfactory (*dukkha*) nature of all that is conditioned.

For a full cultivation of the liberating potential of the instructions on mindfulness of breathing, it is crucial that we fully allow dispassion to do its work. The *Ānāpānasati-sutta* has very little emphasis on the characteristic of *dukkha*, being mostly concerned with impermanence as the foundation for insight. The present step is therefore of particular importance for ensuring a comprehensive development of insight.

The relatively little emphasis on *dukkha* in the *Ānāpānasati-sutta* contrasts with the *Satipaṭṭhāna-sutta*, where two of the body contemplations common to the three discourse versions drive home the body's lack of inherent beauty and its mortality. One of the three feeling tones to be contemplated concerns painful ones, and several of the mental states under the third *satipaṭṭhāna*, as well as hindrances in the fourth *satipaṭṭhāna*, are not particularly pleasant. The *Ānāpānasati-sutta* does not explicitly deconstruct notions of bodily beauty, painful feeling tones are not mentioned, and neither defiled states of mind nor the hindrances come up explicitly for contemplation.

The contrast between the *Ānāpānasati-sutta* and the *Satipaṭṭhāna-sutta* becomes even more pronounced with the story of the mass suicide of monastics after excessive and unbalanced contemplation of the body's lack of inherent beauty (see below p. 198). When informed of what has happened, the Buddha is on record for recommending the practice of mindfulness of breathing in sixteen steps. This practice apparently served as a skilful means for establishing a balanced attitude.

In the approach to mindfulness of breathing presented here, the characteristic of not-self can be cultivated with the last step of the preceding tetrad on contemplation of the mind; it also comes up again to some degree in the final two steps of the present tetrad, contemplation of cessation and of letting go, both of which require relinquishing all identification and appropriation.

For a balanced cultivation of insight, including all three characteristics in one way or another is highly advisable. It is perfectly fine and perhaps even natural to give prominence to one of these, in line with personal preferences and inclinations.

Nevertheless, for balanced and swift progress to liberation, such emphasis is best complemented by giving some room also to the other characteristics. For the characteristic of *dukkha*, the appreciation of the ultimately unsatisfactory nature of all that is conditioned, contemplating dispassion affords a convenient opportunity to cover what the *Satipaṭṭhāna-sutta* accomplishes with several contemplations. The chief task here is to let the implications of impermanence really sink in and transform our mental attitudes. We allow the flow of impermanence to wash out our passions and attachments, generating a genuine thrust towards liberation, rather than letting them be watered down to become an enjoyment of ephemeral pleasures as long as they last.

A discourse in the *Saṃyutta-nikāya* clarifies that the very purpose of dispassion is liberation (SN 23.1). Progress towards liberation clearly underlies the present tetrad on contemplation of dharmas, as dispassion leads on to cessation and eventually to the culmination point of letting go.

CESSATION

The next step of cessation, *nirodha*, complements the thrust of dispassion. Viewed from the perspective of the other meaning of the term *virāga* as "fading away", things that fade away will eventually cease. All conditioned phenomena will certainly cease sooner or later. This in turn brings out their empty nature. Had they been endowed with some perdurable essence, they would not be bound to cease completely. By understanding cessation as an implicit pointer to emptiness, the meditative progression from impermanence to dispassion and cessation can be seen as touching, in its own specific manner, on the three characteristics (impermanence, *dukkha*, and not-self). On this understanding, the present tetrad can be viewed as a brief tour through the essentials of insight, leading up to inclining the mind towards the final goal of liberation.

The fact of eventual complete cessation is of particular relevance to the breath, as the continuity of breathing ensures the continuity of life. It is for this reason that an alternative use of the breath for meditation purposes is precisely by way of recollection of death. Here awareness turns to the fact that we cannot be completely sure even that the next breath will take place (see below p. 242; Anālayo 2016b: 200–207 and 2018d: 90–95). To breathe is to be alive; with the ending of life, breathing comes to an end (see below p. 159). Death will certainly come, yet we do not know when. It could even be very soon that we breathe our last breath. With every breath we take, the time of our death is coming one breath closer.

In the present context the question of death is not at the foreground of meditative attention, although previous practice of recollection of death would certainly enhance our contemplation of cessation and provide it with additional depth. As part of mindfulness of breathing, the task is simply to be aware of the fact that every inhalation and exhalation ceases. Just as the continuity of breathing involves the recurrent event of a cessation, so the continuity of life can be seen as a stringing together of events, each of which involves some cessation. Paying attention to this dimension counters the ingrained tendency of the mind to be on the lookout only for what is new and beginning, what is fresh and young, at the cost of ignoring what grows old and comes to an end.

The supreme converging point and final peak of dispassion and cessation is the realization of Nirvāṇa. In the *Girimānanda-sutta* this finds expression in a maxim employed for the perceptions of dispassion and cessation respectively, which serves to incline the mind towards this final converging point (AN 10.60; Anālayo 2016b: 103). The maxim used for this purpose also occurs elsewhere in the discourses (MN 64; Anālayo 2015a: 169), taking the following form:

> This is peaceful, this is sublime, namely: the calming of all constructions, the letting go of all supports, the extinguishing of craving, dispassion, cessation, Nirvāṇa.

The first of the actual epithets listed after the qualification of being peaceful and sublime is "the calming of all constructions". This expression involves the Pāli term *samatha*, "calming" or "tranquillity". The occurrence of a direct reference to tranquillity in this context shows that the peak of dispassion and cessation, the culmination of insight, has at the same time a relationship to tranquillity. In this way, in spite of an indubitably strong emphasis on the cultivation of insight, tranquillity is not entirely absent. It makes its appearance not so much in the form of temporary experiences of deep concentrative calm, but rather in the form of leading up to a state of mind that, due to having eradicated defilements for good, is by its very nature tranquil. The realization of Nirvāṇa is the supreme tranquillity indeed. The ending of all unwholesomeness in the mind yields an inner calm that will no longer be perturbed by anything that happens.

LETTING GO

The next epithet in the above maxim concerns "letting go". The consummation of the convergence of tranquillity and insight, which has been a continuous theme throughout the sixteen steps in the form presented here, comes within reach through letting go, the final step in the practice of mindfulness of breathing.

The Pāli term translated in the above maxim and in the last step of the present tetrad as "letting go" is *paṭinissagga*. A term with very similar connotations is *vossagga* (Anālayo 2009c), which refers to the "letting go" that is to occur once the awakening factors are being cultivated in dependence on seclusion, in dependence on dispassion, and in dependence on cessation. Both terms can be taken to convey an inclining of the mind towards the realization of Nirvāṇa.

Inspiration for inclining the mind in such a way can be gained from the *Girimānanda-sutta* (AN 10.60; Anālayo 2016b: 226–229), already mentioned above. The relevant part from the discourse concerns a set of four perceptions. The first two employ the maxim translated above to flesh out the perceptions of dispassion and of cessation. The final goal is indeed supreme dispassion in the sense of freedom from all passion, lust, and attachment. It is at the same time also supreme cessation in the related sense of the complete ending of all defilements and traces of unwholesomeness in the mind.

The third of the four perceptions in the *Girimānanda-sutta* shows that the true aim of the practice is to go beyond delighting in anything whatsoever in the whole world, particularly in the sense of going beyond the tendency to hold on to our cherished views, preferences, and opinions. According to the fourth perception, with a keen appreciation of the impermanent nature of all formations the mind becomes thoroughly disenchanted with all that is conditioned and inclines fully towards the unconditioned. Any of these four perceptions, singly or intertwined, could inform our letting go as the final step in the mode of practice described in the *Ānāpānasati-sutta*. Throughout, the basic principle holds that the commendable type of letting go is one that leads to the diminishing of unwholesome qualities (AN 10.94).

PROGRESS OF INSIGHT

The insight progression that underlies the present tetrad on contemplation of dharmas could be illustrated with the example of standing on the bank of a river. Facing the water and looking at its flow corresponds to contemplation of impermanence. Suppose now we step on a bridge that spans over the river and face the direction in which the water flows, whereby our perspective will be with more emphasis on the motion of the water away from us. This change of position illustrates contemplation of dispassion, when emphasis is on the moving away and eventual disappearance of contemplated phenomena. Next we might turn around on the bridge and face the direction from which the river comes. Instead of looking out to the far distance, we look straight down to see how the water disappears from view right at the edge of the bridge. This illustrates contemplation of cessation, when the disappearance and ending of things stands out prominently. Finally we might let ourselves plunge into the river itself. This illustrates the final step in the present tetrad, letting go.

Beside attempting to convey a practical flavour of each of the four insight themes, the simile of the river is also meant to point to their interrelation. At first sight, it might seem

that impermanence is a quality of the object and dispassion a subjective response to it. Again, cessation can appear a quality of the object and letting go a subjective reaction to it. Although this is indeed a way of reading the insight progression described here, such a distinction between subject and object does not do full justice to the insight dynamics that can unfold here. Impermanence and cessation need to be applied as well to the subjective. Conversely, *virāga* in its alternative sense of fading away can be a dimension of the object. Letting go needs to be comprehensive, comprising object and subject. From this viewpoint, each of the four insight contemplations can have a broad range of possible applications.

The set of four insight contemplations that culminates in letting go occurs in other Pāli discourses in relation to feeling tones. One type of occurrence features in an explanation of how to reach the complete destruction of craving (MN 37 and AN 7.58). The instruction is that any type of feeling tone, be it pleasant, unpleasant, or neutral, should be contemplated from the viewpoint of impermanence, dispassion, cessation, and letting go. Such contemplation leads to not clinging to anything. One who does not cling is not agitated, and not being agitated one attains Nirvāṇa.

Another type of occurrence, featuring in instructions given to the sick (SN 36.7 and SN 36.8; Anālayo 2016b: 162), adds contemplation of "passing away" to the set of four insight contemplations (placed between impermanence and dispassion; the Chinese parallel also mentions "arising"). Here these insight contemplations fall into place after cultivation of the four *satipaṭṭhāna*s and of clear knowing, in the sense of possessing circumspection, in relation to various bodily activities. These practices serve in particular as a preparation for the time of death.

If during such practice a pleasant, unpleasant, or neutral feeling tone arises, it should be seen as dependently arisen. Such seeing could attend to the feeling tone as being dependent on the body (SN 36.7) or else as being dependent on contact (SN 36.8). In each of the two alternative cases, the impermanence and passing away of the respective condition (the body or contact) should be contemplated, with the understanding that the same impermanent nature applies to feeling tones arisen in dependence on that condition. Such understanding then leads over to contemplating dispassion, cessation, and letting go. In this way the underlying tendency to lust in relation to pleasant feeling tones can be abandoned, just as the underlying tendencies to aversion in relation to unpleasant feeling tones and to ignorance in relation to neutral feeling tones. As a result, attachment in relation to any of these three types of feeling tones can be overcome.

The two employments of the four insight contemplations, mentioned above, provide additional perspectives for the present tetrad of contemplation of dharmas. Each can be taken to point to the potential of undertaking the four insight contemplations, described in this part of the *Ānāpānasati-sutta*, with a specific focus on the felt aspect of experience. In the present context, this is first of all the breath. The continuity of breathing is perhaps the most convenient aspect to be taken up for contemplating the dependent nature of present-moment experience. Such contemplation brings into sharp relief the fact of impermanence, especially if the breath's eventual passing away is taken into account, perhaps even to the extent of acknowledging that, once breathing stops for good, the body will pass away and fall apart. The resultant dispassion could then find expression in not clinging to anything and moving beyond any agitation.

THE UNDERLYING TENDENCIES

For those who like to work with additional details, an option would be to relate dispassion more specifically to one of the three underlying tendencies of sensual lust, aversion, and ignorance. Such specific relating could be based on having earlier ascertained whether sensuality is a prominent issue for us, or else whether anger manifests recurrently, or else whether we often dwell in delusion.

In the case of the *Satipaṭṭhāna-sutta*, working with these three basic types of personal propensities can take the form of giving special emphasis to particular exercises (Anālayo 2018d: 209f). In the case of the present tetrad of mindfulness of breathing, such working with a particular type could take place at a subtler level, as for each type the same four insight contemplations are to be undertaken by moving from impermanence to dispassion, cessation, and letting go.

The above-mentioned instructions for the sick relate each of the three underlying tendencies to the corresponding feeling. On being applied to mindfulness of breathing meditation, this need not be taken to mean that we should wait for the particular feeling tone to manifest before we do something about the corresponding underlying tendency. Suppose our main problem is lust, be it our character type in general or something that recently manifested strongly. Suppose also that right now we are experiencing neutral feeling tones. Contemplating these feeling tones as impermanent could be undertaken while keeping in mind that pleasant feeling tones, in particular those related to sensual gratification, are similarly impermanent and of a nature to pass away. In this way, dispassion, cessation, and letting go can be related to those pleasant feeling tones that tend to trigger our lust, even if we are not experiencing them right now.

If instead anger is our main challenge, again any feeling tone that manifests can be a reminder of the impermanent nature of feeling tones in general. For this reason, it can serve as a pointer to the changing nature of whatever unpleasantness or pain usually causes our irritation. This is certainly bound to pass away sooner or later. Dispassion, cessation, and letting go can in this way become directly relevant to whatever tends to trigger our anger and irritation.

Should delusion be what we need to face, then we could target in particular the cosy sense of dullness and the temptation to switch off and have an easy time. Instead, we emphasize alertness and becoming fully alive to the changing nature of the present moment, such that any dullness is overcome. Based on that, we cultivate dispassion, cessation, and letting go in relation to the deluding comfort of a cloudy mind that is adrift with no purpose.

If none of these three chief topics should fit our case at present, further inspection can be undertaken along the lines of the above-mentioned passage on reaching the complete destruction of craving. This passage, the first of the two types of occurrences of the four insight contemplations, relates the absence of clinging to not being agitated. Wherever and whenever agitation manifests, right there mindfulness and investigation are required to discern the underlying clinging that must be there for agitation to arise. This could be, for example, conceit. Once clinging to our ego or any other clinging has been identified, we know how to direct our contemplation of impermanence, dispassion, cessation, and letting go.

THE BREATH AND INSIGHT

Besides these alternative modes of discerning how to provide a sense of direction to the four insight contemplations of the present tetrad of mindfulness of breathing, the experience of the breath can be used as a reference point for these four steps. This can take the form of relating the four insight contemplations more closely to aspects of the breath, which for this purpose can become more prominent in the field of our awareness. We now give the breath just a bit more attention in order to be able to discern clearly the beginning, middle, and end of each inhalation and exhalation. Such a shift of paying attention to aspects of the breath is best done without influencing the breath itself. It just entails an unobtrusive mode of paying attention that need not become in any way forced or stilted.

With the first step on contemplating impermanence, we could remain continuously aware of the beginning, middle, and end of each inhalation and exhalation. As mentioned in the first chapter (see above p. 22), this neatly exemplifies the early Buddhist conception of impermanence, according to which things arise, may persist for some time as a continuously changing process, and sooner or later cease.

Based on the continuity of well-established mindfulness, we move on to contemplating dispassion as the second step. Here we might give more importance to the middle and the ending part of each inhalation and exhalation, to their change while persisting and eventual disappearance. These are the two aspects of impermanence that undermine attachment and passion: the fact that things change and that sooner or later they end. Countering the innate tendency to pay attention only to beginnings and to what is new, we learn to notice the changing nature of whatever manifests and to acknowledge fully its eventual passing away.

This acknowledgement can then become the sole object of practice when proceeding to contemplation of cessation, the third step in this last tetrad of mindfulness of breathing. Although we still experience each inhalation and exhalation fully, our attention is directed to their disappearance, their passing away and ending. Breathing remains natural throughout; the suggestions presented here should not lead to changing the breath in any way. The issue at stake is only a shift of emphasis in attention by noticing how each breath ends and vanishes.

With the final step of letting go, we could give importance to the gap between inhalation and exhalation or between exhalation and inhalation. Between each of these, there is a moment of stillness, when one has just ended and the next not yet started. Paying attention to the stillness of this gap, we in a way let go into this gap, let go into this peaceful moment of quietness between the activity of inhalations and exhalations (see also below p. 236).

At times we might just rest in that peaceful moment of quietness and wait for the breath to start on its own. This is not to encourage in any way some form of breath retention. The idea is only to relax into that gap and, rather than initiating the next inhalation or exhalation, just wait for it to manifest of its own accord.

Due to the subtlety reached at this stage of practice, at times the breath can become so refined that it can no longer be discerned distinctly. Such disappearance, due to the mind becoming deeply concentrated, needs to be distinguished from the breath being actually still perceptible but only not manifesting in gross physical sensations. In such a situation, as discussed in an earlier chapter (see above p. 20), we only need to remind ourselves that the breath itself is the object of attention and not any particular physical sensation. This will enable finding ways of observing the breath independent of the particular physical sensation used earlier, which in the meantime has become too subtle to be distinctly perceived.

The disappearance discussed here, however, usually occurs only after considerable refinement of the practice. Gradually the breath becomes more and more refined and subtle. On noticing that, we might adjust our progression through the sixteen steps in such a way that the alternation between inhalation and exhalation still accompanies our practice of the preceding steps until we reach the contemplation of letting go. This theme could then be allowed to occupy the entire field of perception, without further attention being paid to the inhalations and exhalations that by now have become too faint to be discernible. The same pattern can be applied to the cultivation of tranquillity, by way of proceeding through the first twelve steps until, with liberating the mind, entry into absorption can take place, without further attention being paid to inhalations and exhalations. In both cases, the increasing subtlety of the breathing leads over to something still subtler (see also below p. 195).

CONTEMPLATION OF DHARMAS

The present tetrad corresponds to contemplation of dharmas, which in the *Satipaṭṭhāna-sutta* comprises a range of different exercises. Based on a comparative study of the parallel versions (Anālayo 2013b: 174–176 and 2018d: 28), what emerges as the common core of this *satipaṭṭhāna* is the contemplation of the awakening factors (and to some degree also contemplation of the hindrances). This suggests that contemplation of dharmas is about monitoring those mental qualities that lead forwards on the path to liberation.

Cultivating the awakening factors in such a way that their awakening potential is fully actualized requires doing so in dependence on seclusion, dispassion, and cessation, culminating in letting go. The last three of these correspond to the last three steps in the present tetrad, a correspondence that I will be taking up for further discussion in the next chapter. Thus contemplation of dharmas in the *Satipaṭṭhāna-sutta* concerns the mental qualities and in the *Ānāpānasati-sutta* the insight topics which, on being combined with each other, are particularly helpful for progressing to the realization of Nirvāṇa.

This correspondence concords with a general pattern, where each of the four tetrads in the *Ānāpānasati-sutta* seems to take off from what the corresponding *satipaṭṭhāna* in the *Satipaṭṭhāna-sutta* has established. The insights into the true nature of the body gained by implementing those exercises common to the parallel versions of the *Satipaṭṭhāna-sutta* can provide support for the calming of bodily activity, being cultivated with the first tetrad on contemplation of the body in the *Ānāpānasati-sutta*. The instructions in the *Satipaṭṭhāna-sutta* help in discerning the conditionality of feeling tones. The second tetrad of mindfulness of breathing on contemplation of feeling tones puts this to good use through its emphasis on joy and happiness, which serve as conditions for progressing to the calming of mental activity. Contemplation of the mind in the *Satipaṭṭhāna-sutta* requires the clear recognition of the concentrated and the liberated mind in contrast to their opposites. Building on such recognition, the third tetrad of mindfulness of breathing leads via concentrating to liberating the mind. In the present case, the establishing of the awakening factors is a chief concern of the instructions in the *Satipaṭṭhāna-sutta*. Cultivating themes that will actualize their awakening potential corresponds to the last three steps in the fourth tetrad of mindfulness of breathing concerned with contemplation of dharmas: dispassion, cessation, and letting go.

These correspondences give the impression that, in general terms, mindfulness of breathing sets in at a comparatively more advanced level of practice than *satipaṭṭhāna* in the form in which it is described in the *Satipaṭṭhāna-sutta*. The same is to some degree also evident from the exclusive association of mindfulness of breathing with the sitting posture, whereas meditation in the *Satipaṭṭhāna-sutta* is not confined to any posture and thus is more easily applied to daily-life situations. Again, whereas the *Satipaṭṭhāna-sutta* covers the presence of the hindrances, successfully overcoming them appears to be a precondition for the practice of mindfulness of breathing, as in fact indicated explicitly in the parallels to the *Ānāpānasati-sutta* (see below p. 183). In sum, the contemplations described in the *Satipaṭṭhāna-sutta* could be seen to build a foundation for then engaging in the more specific practice of the sixteen steps of mindfulness of breathing.

SUMMARY

From whatever approach we have adopted for the last step of the third tetrad, concerned with liberating the mind, practice proceeds to contemplation of impermanence. This is a theme that has been present throughout the entire trajectory of mindfulness of breathing, evident in the alternation between inhalations and exhalations as well as in whatever changes have become apparent during a single inhalation or exhalation. At the present juncture this theme comes right to the forefront of attention and is allowed to display all of its implications. It becomes increasingly clear that, just as the breath is impermanent, so body and mind must also be impermanent.

Insight into impermanence can be strengthened by being applied to each of the five aggregates of form, feeling tone, perception, volitional formations, and consciousness. In the context of mindfulness of breathing, form is experienced as the body engaged in breathing, feeling tone takes the form of sensations caused by the breath, perception corresponds to the cognizing of the inhalations and exhalations, volitional formations are the intentions to direct attention to the breath and stay with it rather than letting the mind wander off, and consciousness takes the form of knowing receptively all of the aforementioned aspects.

From contemplating impermanence, practice shifts to letting the implications of impermanence sink into the mind and transform its affective disposition. We allow the flow of impermanence to wash out our passions and attachments by becoming dispassionate towards what in the final count is merely *dukkha*. With the transformation effected by dispassion, we apperceive cessation more fully and learn to be at ease with the fact that all things eventually end and disappear. The resultant deepening appreciation of emptiness in turn strengthens our ability to let go and incline the mind towards the supreme freedom possible with the realization of Nirvāṇa.

The progression in the present tetrad can at times be related more closely to aspects of the breath itself. Contemplating impermanence could come with attention paid to the beginning, middle, and end of each inhalation and exhalation. Moving on to dispassion, more importance can be accorded to noting the middle and the end part of each inhalation and exhalation, so that their change while persisting and their eventual disappearance stand out more distinctly. Contemplating cessation can be combined with attention directed to disappearance only, to the passing away and ending of each inhalation and each exhalation. Proceeding to the final step in this tetrad, attention can turn to the gap between inhalation and exhalation or exhalation and inhalation by way of letting go in the most thorough manner possible.

VI

AWAKENING

With all awakening factors established and balanced, the condor and the mountains can eventually become entirely transparent, symbolizing the complete letting go into the experience of the unconditioned.

In this chapter I discuss the final section in the *Ānāpānasati-sutta* (MN 118), which clarifies the overall purpose and potential of cultivating mindfulness of breathing in sixteen steps. This clarification begins by correlating the four tetrads to the four *satipaṭṭhāna*s. Based on this correlation, the *Ānāpānasati-sutta* then shows how the awakening factors can be aroused and how they lead to knowledge and liberation.

I begin by briefly surveying the correlation between the four tetrads and the four *satipaṭṭhāna*s and then take up the prominence of the awakening factors in the practice of mindfulness of breathing. Then I examine in detail the implicit and explicit indications provided in the *Ānāpānasati-sutta* regarding the cultivation of the seven awakening factors. Next I turn to the need for balancing the awakening factors, and then take up their inclining towards awakening in such a way that they lead to knowledge and liberation.

THE AWAKENING FACTORS AND THE FOUR *SATIPAṬṬHĀNAS*

After its exposition of the sixteen steps, the *Ānāpānasati-sutta* continues by relating the resulting four tetrads to the four *satipaṭṭhāna*s (Anālayo 2013b: 233–235) as follows:

- contemplation of the body: understand long breath (1), understand short breath (2), experience the whole body (3), calm bodily activity (4);
- contemplation of feeling tones: experience joy (5), experience happiness (6), experience mental activity (7), calm mental activity (8);
- contemplation of the mind: experience the mind (9), gladden the mind (10), concentrate the mind (11), liberate the mind (12);
- contemplation of dharmas: contemplate impermanence (13), contemplate dispassion/fading away (14), contemplate cessation (15), and contemplate letting go (16).

The main rationale for this correlation appears to be simply that with the first tetrad aspects of the body are contemplated, with the second tetrad feeling tones are a prominent theme, the third tetrad turns to the mind, and the fourth tetrad takes up central aspects of the Dharma (see below p. 203).

In the course of establishing this correlation, the *Ānāpānasati-sutta* indicates that each tetrad of mindfulness of breathing leads to dwelling "diligent, clearly comprehending, and mindful, free from desire and discontent with regard to the world". The same phrase occurs in the *Satipaṭṭhāna-sutta* in relation to each *satipaṭṭhāna* (MN 10; Anālayo 2003b: 31–43 and 2013b: 12–15). This goes to show that each tetrad of mindfulness of breathing functions in the same basic mode as the corresponding *satipaṭṭhāna* in the *Satipaṭṭhāna-sutta*.

A simile found in a discourse in the *Saṃyutta-nikāya* and its parallel illustrates the potential of each tetrad for diminishing unwholesome states with the example of a chariot that drives over a mound of soil at a crossroads (SN 54.10; see below p. 211). No matter from which of the four directions the chariot comes, it will flatten the mound. Similarly, no matter which of the four *satipaṭṭhāna*s is being cultivated with the help of the corresponding tetrad, it will flatten the mound of unwholesomeness in the mind (presumably in the sense of removing even the last traces of unwholesome tendencies).

This conveys the impression that each tetrad can lead to liberation. From a practical viewpoint, this leaves open the possibility of giving emphasis to one particular tetrad during one's practice. At the same time, however, the dynamics of the whole scheme of sixteen steps would make it preferable if we proceed at least once through all four tetrads one after the other before taking up a single tetrad for further practice. The commendability of such an approach becomes evident on closer inspection of the dynamics of the whole scheme and its relationship to an arousal of the awakening factors. Before turning to that topic, however, I briefly want to set the scene by discussing the prominence of the awakening factors in the mode of practice presented in the *Ānāpānasati-sutta*.

PROMINENCE OF THE AWAKENING FACTORS

In the *Satipaṭṭhāna-sutta* the contemplation of the awakening factors features as one of a range of different exercises and comes up only under the fourth *satipaṭṭhāna*. In the progression of practice described in the *Ānāpānasati-sutta*, rather than being the domain of contemplation of dharmas only, their cultivation relates to each of the four tetrads. In this way, the *Ānāpānasati-sutta* places considerable emphasis on the awakening factors, which clearly reflects a distinct concern of mindfulness of breathing in sixteen steps.

This apparent emphasis on the awakening factors might explain the function of mindfulness of breathing in the *Girimānanda-sutta* as the last of a series of ten perceptions (AN 10.60; Anālayo 2016b: 229–236). Hearing a recitation of the entire set of ten perceptions led to Girimānanda's recovery from disease. According to another set of three discourses in the *Bojjhaṅga-saṃyutta*, a recitation of the awakening factors had the similar effect of bringing about a cure of illness (SN 46.14–16; Anālayo 2016b: 43–50). In each case, it can safely be assumed that the respective recitations led to corresponding mental cultivation by the listener. Perhaps the case of Girimānanda is similar to these three other discourses, in that, as a climax of the different perceptions he was taught, it could have been in particular the arousing and cultivation of the awakening factors through the sixteen steps of mindfulness of breathing that served to enable his return to health.

An emphasis on the awakening factors could also explain the Buddha's apparent predilection for the practice of mindfulness of breathing, already mentioned in the introduction, to the extent that he would spend a whole retreat dedicated to its practice. Given that the cultivation of the awakening factors is considered a distinct discovery of the Buddha (SN 46.42; Anālayo 2003b: 240f and 2013b: 218f), it would be natural for him to engage in a form of meditation practice that stands out for its close relationship to these seven mental qualities.

The significance of mindfulness of breathing that emerges in this way could also provide a context to the introductory narration to the *Ānāpānasati-sutta*. This narration depicts an assembly of monastics engaged in meditation practices of various types. In this setting of earnest practitioners, the Buddha is on record as expounding the sixteen steps of mindfulness of breathing (see below p. 220). This points to the eminent role of this particular meditation practice and perhaps also to its potential to enhance other meditation practices through training the skill of remaining well anchored in the present moment. In the approach to practice presented here, this takes place through peripheral awareness of the process of breathing and the skilful employment of wholesome types of joy.

AROUSING THE AWAKENING FACTORS

The instructions on mindfulness of breathing in the *Ānāpānasati-sutta* lead up to an exposition on how the whole set of seven awakening factors can be developed with each of the four tetrads, which comes with helpful information on the nature of each awakening factor. The passage in question specifies that, by working with any tetrad and thereby cultivating the respective *satipaṭṭhāna*, the following takes place:

> One dwells contemplating diligent, clearly comprehending, and mindful, free from desire and discontent with regard to the world. At that time mindfulness is established continuously. At a time when mindfulness is established in one continuously, at that time the awakening factor of mindfulness is aroused in one, at that time one cultivates the awakening factor of mindfulness, at that time the awakening factor of mindfulness comes to be accomplished in one by cultivation.
>
> Dwelling mindfully in this way, one discerns, investigates, and makes an examination of that state with wisdom. At a time when, dwelling mindfully in this way, one discerns, investigates, and makes an examination of that state with wisdom, at that time the awakening factor of investigation-of-dharmas is aroused in one, at that time one cultivates the awakening factor of investigation-of-dharmas, at that time the awakening factor of investigation-of-dharmas comes to be accomplished in one by cultivation.
>
> In one who discerns, investigates, and makes an examination of that state with wisdom, unwavering energy is aroused. At a time when unwavering energy is aroused in one who discerns, investigates, and makes an examination of that state with wisdom, at that time the awakening factor of energy is aroused in one, at that time one

> cultivates the awakening factor of energy, at that time the awakening factor of energy comes to be accomplished in one by cultivation.
>
> In one who has aroused energy, unworldly joy arises. At a time when unworldly joy arises in one who has aroused energy, at that time the awakening factor of joy is aroused in one, at that time one cultivates the awakening factor of joy, at that time the awakening factor of joy comes to be accomplished in one by cultivation.
>
> In one who is joyous, the body becomes tranquil and the mind becomes tranquil. At a time when, in one who is joyous, the body becomes tranquil and the mind becomes tranquil, at that time the awakening factor of tranquillity is aroused in one, at that time one cultivates the awakening factor of tranquillity, at that time the awakening factor of tranquillity comes to be accomplished in one by cultivation.
>
> In one whose body is tranquil and who is happy, the mind becomes concentrated. At a time when, in one whose body is tranquil and who is happy, the mind becomes concentrated, at that time the awakening factor of concentration is aroused in one, at that time one cultivates the awakening factor of concentration, at that time the awakening factor of concentration comes to be accomplished in one by cultivation.
>
> One carefully oversees, without interfering, the mind that has become concentrated in this way. At a time when one carefully oversees, without interfering, the mind that has become concentrated in this way, at that time the awakening factor of equipoise is aroused in one, at that time one cultivates the awakening factor of equipoise, at that time the awakening factor of equipoise comes to be accomplished in one by cultivation.

Although this passage relates the arousing of the awakening factors to a single of the four tetrads of mindfulness of breathing, this does not amount to a recommendation to limit practice in principle to one tetrad only. In fact, closer inspection of the sixteen steps described in the *Ānāpānasati-sutta* reveals potential stimulants for these awakening factors that are implicitly built into the preliminaries and the steps in the first three tetrads. This potential makes it indeed preferable, as briefly mentioned above, to proceed at least once through the entire set of sixteen steps and only then turn to a cultivation of the awakening factors in relation to individual tetrads.

In what follows, I will first survey the awakening factors individually and discuss how they can be cultivated during an initial progression through the sixteen steps. Then I will relate their cultivation to individual tetrads as a mode of practice that can be adopted after having once progressed through the entire scheme. Before delving into such details, however, I would like to present a simile as a way of conveying a general sense of the type of practice I will be describing.

MOUNTAIN SIMILE

A cultivation of the seven awakening factors by first proceeding through all sixteen steps and then taking up individual tetrads could be illustrated with the example of walking up a mountain, with benches that afford beautiful views, situated at roughly equal distances on three spots along the trail and a fourth bench on top of the mountain for viewing the whole panorama. The walking up corresponds to the different steps of mindfulness of breathing, the enjoying of the scenery while seated on one of the benches represents the presence of the awakening factors while dwelling in the last step of one of the four tetrads.

At first we can walk straight up all the way to the mountaintop and there sit down to enjoy the scenery. Similarly, to get started it is preferable to proceed once through the whole series of sixteen steps. After having worked through the entire scheme of four tetrads once, we could choose one of the tetrads, according to what appears to fit our present condition best. In terms of the mountain simile, after having had an overview of the scenery from the top of the mountain, we can walk over to any of the other benches in order to sit there and enjoy the distinct view of the surroundings that each of them can offer.

Throughout the walk we are free to decide at what speed to proceed and how much time to spend on each bench. Similarly, we are free to decide at what speed to proceed through a tetrad of mindfulness of breathing. After proceeding through a tetrad at whatever speed we find appropriate we could then combine its last step with cultivating all of the awakening factors. Having dwelled for some time in this mode of practice, it might be opportune to take up another tetrad for practice or else to repeat the present one over again.

When proceeding through any of the four tetrads, we might either stay for quite some time with each individual step or else proceed swiftly in order to reach the final step in the tetrad and then remain dwelling in the corresponding meditative theme. Throughout, the main concern is maintaining the awakening factors in balance.

In what follows, I proceed from the general illustration of the practice with the help of the mountain simile to an examination of individual awakening factors and of potential stimulants for each that are implicit in the preliminaries and individual steps in the first three tetrads. After summarizing the relationship that emerges in this way, in a subsequent part I will then discuss the cultivation of the awakening factors in relation to single tetrads.

MINDFULNESS

In order for mindfulness as the first awakening factor to be "established continuously", we need to dwell "contemplating diligent, clearly comprehending, and mindful, free from desire and discontent with regard to the world". In the *Ānāpānasati-sutta* such establishing of mindfulness has its starting place in the preliminary practice of "having established mindfulness to the fore", following which "mindful one breathes in and mindful one breathes out." Already at this stage in the mode of practice presented here, we have gained some degree of freedom from desires and discontent through working with the preliminaries in the way described in the first chapter. Ongoing practice of the subsequent steps of mindfulness of breathing will keep strengthening this type of freedom.

The cultivation of mindfulness can be seen to go through a gradual process of maturation with the ensuing steps. From just being mindful of inhalations and exhalations, the first two steps combine mindfulness with a stronger focus on the length of the breath. In the remaining steps, mindfulness needs to encompass peripheral awareness of the breath and other meditative topics. The gradual maturation of mindfulness that takes place in this way corresponds to the meditative evolution that underlies the four *satipaṭṭhāna*s, from body via feeling tone and mind to dharmas.

INVESTIGATION

For engendering a cultivation of the other awakening factors, being mindful of the breath needs to be combined with an element of enquiry or investigation. This first of all results in a clear distinction between inhalations and exhalations, which can already serve to arouse the second awakening factor, investigation-of-dharmas, in an incipient stage. The same factor then more fully manifests when investigating the length of the breath in order to determine if it is long or short.

According to the description in the *Ānāpānasati-sutta*, this awakening factor arises when "one discerns, investigates, and makes an examination of that state with wisdom." Here the mention of examining with wisdom "that state", *taṃ dhammaṃ*, need not be taken as referring to the breath only. Instead, it seems preferable to understand this expression as covering also the "state" of the mind brought into being through whichever step is being practised.

Directing investigation towards our overall condition has an immediate benefit in so far as it supports the continuity of mindfulness, simply because any tendency towards distraction will more easily and quickly be noticed. It also offers a field of examination of added interest, as our overall condition exhibits further diversity than the breath alone.

Another advantage of such an understanding of the scope of investigation-of-dharmas is that it accords better with the indication made elsewhere in the Pāli discourses that distinguishing between what is wholesome/skilful and what is unwholesome/unskilful serves as nourishment for this awakening factor (SN 46.51; Anālayo 2013b: 207). Such a distinction makes considerably more sense in relation to the overall state of the mind than in relation to the breath. After all, however thoroughly it is explored, from the viewpoint of the overarching goal of gaining liberating insight there is little to be learned about the breath, apart from the fact that it is impermanent. A more fruitful arena for the deployment of investigation would be our present overall condition. This does have an evident relationship to the wisdom mentioned in the instruction ("one discerns, investigates, and makes an examination of that state with wisdom"), since such investigating has a greater potential to generate wisdom than examining just our breathing.

In practical terms, already when discerning the length of the breath, investigation can also scrutinize the condition of the mind, discerning how the modality of more focused attention affects our mental condition. This helps to decide when it is opportune to turn to the whole body with the next two steps, and proceed in the ensuing two tetrads to feeling tones and the mind, respectively. With the final tetrad on contemplation of dharmas, the progression of insight (starting off with impermanence) becomes the object of investigation.

In this way, the investigative wisdom is at first somewhat rudimentary, as it is merely concerned with discerning aspects of the breath and how attending to them impacts the mind. But with subsequent steps the same basic activity of discerning, investigating, and making an examination comes to encompass other dimensions of the meditative experience that have a more prominent relationship to wisdom. This is particularly evident with the insight perspectives in the final tetrad on contemplation of dharmas. In a way, investigating and examining the breath could be considered to sharpen the sword of wisdom, as it were, preparing it for the tasks that lie ahead. These tasks become gradually more refined and eventually lead all the way up to the brink of liberating wisdom. In this way, a gradual maturation of investigation-of-dharmas is possible in the course of progressing through the tetrads.

ENERGY

In order for such an investigation to bear its potential fruits, it needs to be sustained. This is where energy comes in, which inspires and sustains the process of examination. Energy in turn is generated by the interest stimulated by investigation. According to the *Ānāpānasati-sutta*, "in one who discerns, investigates, and makes an examination of that state with wisdom, unwavering energy is aroused."

In the approach to practice described here, the degree of mental stability that has resulted from the investigative focus on the breath during the first two steps becomes a continuous element in the background of the remaining steps, maintained by keeping the breath in peripheral awareness. This is where the awakening factor of energy comes in, namely by ensuring that such peripheral awareness of the breath is sustained alongside the main steps of practice. It is in this way that the investigation of inhalations and exhalations, carried out during the first two steps, serves to arouse the energy required for maintaining peripheral awareness of inhalations and exhalations during the ensuing progression. Here energy needs to be indeed "unwavering" in order to fulfil its task, which is in particular to ensure that the hindrances are kept at bay (see below p. 196).

The task of energy continues to evolve as we progress through the ensuing steps. Whereas maintaining awareness of the alternation between inhalations and exhalations alongside "experiencing the whole body" (3) is fairly simple, with ensuing tetrads the task expands to bridging the bodily phenomenon of the breath and experiences of feeling tones and mental states. With "liberating the mind" (12) a level of practice is eventually reached where energy has become very subtle, yet nevertheless present. Even the smallest amount of active interference would run counter to the thrust of this step. At the same time, a loss of energy would result in distraction. The balance of energy achieved at this juncture then sustains the insight contemplations in the last tetrad.

JOY

The gradual building up of the practice during the first tetrad on contemplation of the body leads over to experiencing joy (5) as the first step in the second tetrad on contemplation of feeling tones. The energy aroused earlier needs to be steady without becoming forceful or leading to tenseness, as this would prevent joy from arising. This joy arises when bodily activity has become calm but the alternation between inhalations and exhalations is still kept continuously in peripheral awareness. It is in this way that "in one who has aroused energy, unworldly joy arises."

As mentioned previously, such joy is the maturation of the pleasant feeling tone of being in the present moment (combined with the bodily tranquillity reached in the previous step). Similar to the other awakening factors discussed so far, joy also goes through a process of gradual maturation by leading on to happiness (6) in the next step. In a way, happiness could be considered as providing a transition from the full experience of joy in the preceding step (5) to shifting the pleasant feeling tone of being in the present moment to peripheral awareness with the next step (7) of this tetrad. The same continues and eventually flowers into the more profound gladdening of the mind (10) in the second step of the third tetrad on contemplation of the mind. Throughout the remainder of the practice, the pleasant feeling tone that results from being in the here and now continues to counter the mind's tendency to distraction.

TRANQUILLITY

The *Ānāpānasati-sutta* explains that "in one who is joyous, the body becomes tranquil and the mind becomes tranquil." In the progression of sixteen steps, bodily tranquillity actually precedes joy and serves as its proximate condition in the form of "calming bodily activity" (4). This reveals that the relationship between joy and tranquillity is not just about the former serving as a condition for the latter. Instead, there is some degree of interrelation between joy and tranquillity. A basis in bodily tranquillity directly feeds joy. Such joy then leads, via two intermediate steps, to the eventual experience of mental tranquillity, when the completion of the second tetrad on contemplation of feeling tones results in "calming mental activity" (8).

CONCENTRATION

The tranquillity of body and mind, established with the completion of the second tetrad on contemplation of feeling tones, provides a foundation for the gaining of concentration with the third tetrad on contemplation of the mind. This is in line with the indication that "in one whose body is tranquil and who is happy, the mind becomes concentrated."

The reference to being happy in this statement could best be related to "gladdening the mind" (10), the step that directly precedes "concentrating the mind" (11). Perhaps this is why gladdening needs to be brought in at this stage of practice as a proximate cause for concentration, even though joy (5) and happiness (6) had already been aroused with the previous tetrad on contemplation of feeling tones. Whereas joy and happiness functioned as aids for progressing from bodily tranquillity to its mental counterpart in "calming mental activity", at the present juncture "gladdening the mind" serves to ripen tranquillity into concentration. In this way, "gladdening the mind" appears to have the task of ensuring a deepening of concentration.

Although some degree of concentration has been established right at the outset when focusing on the length of the breath, it is with the third step in the third tetrad on contemplation of the mind that it comes to the fore with the explicit injunction to "concentrate" the mind. The degree of concentration achieved in this way ensures firm stability of the mind for what comes next.

EQUIPOISE

This holds particularly for the next step that completes the third tetrad on contemplation of the mind, which is "liberating the mind" (12). Such liberating of the mind requires indeed that "one carefully oversees, without interfering, the mind that has become concentrated in this way." Regardless of whether we take this step as a basis for entry into absorption or for cultivating insight, such careful overseeing, without interfering, is what this particular step requires above all.

In this way, the continuity of mindful investigation that is supported by the steadiness of energy, the inspiration of joy, the grounding of tranquillity, and the composure of concentration eventually converges into carefully overseeing the concentrated mind without interfering. In the case of this last awakening factor, the Chinese parallel offers the additional information that the required mental condition of balance and equipoise is reached due to completely leaving behind desire and discontent (see below p. 208). Although these have already been set aside at the outset of the practice, at the present juncture any remaining trace of inclining towards desire or discontent, however subtle, is definitely left behind.

A build-up to this level of equipoise occurs during the progression through the previous two tetrads on contemplation of the body and feeling tones. The steps in these two tetrads follow a pattern where one step that is more energizing is followed by one step that is more tranquil, a constant alternation that can be understood to build up and gradually fortify the balance of equipoise (see above p. 82). This alternation takes the following form:

- long breath (1) leads to short breath (2),
- experiencing the whole body (3) leads to calming bodily activity (4),
- experiencing joy (5) leads to the (comparatively calmer) happiness (6),
- experiencing mental activity (7) leads to its calming (8).

The third tetrad on contemplation of the mind then serves to build up to a level of equipoise that facilitates the mind becoming liberated. This tetrad differs from the previous two, in which the progression from the first two steps to the third and fourth step involves some degree of thematic shift. In the first tetrad on contemplation of the body this is a shift from the breath to the body (and its activity). In the second tetrad on contemplation of feeling tones this is a shift from pleasant mental states (joy and happiness) to mental activity.

In the third tetrad on contemplation of the mind, however, a single theme continues throughout: the mind. It is the mind which is to be experienced (9), gladdened (10), concentrated (11), and liberated (12). This meditative progression leads up to a peak of equipoise with the final step of liberating the mind. It is based on this peak of equipoise that the insight contemplations in the last tetrad can unfold their full potential.

THE AWAKENING FACTORS AND INDIVIDUAL STEPS

The above survey of each individual awakening factor shows how a progression from the preliminaries to the conclusion of the third tetrad can actualize each of these seven qualities. Due to the importance of this aspect of the practice, in what follows I briefly summarize the relationships between individual steps and awakening factors that have emerged in this way.

The practice begins with the initial practice of establishing *mindfulness* to the fore such that we mindfully breathe in and out. The distinction to be drawn between inhalations and exhalations already requires some degree of *investigation*, which becomes fully prominent with the first two steps by investigating the length of the breath in order to discern long and short breaths.

The remainder of the instructions comes with the injunction to "train". Such training requires the arousal of *energy*. In the way of practice presented here, it involves combining the individual step to be executed with maintaining peripheral awareness of the breath.

The first step of the second tetrad on contemplation of feeling tones explicitly refers to *joy* (5). Although in the mode of practice suggested here some subtle pleasant feeling tone has been aroused right at the outset when establishing mindfulness, it comes into full bloom in the form of joy with the onset of the second tetrad.

Already with the final step of the first tetrad on contemplation of the body, tranquillity of the body came to the forefront through calming bodily activity (4). The final step of the second tetrad on contemplation of feeling tones involves precisely the same calming but with mental activity (8). This neatly mirrors the fact that the awakening factor of *tranquillity* has a bodily and a mental dimension.

The combination of joy (together with happiness and gladness) with tranquillity of body and mind naturally leads over to *concentration* (11), which forms the third step in the third tetrad on contemplation of the mind.

Although not explicitly mentioned, the last awakening factor of *equipoise* can be understood as underlying the last step in the third tetrad on contemplation of the mind, where with liberating the mind (12) a supreme degree of inner balance is reached. The *Ānāpānasati-sutta* describes the actual activity of the awakening factor of equipoise with the term *ajjhupekkhati*, which I understand to mean "to oversee without interfering". This is precisely what is required when liberating the mind: not interfering, while at the same time still having a full overview of the situation. It is in this way that either entry into absorption can take place or else the mind can be liberated from any self-referentiality and from any I-making and my-making.

These implicit cross-relations between individual steps and awakening factors complement two similar cross-relations, noted in previous chapters. One of these obtains between individual steps and the factors of absorption (see above p. 92). The other concerns precedents among individual steps to discerning the impermanent nature of each of the five aggregates (see above p. 103). In this way, the cultivation of tranquillity and insight can build on groundwork already established during the progression through the first three tetrads. Adding to these the possibility that each of the seven awakening factors can be stimulated in the way described above, the profundity of the instructions in the *Ānāpānasati-sutta* becomes readily apparent.

For ease of reference, below I present these cross-relations in a graphic manner. The left side has the step particularly relevant for arousing or fully cultivating a particular factor or perspective, which is found on the right side.

Steps:		**Absorption factors:**
1	(long breath)	*vitakka* (application of the mind)
3	(whole body)	*vicāra* (sustaining of the mind)
5	(joy)	joy
6	(happiness)	happiness
11	(concentrate mind)	unification

Steps:		**Five aggregates:**
3	(whole body)	form
5	(joy)	feeling tone
7	(experience mental activity)	perception and intentions
9	(experience mind)	consciousness

Steps:		**Awakening factors:**
0	(mindfulness to the fore)	mindfulness
1	(long breath)	investigation
3	(whole body)	energy
5	(joy)	joy
8	(calm mental activity)	tranquillity
11	(concentrate mind)	concentration
12	(liberate mind)	equipoise

EMPHASIS ON INDIVIDUAL AWAKENING FACTORS

Based on the correlations between individual steps and awakening factors, described above, a progression through the preliminaries and the first three tetrads can be employed to arouse the awakening factors or to maintain and strengthen their presence. Once this has been accomplished, it can be helpful for a moment to become fully aware of the quality of the mind when it is being enriched by all of these seven awakening factors. This is similar to the suggestion, in relation to the preliminaries to mindfulness of breathing, to take a moment for just being with the quality of the mind in which mindfulness has come to the fore, similar to meeting a good old friend whom we are going to be working with on some project (see above p. 19). In the same way, shining the light of awareness on the rich condition of our mind at the present juncture of practice will strengthen our ability to maintain the presence of the awakening factors during ensuing practice.

The meditative progression of arousing the seven awakening factors one after the other could at times be undertaken with an emphasis on a particular one of these factors. Working with an individual awakening factor in such a way could take the form of moving continuously through whatever steps precede the step that is particularly prone to arousing the chosen awakening factor, in clear awareness of their contribution to its eventual arising. Reaching the specific step in question can lead to dwelling at length in the experience of the full arousal of the chosen awakening factor. The ensuing progression through the remaining steps could then take place with an eye on the contribution made by this awakening factor to their smooth unfolding. Such a mode of practice can help to arrive at a clear practical understanding of the nature of an individual awakening factor, of how it can be aroused and how it can be gradually matured.

A discourse in the *Bojjhaṅga-saṃyutta* reports Sāriputta's ability to remain established in one particular awakening factor of his choice even for a third part of a day (SN 46.4; Anālayo 2013b: 205). This shows that there is nothing wrong in dedicating some time to familiarizing ourselves with the specific flavour and distinct characteristics of one awakening factor through its individual cultivation, before moving on to the others.

In this way a lively form of practice can ensue, where we keep freely choosing how much time to accord to individual steps as well as to individual awakening factors, in keeping with what seems to fit our situation best, guided by the overarching concern of cultivating all of the seven awakening factors alongside remaining aware of the impermanent nature of the breath.

THE INDIVIDUAL TETRADS AND THE AWAKENING FACTORS

Besides the implicit relationship between individual awakening factors and particular steps, the *Ānāpānasati-sutta* explicitly describes a cultivation of all seven awakening factors based on each of the four tetrads. In what follows I apply this to actual practice.

If we turn to the first tetrad on contemplation of the body after having once proceeded through all sixteen steps, practice can start off by just attending to the distinction between inhalations and exhalations and then discerning if these are long or else short, followed by experiencing the whole body, and calming bodily activity. Proceeding through these at whatever speed appears appropriate for this particular sitting, contemplation of the body through mindfulness of breathing has been completed. Based on the condition of deep bodily relaxation and calmness of bodily activity that has been established with the last step of this first tetrad, the awakening factors can be cultivated, alongside continuous awareness of the process of breathing, in the following manner:

Mindfulness furnishes the basic presence of the mind. As we are mindfully aware of the calmness of bodily activity, investigation-of-dharmas can serve to scrutinize for any possible remainder of tension that can still be calmed. Such investigation leads to, and is sustained by, unwavering energy. Energy in turn has the task of ensuring continuity, in particular of peripheral awareness of the breath alongside bodily calmness. From having established energy in this way, next we need to make sure that unworldly joy can arise out of the experience of bodily tranquillity, avoiding any tenseness or pushiness. Such joy provides the finishing touch to our ability to stay in the present moment by endowing it with the natural attraction that pleasant experiences have to keep the mind in place and avoid it becoming distracted.

Once we have become joyous, bodily tranquillity naturally leads to resting bodily and mentally grounded in the present experience. As a result of such resting, happiness arises and the mind becomes effortlessly concentrated. It simply wants to remain in the wholeness of composure, rather than chasing after this or that and thereby get involved again in the fragmentation characteristic of ordinary experience. All we need to do is to oversee carefully the concentrated mind without interfering.

While gradually proceeding through the awakening factors in this way, we might deliberately formulate the notion of the specific awakening factor once and then just rest in the resulting experience without further formulating concepts for another two, three, or more breaths. This helps to avoid being lost in mental fabrication without actually experiencing the distinct flavour of the respective awakening factor.

Once each awakening factor has been well established, we just dwell with all seven awakening factors present in a condition of the mind that is characterized by the calmness of bodily activity, all the while remaining aware of the changing nature of the inhalations and exhalations.

Before turning to the next tetrad, I would like to note that the presentation in the *Ānāpānasati-sutta* clearly envisages the cultivation of all awakening factors to be possible based on the first tetrad of body contemplation only. For that purpose, however, it would be advisable to proceed once through the entire scheme of sixteen steps. Having progressed once through the whole scheme will make it much easier to cultivate all of the awakening factors with the first four steps, since these have already been previously aroused during the earlier progression through the first three tetrads.

In the case of the second tetrad on contemplation of feeling tones, attending to the pleasant feeling tone of being in the present moment can lead to the arousal of joy and the experience of happiness, leading to experiencing and calming mental activity. The resultant still mind is now the condition or state (*dhamma*) that serves as the reference point for the cultivation of the awakening factors. Given that this tetrad corresponds to contemplation of feeling tone, it is in particular the subtle pleasant feeling tone of the still mind that can be allowed to stand out prominently.

Mindfulness is aware of the condition of mental calmness, investigation of it engenders energy and joy, which in turn lead to tranquillity, concentration, and equipoise. Each of these functions in ways comparable to the description given above in relation to the first tetrad of contemplation of the body. With all of the awakening factors present in the mind, we continue to dwell for as long as seems appropriate in the pleasant experience of the still mind, keeping the alternation between inhalations and exhalations in the periphery of our field of attention throughout.

Getting started on the third tetrad on contemplation of the mind can take place by turning to the knowing of the breath and from that to experiencing the mind. This then leads to gladdening, concentrating, and liberating the mind, dedicating as much time as seems appropriate to each of these four steps. Once the mind has been temporarily liberated from self-referentiality, the awakening factors take this mental condition as their reference point. Their gradual growth culminates in a state of mind well liberated from self-referentiality and endowed with all seven awakening factors, while at the same time we remain aware of inhalations and exhalations.

The same basic pattern applies to the fourth tetrad on contemplation of dharmas, which can take the alternation between inhalations and exhalations as its starting point to contemplate impermanence, followed by dispassion/fading away, cessation, and letting go as completely as possible. This is now the mental condition that serves as the reference point for the awakening factors, in combination with continuous awareness of the process of breathing. The fourth tetrad is also the one best suited to serve as the final one after working flexibly with various tetrads, in order to ensure that the finishing touch of insight falls into place.

In this way, the overall state of our mind after the completion of each tetrad can become the reference point for the cultivation of the awakening factors as follows:

- 1st tetrad (contemplation of the body): deep bodily relaxation,
- 2nd tetrad (contemplation of feeling tone): the pleasant feeling tone of the still mind,
- 3rd tetrad (contemplation of the mind): the mind liberated from self-referentiality,
- 4th tetrad (contemplation of dharmas): letting go by inclining towards Nirvāṇa.

The above presentation is only meant to depict a possible mode of practice and not to restrict a cultivation of the awakening factors to the last step of each tetrad only; in fact the same can be done with each step. This is particularly the case for the insight perspectives in the last tetrad on contemplation of dharmas, each of which can be taken up on its own for a sustained cultivation of the awakening factors.

BALANCING THE AWAKENING FACTORS

Once the awakening factors have been established, they need to be balanced with each other (Anālayo 2013b: 201–205). Mindfulness serves as a foundation that is required throughout. Based on mindfulness being well established, the more energetic awakening factors of investigation-of-dharmas, energy, and joy need to be brought into harmonious balance with the more calming awakening factors of concentration, tranquillity, and equipoise. Mindfulness monitors this balance of the awakening factors.

The monitoring function of mindfulness is relevant for the entire scheme of practice; in fact it is even needed if we head for absorption attainment with "liberating the mind", the last step of the third tetrad on contemplation of the mind. Here mindfulness takes the role of supervising the presence and continuity of the absorption factors and their balanced cooperation to bring about and maintain the actual experience of absorption.

Balancing the awakening factors while practising different steps of mindfulness of breathing (or alongside other types of meditation practices) is a bit like driving a car with manual transmission in a town. Most of our attention is on what is happening outside – we keep in mind the direction we want to go in and continue to observe the condition of the traffic. But part of our attention is also on the car itself, so that we notice when we need to change gears. This awareness of how the engine is doing in relation to the overall traffic situation is similar to the awareness of how the mind is doing in relation to the overall situation of our meditation practice. Just as we keep noting if we need to change gear in order to drive smoothly, so we keep noting which of these awakening factors needs to be strengthened so that our practice continues smoothly.

BALANCING WITH INDIVIDUAL STEPS

What follows is meant to provide some additional tools, which are not necessarily relevant for each meditator. A possible tool to achieve a balancing of the awakening factors during the practice of mindfulness of breathing, in the way presented here, relates to individual steps in each tetrad. Closer examination shows that in each tetrad one of the first two steps tends to have somewhat more affinity with the three energizing awakening factors, whereas one of the remaining two steps tends to have a bit more affinity with the calming awakening factors.

The steps that can be given more emphasis to bring about an energizing effect and thus to strengthen in particular the cultivation of the three awakening factors of investigation-of-dharmas, energy, and joy are the effort to focus on the length of the breath at the outset of the first tetrad (contemplation of the body), the experiencing of joy at the outset of the second tetrad (contemplation of feeling tones), the gladdening of the mind as the second step in the third tetrad (contemplation of the mind), and the contemplative investigation of impermanence at the outset of the fourth tetrad (contemplation of dharmas). In this way, energizing steps that could be related to investigation-of-dharmas, energy, and joy are:

- understand length of breath (1 and 2),
- experience joy (5),
- gladden the mind (10),
- contemplate impermanence (13).

Other steps can be given special attention to bring about a more calming effect and thereby strengthen the cultivation of the three awakening factors of concentration, tranquillity, and equipoise. These are calming bodily activity as the last step in the first tetrad (contemplation of the body), calming mental activity as the last step in the second tetrad (contemplation of feeling tones), concentrating the mind as the third step in the third tetrad (contemplation of the mind), and contemplating letting go as the last step in the fourth tetrad (contemplation of dharmas). In this way, calming steps that could be related to concentration, tranquillity, and equipoise are:

- calm bodily activity (4),
- calm mental activity (8),
- concentrate the mind (11),
- contemplate letting go (16).

In this way, strengthening one of the two groups of three awakening factors could be related to a particular step in whichever of the four tetrads we are currently practising. Such emphasis could take the form either of an increase of mental attention or of remaining with this particular step for longer than the time dedicated to other steps in this tetrad. Suppose more energy is required, then the energizing steps of focusing on the length of the breath, experiencing joy and gladness, and contemplating impermanence could receive more room or emphasis in our practice. Suppose calmness is required, then the tranquillizing steps of calming the activity of body and mind, concentrating the mind, and contemplating letting go could be those in which we dwell a little longer or to which we give particular attention.

BALANCING WITH THE BREATH

Besides working with a particular step in one of the tetrads, balance can also be achieved and maintained by attending to the alternation between inhalations and exhalations. The basic principle here is that attention given to the slightly more energizing inhalation can be associated with the energizing awakening factors, whereas attention given to the exhalation, which is a little more relaxing, can be associated with the calming awakening factors.

This suggestion is just about directing attention and should be implemented without influencing or changing the breath itself. Such a mode of paying attention would be particularly relevant when, after having proceeded through one of the tetrads, we are just dwelling with continuous awareness of the final theme aroused through this tetrad.

Applying this to actual practice, first of all one or more cycles of the breath can be used to strengthen the grounding of the awakening factor of mindfulness in proprioceptive awareness of the body. Next, based on the continuity of being mindful of the alternation between inhalations and exhalations, during the inhalation attention can be directed to strengthening the three energizing awakening factors of investigation-of-dharmas, energy, and joy. During the exhalation attention can strengthen the three calming awakening factors of tranquillity, concentration, and equipoise. The resulting themes that emerge with the inhalation and the exhalation respectively are:

- inhalation: joyfully sustained interest,
- exhalation: calmly composed balance.

In this way, being mindful of the natural alternation between inhalation and exhalation can serve as a reminder of the balance required between these two sets of three awakening factors. When mindfulness notices that practice has become a bit sluggish, more attention to the inhalation and the awakening factors of investigation-of-dharmas, energy, and joy can help to recover balance. If mindfulness notices that practice has become a bit agitated, more attention to the exhalation and the awakening factors of tranquillity, concentration, and equipoise can likewise serve to balance.

At times practice may evolve based on a particular basic rhythm of several cycles of breaths. For the duration of one such cycle, we could emphasize keeping mindfulness established in relation to what has emerged with the conclusion of the tetrad we have been working with. Once the cycle is over, we check in on the condition of the mind in order to see if it needs to be slightly more energized or else a little more calmed. Depending on what seems appropriate, we then cultivate the three energizers (investigation, energy, joy) or the three calmers (tranquillity, concentration, equipoise). If checking in on the condition of the mind has not revealed any discernible indication that would make one of these two groupings appear preferable, we might just give emphasis to mindfulness. Throughout, mindfulness remains the foundation for each of these alternative approaches to balance.

In addition to being helpful for maintaining balance, the mode of practice described above also prevents the mind from going into autopilot mode. Checking in at regular intervals and then deciding what to do next, based on having discerned the present condition of the mind, keeps us interested and introduces an element of liveliness into the practice.

The main theme throughout remains impermanence, inculcated primarily through being continuously mindful of the breath. At the same time, the fact of impermanence can also find reflection in this practice of monitoring current conditions and, as they change, adjusting to them.

INCLINING TOWARDS AWAKENING

After depicting the arousing of the awakening factors with each tetrad of practice, the *Ānāpānasati-sutta* continues by explaining how cultivation of mindfulness of breathing can lead to knowledge and liberation. This explanation takes the following form:

> One develops the mindfulness awakening factor *in dependence on seclusion, in dependence on dispassion, and in dependence on cessation, culminating in letting go.*
>
> One develops the investigation-of-dharmas awakening factor in dependence on seclusion, in dependence on dispassion, and in dependence on cessation, culminating in letting go.
>
> One develops the energy awakening factor *in dependence on seclusion, in dependence on dispassion, and in dependence on cessation, culminating in letting go.*
>
> One develops the joy awakening factor *in dependence on seclusion, in dependence on dispassion, and in dependence on cessation, culminating in letting go.*
>
> One develops the tranquillity awakening factor *in dependence on seclusion, in dependence on dispassion, and in dependence on cessation, culminating in letting go.*
>
> One develops the concentration awakening factor *in dependence on seclusion, in dependence on dispassion, and in dependence on cessation, culminating in letting go.*
>
> One develops the equipoise awakening factor in dependence on seclusion, in dependence on dispassion, and in dependence on cessation, culminating in letting go.

In what follows, I will refer to the mention of seclusion, dispassion, cessation, and letting go in this instruction as the "awakening themes" that are to be cultivated, once the awakening factors have been established. Stated in brief, I take these awakening themes to point to *seclusion* from all that is unwholesome, *dispassion* as the fading away of craving, and the gradual *cessation* of all that is *dukkha* (Anālayo 2013b: 219–221). In dependence on these three, the mind increasingly learns to *let go* in the sense of inclining towards Nirvāṇa.

In this way, based on being mindful of the flow of impermanent experience, investigation supported by energy could check if *seclusion* from all that is unwholesome is firmly established, if there is any trace of passion that could be turned into *dispassion* or any trace of craving that can be allowed to *cease*, and perhaps most importantly if there is any trace of I-making or my-making, however subtle, that can be *let go* of. Each of these investigations is productive of joy and tranquillity, they lead to the mind becoming concentrated and balanced, ready for the plunge into the unconditioned.

From the viewpoint of knowledge and liberation as the final goal of mindfulness of breathing, the three awakening themes of seclusion, dispassion, and cessation could be seen as establishing the required *knowledge*. With the awakening theme of letting go, *liberation* can take place.

THE FOURTH TETRAD

Regarding this overall aim of knowledge and liberation, it is noteworthy that, as already mentioned in the previous chapter (see above p. 100), the four awakening themes to be related to each awakening factor closely resemble the four steps in the final tetrad of the instructions for mindfulness of breathing. Here is a correlation of the awakening themes (on the left side) and the fourth tetrad on contemplation of dharmas (on the right side):

seclusion	≠	impermanence (13)
dispassion/fading away	=	dispassion/fading away (14)
cessation	=	cessation (15)
letting go (*vossagga*)	≈	letting go (*paṭinissagga*) (16)

The main difference is that, instead of seclusion, the first step in the fourth tetrad is impermanence. Given that temporary seclusion from the hindrances is to be established already at the outset of the scheme of sixteen steps, it is perhaps only natural that this aspect is replaced by highlighting the insight that forms the undercurrent of the entire scheme, which is impermanence. In this way impermanence comes right to the forefront of attention and serves as an entry into dispassion and cessation, culminating in letting go.

This similarity between the four awakening themes and the final four steps shows that, whereas with the first three tetrads the seven awakening factors can be aroused, the final tetrad can bring them to maturation by moving through the awakening themes. In other words, a progression through these sixteen steps of mindfulness of breathing covers all that is needed for progress to awakening, as it implements the four *satipaṭṭhāna*s, enables the arousal of each of the seven awakening factors, and activates their awakening potential.

TRANQUILLITY AND INSIGHT

The first step of impermanence comes in particularly handy if the previous tetrad on contemplation of the mind has been employed as an avenue for entry into absorption. On emergence, contemplation of impermanence is the most appropriate way of continuing meditation, thereby making sure that the strength of concentration still present is put to good use and that the experience of absorption is divested of any potential clinging and attachment.

If we have instead opted for the cultivation of insight in terms of emptiness as a way of implementing the injunction to liberate the mind, contemplation of impermanence rounds off such insight by strengthening its foundation. It is precisely because all aspects of personal experience are changing that they are not fit to be clung to as a self or to be appropriated as belonging to a self.

THE AWAKENING FACTORS AND THEMES

Whether we conclude the previous third tetrad on contemplation of the mind with an emphasis on tranquillity or on insight, actualizing the awakening themes simply requires progressing through the fourth tetrad on contemplation of dharmas. Due to previous practice of the other tetrads, by this time the awakening factors will have been established.

Comparable to the simplified approach of relating the balancing of the awakening factors to the alternation between inhalation and exhalation, suggested above, a similarly simplified approach is possible with the awakening themes. Once all awakening factors have been established, we might relate seclusion, dispassion, and cessation to the three stages of a single inhalation (its beginning, middle, and end) and letting go to the whole of the exhalation.

At other times, when practice requires still more simplicity, we might just give emphasis to letting go, as long as we are fairly sure that our previous meditative progression has already successfully established the other three awakening themes of seclusion, dispassion, and cessation. In this way the momentum can be maintained by adjusting to different situations, ensuring that the practice remains lively rather than becoming mechanical.

LETTING GO

Of central importance in the cultivation of mindfulness of breathing is the final step and the last of the awakening themes: letting go. Its relevance is similar to the last section of the part of the *Satipaṭṭhāna-sutta* that I have dubbed the "refrain". According to this last section, with any *satipaṭṭhāna* contemplation we should "abide independently, without clinging to anything in the world". In the *Ānāpānasati-sutta*, this injunction appears to have its counterpart in letting go as the culmination point of the sixteen steps. The gradual building up to such letting go can be appreciated by taking a closer look at how it relates to each of the tetrads.

The whole practice starts off with seclusion from the hindrances, which enables establishing a focus on the long breath without being carried away by distraction (1). Increasing aloofness from the hindrances achieved in this way facilitates remaining aware of the comparatively subtler short breath (2). A reduced need for vigilance regarding potential distraction through a recurrence of the hindrances allows us to progress from a focus on the breath to the more relaxed and broad awareness of the whole body, with the breath kept in peripheral awareness (3). At this stage anything that might agitate the body is left behind for good, leading to a deep relaxing and calming of any bodily activity (4).

The completion of the first tetrad on contemplation of the body results in a peaceful and calm condition of the body as the fruition of having left behind any of the hindrances that might lead to tension at the bodily level. The culmination point of this tetrad could be seen as a thorough *letting go* of any bodily tension.

The experience of joy (5) relies on the mind being at least temporarily aloof from complete immersion in thinking and reflection. With attachment to the exhilaration of joy left behind, the comparatively calmer experience of happiness (6) can arise. A further diminishing of attachment makes it possible to step back, as it were, and view anything that happens in the mind as simply manifestations of mental activity (7). Letting go of any involvement with whatever happens in the mind eventually results in calming mental activity (8).

The completion of the second tetrad on contemplation of feeling tones leads to a peaceful and calm condition of the mind, due to having left behind involvement in mental activity. As the fruition of a gradual diminishing of attachment and involvement, a culmination point is reached by *letting go* of thought activity.

Being able to experience the mind (9) relies on having let go of mental activity and thereby what provides a prominent base for our sense of identity. The deepening of this experience naturally leads to the experience of gladness (10) and to the mind becoming effortlessly concentrated (11). In the mode of practice presented here, liberating the mind then requires letting go of all conceit of "I" and appropriation as "mine" (12).

The completion of the third tetrad on contemplation of the mind yields a profoundly peaceful dwelling in emptiness, due to having left behind all identification with, and appropriation of, any aspect of experience. Its culmination point is the *letting go* of all selfing.

Building on this groundwork in modes of letting go, achieved through the previous three tetrads in this way, the fourth tetrad on contemplation of dharmas complements the cultivation of insight by bringing impermanence (13) right to the forefront of meditative attention and thereby arousing knowledge, *vijjā*, and countering ignorance, *avijjā*. Countering the current of ignorance, we cultivate the steps that correspond to the three awakening themes of dispassion (14) and cessation (15), culminating in letting go (16). In this way, our knowledge becomes increasingly liberating.

The correlations suggested here are meant to help accentuate the gradual deepening of letting go during a progression through the sixteen steps. Presented in summary, the proposed correlations are:

- 1st tetrad (body): let go of tension,
- 2nd tetrad (feeling tones): let go of thought,
- 3rd tetrad (mind): let go of selfing,
- 4th tetrad (dharmas): totally let go.

This can serve as a complement to the main theme set by the last step of each tetrad as a reference point for cultivating the awakening factors. In this way, calming bodily activity (4) can come to be invested with a sense of freedom from tension. Calming mental activity (8) can be associated with the beauty of a silent mind free from thought. Liberating the mind (12) can find its expression in emptying the mind from the burden of selfing. Letting go (16) as the culmination point of the sixteen steps and the four awakening themes can serve to incline the mind towards the unconditioned.

The same modalities of letting go can also be cultivated during walking meditation. Fully embodied walking can lead to *letting go* of bodily tension, corresponding to an implementation of steps 3 and 4 (experiencing the whole body and calming bodily activity). Awareness of mental activity while walking can lead to *letting go* of thought activity, corresponding to an implementation of steps 7 and 8 (experiencing and calming mental activity). Turning inwards to the knowing quality can lead to *letting go* of selfing in relation to the activity of walking, corresponding to an implementation of steps 9 and 12 (experiencing and liberating the mind). Giving full importance to the process character of walking as a manifestation of impermanence can lead to *letting go* of all that is subject to the law of change, corresponding to an implementation of steps 13 and 16 (contemplating impermanence and letting go).

On a side note, the steps chosen for walking meditation reflect the somewhat different character of the first and second tetrad (body and feeling tones) compared to the third and fourth tetrad (mind and dharmas). As mentioned earlier (see above p. 82), the first and second tetrad proceed through two distinct themes, which are introduced with the respective first and third step, whereas the third and fourth tetrad have a single theme, introduced with their first step. For this same reason, the above suggested application of letting go to walking meditation can combine the third and the fourth steps of the first two tetrads but instead relates the first to the fourth steps of the last two tetrads.

In this way, with walking meditation the same free choosing of a particular theme from one of the four tetrads could be practised as with the sixteen steps during sitting meditation. In each case, one topic can be the foundation for walking, namely embodied walking, walking aware of thoughts, turning inwards to the knowing of the walking, and attending to the process character of the experience of walking. Whenever possible, these can lead on to the respective types of letting go.

THE CONDOR SIMILE

At the beginning of each chapter, I illustrated a progression through the sixteen steps of mindfulness of breathing with the example of a condor. In what follows I bring together the different aspects of this imagery.

The preliminaries discussed in the first chapter correspond to the condor getting high into the air. With the body-contemplation tetrad the condor reaches sufficient height and only very minor adjustments of the wings' positions are needed to keep balance while gliding along, which corresponds to the process of breathing that we keep in peripheral awareness throughout. Flying effortlessly over mountaintop after mountaintop, the bodily stillness of the condor illustrates the bodily tranquillity achieved with the completion of the first tetrad of contemplation of the body. The continuously changing scenery through which the condor flies stands for the continuous awareness of impermanence that pervades the whole practice of mindfulness of breathing.

With the conclusion of the second tetrad on contemplation of feeling tones, leading up to a calming of mental activity, the head of the condor becomes transparent. The transparency of the head symbolizes the clarity of the mind free of mental chatter, once thought activity has gone into abeyance. The changing scenery continues to represent awareness of impermanence that has become more apparent due to the transparency of the head.

As the third tetrad on contemplation of the mind comes to completion in the way described here, with liberating the mind understood as pointing in particular to freedom from self-referentiality, the torso of the condor also becomes transparent. The transparency of the condor's torso signifies that the conceit of an "I" has gone into abeyance. Due to the increasing transparency of the condor, the changing scenery becomes still more visible, reflecting an increasingly comprehensive vision of impermanence as a result of relinquishing all self-notions.

At this point of practice, when the awakening factors have been established, the torso of the condor can come to represent mindfulness and the wings the other six awakening factors, with one wing standing for the three that energize and the other wing for the three that calm. The minimal adjustments of the condor's wings when gliding along represent the need for similarly minimal adjustments to keep the awakening factors in balance.

With the onset of the fourth tetrad, the condor becomes completely transparent, as its wings also become invisible. In this way, the gradual transparency of the condor reflects the gradual progression in the cultivation of the awakening factors.

The condor still keeps flying effortlessly over mountaintop after mountaintop, but it is no longer visible (similar to the Cheshire Cat in *Alice in Wonderland*, which gradually disappears until only its smile remains). As the condor has become completely transparent, the changing scenery is in turn completely visible. This corresponds to bringing impermanence right to the forefront of attention at the outset of the present tetrad on contemplation of dharmas.

All that remains to be seen is a superb letting go, with whose complete implementation even the mountains vanish. The invisibility of both the condor and the mountains then symbolizes the superb letting go of all conditioned phenomena that can take place with the completion of the sixteen steps of mindfulness of breathing.

SUMMARY

Proceeding once through the sixteen steps can implicitly touch on each of the seven awakening factors during the first three tetrads on contemplation of the body, feeling tones, and the mind. The last tetrad on contemplation of dharmas relates to the awakening themes. Based on *seclusion* from all that is unwholesome, we cultivate *dispassion* as the fading away of craving and the gradual *cessation* of all that is *dukkha*. In dependence on these three, the mind becomes ready to *let go* by inclining towards Nirvāṇa.

Based on having once gone through the entire scheme, any of the tetrads can be taken up individually, with the respective last step serving as a reference point for the awakening factors. Their cultivation requires balancing, based on mindfulness. Lack of energy can be countered by more emphasis on investigation–energy–joy, excess of energy by instead giving attention to tranquillity–concentration–equipoise.

The main goal of the approach to mindfulness of breathing presented here remains throughout to arouse and cultivate the awakening factors, based on being continuously aware of the changing nature of the breath, with the final aim of letting go as completely as possible.

VII

TRANSLATIONS FROM THE *DĪRGHA-ĀGAMA*

With the present chapter, my presentation shifts from practical instructions to providing a more scholarly perspective as a support for the preceding six chapters. The next four chapters are intended to supplement my practice guide to mindfulness of breathing with more detailed information based on annotated excerpts, translated from the four Chinese *Āgamas*, that are in some way or another relevant to the breath or its meditative contemplation. Readers interested predominantly in matters of practice might prefer to skip these chapters or just browse through them lightly, perhaps based on first reading the summary at the end of a chapter in order to see what topic might seem worth following up. Other readers might prefer to examine the material in more detail by reading through the entire chapter and thereby appreciate more deeply central aspects of the early Buddhist teachings that underlie and inform the actual cultivation of mindfulness of breathing.

My survey of material alternates between translations, which I present in the sequence in which they are found in the Taishō edition of the Chinese canon, and my comments on the translated excerpts in the light of their Pāli discourse parallels. The survey in the following pages includes material from the Chinese *Āgamas* that does not have a Pāli counterpart. I begin in the present chapter with extracts from the *Dīrgha-āgama* collection (T 1), which was probably transmitted by Dharmaguptaka reciters. Here and elsewhere, for indicating supplementations of abbreviated passages in the translations I employ italics (which is why I do not use italics for Pāli terms that occur in a translation). I also replace references to a *bhikkhu* with "one", in order to make it clear that the instructions are not meant only for male monastics. Subtitles are my own and do not reflect discourse titles in the originals.

DYING AND THE WIND ELEMENT (DĀ 1)

The first passage to be taken up is part of the account of a former Buddha's going forth. During outings from his palace, the one who eventually became the Buddha Vipassin happened to see someone old, someone sick, and eventually someone who was dead. In the narrative setting, Vipassin needs to be told by his attendant what old age, disease, and death imply. In the case of seeing someone dead, according to the *Dīrgha-āgama* account the future Buddha was informed by his attendant about what it means to be dead in the following words:[1]

> For one who is dead, first there is indeed a termination of his winds and next of his heat.

This statement does not have a counterpart in the Pāli parallel, the *Mahāpadāna-sutta* (DN 14), and in another parallel extant in Sanskrit fragments. In both cases, the explanation about the significance of being dead does not take up winds, heat, or any other bodily manifestation of death, as these versions are only concerned with the separation from one's relatives that results from passing away.[2] A Chinese parallel preserved as an individual translation, however, mentions that breathing comes to an end at death.[3] Inasmuch as the breath is a manifestation of the wind element (see below p. 163), this presentation corresponds at least in part to the indication in the above *Dīrgha-āgama* passage. Given that in all versions the point of the description is to convey the implications of death to someone who does not know what this means, the

1 DĀ 1 at T I 6c13 (already translated by Ichimura 2015: 35).
2 DN 14 at DN II 27,17 (translated by Walshe 1987: 209) and Waldschmidt 1956: 127 (81.7).
3 T 3 at T I 155b10.

absence of breathing would indeed be an obvious mark.

In addition to the winds, the above passage proceeds to heat and thereby to a manifestation of the fire element. In other words, after first the breath and other bodily manifestations of the wind element in the form of motion have stopped, next bodily heat will become completely dissipated. The *Dīrgha-āgama* discourse does not continue with the other two elements of water and earth but turns to other aspects of the body's death. On pursuing the same with the remaining elements, the next stage would be when the body gradually loses water and then begins to decompose and eventually crumble to dust, thereby losing its solidity, represented by the earth element. Such a gradual dispersal of the elements after death is preceded by the gradual loss of control over them that can occur during the natural process of dying.[4] Here loss over the earth element manifests first, in the sense of the body feeling heavy and more difficult to move. Next loss of water occurs through the orifices, gradual loss of bodily heat manifests particularly at the extremities, and eventually the breathing becomes more and more laboured until it ends. When considered from this perspective, the process that leads up to and the process that sets in after the moment of death converge on the breath. In this way, breathing has indeed a close relationship to death and dying.

THE BUDDHA'S LAST BREATH (DĀ 2)

The close relationship between breath and death comes up again in a description of events related to the Buddha Gotama's demise. When the Buddha had passed away, various eminent witnesses expressed their sentiments in verse. One of these was Anuruddha, a chief monastic disciple of the Buddha, who is on record as having proclaimed a verse that begins as follows:[5]

> So as to dwell in the unconditioned,
> The Buddha did not require inhalations and exhalations.

---

4 See in more detail Anālayo 2018d: 99f.

5 DĀ 2 at T I 26c27 (already translated by Ichimura 2015: 152); a similar formulation can be found in T 6 at T I 188c16.

The first part of the corresponding verse by Anuruddha in the Pāli parallel, the *Mahāparinibbāna-sutta* (DN 16), also refers to the absence of inhalations and exhalations, which here reflect the Buddha's steadiness of mind and imperturbability.[6] The same Pāli verse by Anuruddha recurs in the *Saṃyutta-nikāya*. This has a parallel in the *Saṃyukta-āgama*, which reads:[7]

> Dwelling [mindful of] exhalations and inhalations,
> He had established his mind well-guarded.

In the account leading up to the Buddha's passing away in the *Mahāparinibbāna-sutta* and its parallels, Anuruddha features as the one who knew exactly what type of meditation practice the Buddha was undertaking. This practice involved proceeding through all four absorptions and immaterial attainments up to cessation in forward order and then following the same progression backwards to the first absorption. After advancing again from the first to the fourth absorption, the Buddha passed away. When with the completion of the first progression in forward order he had reached the attainment of cessation, Ānanda thought the Buddha had already passed away. Anuruddha corrected him by clarifying that the Buddha had not yet passed away; instead, he had rather entered the attainment of cessation.[8]

In this way, according to the narrative leading up to the present verse, Anuruddha was the one who best knew about the Buddha's meditation practice at the time just before his passing away. Perhaps the same ability is also reflected in the above verse when he refers to mindfulness of breathing, for which the Buddha had a clear predilection (as evident in other passages, see below p. 192).

The *Dīrgha-āgama* verse translated above could then be taken as making the point that for abiding in the unconditioned the Buddha did not need to rely even on breathing, which otherwise formed the object of the meditation practice he had

---

6 DN 16 at DN II 157,12 (translated by Walshe 1987: 271); see also the reconstruction of his verses in the corresponding Sanskrit fragments, Waldschmidt 1950: 400 (44.9).

7 SĀ 1197 at T II 325b25, parallel to SN 6.15 at SN I 159,3 (translated by Bodhi 2000: 253) and to SĀ[2] 110 at T II 414a7.

8 See Anālayo 2016b: 195 and 2017a: 228 and 243.

frequently engaged in. This could in turn be related to the connection established in other discourses between the fourth absorption and the absence of breath (see below p. 160). On this understanding, just prior to passing away the Buddha had already established a condition of non-reliance on breathing through attaining the fourth absorption. This makes his passing away all the more remarkable. Unlike the average person holding on to the breath until eventually forced to "breathe one's last", so to speak, the Buddha had already deliberately let go of breathing before his passing away.

DEATH AND BREATH (DĀ 7)

The relationship between breathing and being alive recurs in a debate on rebirth between a materialist king and a Buddhist monastic. At the present point in the debate, the Buddhist monastic refers to breathing as part of an explanation of the difference between being alive and being dead.[9]

> Human beings are also like that: When the life faculty and consciousness are there, they breathe in and out, are able to bend and stretch, to look around and speak. When the life faculty and consciousness are no longer there, they do not breathe in and out, do not bend and stretch, and do not look around and speak.

The corresponding descriptions in the Pāli and two Chinese parallels do not mention the process of breathing.[10] As a result, the present *Dīrgha-āgama* discourse stands alone in providing a direct reference to the continuity of breathing as equalling the continuity of life. In the case of the first passage taken up in this chapter, it was also the *Dīrgha-āgama* discourse (and one Chinese parallel) that explicitly referred to the fact that with death the manifestation of the wind element in the form of the process of breathing comes to an end.

The three passages surveyed so far reflect a particular potential of directing mindfulness to the process of breathing, namely insight into the dependency of the human body on a

---

9 DĀ 7 at T I 45a25 to 45a27 (translated by Anālayo 2017a: 315).
10 DN 23 at DN II 338,16 (translated by Walshe 1987: 360), MĀ 71 at T I 528a17 (translated by Bingenheimer et al. 2013: 519), and T 45 at T I 833a17.

continuous supply of oxygen in order to remain alive. This provides an additional perspective on mindfulness of breathing, whose sixteen steps build on a continuous awareness of the impermanent nature of the process of breathing. This becomes evident in the alternations between inhalations and exhalations. Becoming aware of the breath can in fact also be employed to drive home the cutting edge of impermanence in the form of one's own mortality, a topic to be taken up again at the end of my survey of Chinese *Āgama* passages (see below p. 242).

THE FOURTH ABSORPTION (DĀ 10)

The relationship between breathing and the fourth absorption comes up in a listing of various doctrinal items and practices, arranged in a pattern that gradually proceeds from ones to tens.[11] As part of a survey of nine items that are to be realized, the following statement can be found:[12]

> On entering the fourth absorption, the thorn of breathing in and out ceases.

The Pāli parallel, the *Dasottara-sutta* (DN 34), takes the same position but differs in that it does not refer to breathing as a "thorn".[13] The idea that breathing in and out ceases when dwelling in the fourth absorption is also reflected in a discourse

11 See also Anālayo 2017a: 397f.

12 DĀ 10 at T I 57a1 to 57a2 (already translated by Ichimura 2015: 335); the same statement recurs in DĀ 11 at T I 59a8. An entertaining story related to this notion can be found in the Dharmaguptaka *Vinaya*, T 1428 at T XXII 957a28. A boy had the task of shaving the Buddha's head. When asked by the parents about his services, the Buddha replied that, although he shaved very well, the boy's breathing was quite rough. When told by his parents to stop his rough breathing, the boy entered the fourth absorption. As a result, someone else had to be found to shave the Buddha.

13 DN 34 at DN III 290,7 abbreviates and needs to be supplemented from DN III 266,9 (translated by Walshe 1987: 507). The corresponding Sanskrit fragment version, Schlingloff 1962: 23 (IX.9), has unfortunately not preserved the relevant text; another parallel, T 13 at T I 240a24, does not take up any of the absorptions. The absence of breath in the fourth absorption comes up also in the **Śāriputrābhidharma*, T 1548 at T XXVIII 632b20 (or else 643a29), as well as in the *Kathāvatthu*, Kv 573,14 (translated by Shwe Zan Aung and Rhys Davids 1915/1979: 332), where it forms part of a debate concerning the impossibility of hearing sound during the first absorption; on this topic see also Anālayo 2017b: 137–150.

in the *Saṃyutta-nikāya* and in its *Saṃyukta-āgama* parallel.[14] A discourse in the *Aṅguttara-nikāya* and its *Madhyama-āgama* parallel make basically the same point in terms of breathing being a thorn,[15] which is to be overcome in order to dwell in the fourth absorption. All of these discourses converge on the notion that one who has entered the fourth absorption would no longer experience the breath.

This indication, found in a range of early discourses, could be understood literally as implying that the breath has indeed ceased.[16] Alternatively, it could be understood in the sense that, due to the deep degree of mental absorption reached at this point, the breath is no longer being perceived by the meditator.[17] Whichever interpretation one prefers, it seems clear that someone who has attained the fourth absorption would no longer be able to observe the breath. This in turn implies that the sixteen steps of mindfulness of breathing could not be undertaken when one has attained such a level of absorption, as such attainment would make it impossible to contemplate inhalations or exhalations.[18] Given that awareness of inhalations

---

14 SN 36.15 at SN IV 220,15 (to be supplemented from SN IV 217,8; translated by Bodhi 2000: 1272) and its parallel SĀ 474 at T II 121b4.

15 AN 10.72 at AN V 135,3 (translated by Bodhi 2012: 1429) and its parallel MĀ 84 at T I 561a9.

16 Jayatilleke 1948: 217 reasons that from the canonical viewpoint the process of breathing is seen as being "under the control of the will, for breathing is made to stop in the Fourth Jhāna", where "it is likely that breathing is mentioned only as [a] concrete instance typifying a general class of acts, namely bodily reflexes, which are all brought within the control of the agent in this Jhāna."

17 Walshe 1987: 622n1123 understands the passage at DN III 266,9 to imply that the breath "becomes so subtle as to be imperceptible".

18 In his discussion of the cessation of mental activity in the second absorption and of the breath in the fourth absorption, Ṭhānissaro 2012: 99f acknowledges that the question is "how can any of the sixteen steps apply to those attainments or to any of the higher levels of concentrations? After all, all of the steps are done in conjunction with breathing." He then reasons that "the answer is that ... the mind will sometimes have to make a deliberate choice when moving from one attainment to the next (MN 121; AN 9:34; AN 9:41). This will require a moment of reflection in which you step back from full focus before plunging in again ... bodily fabrication [*kāyasaṅkhāra*] will resume during those moments of choice, which means that any of the sixteen steps could also be applied during those moments." Yet, based on this interpretation the training in the relevant step would still only be possible during the moment when the mind is not immersed in absorption. Instead of confining the relevance of the instructions to the time of transition between one absorption and

and exhalations is a continuous feature throughout the entire scheme of sixteen steps,[19] it follows that none of these steps seems to be practicable while being in the attainment of the fourth absorption.

This completes my survey of passages from the *Dīrgha-āgama* that are in some way relevant to the practice of mindfulness of breathing. In the next chapter I will examine similar passages from the *Madhyama-āgama*.

SUMMARY

At the moment of death, the breath comes to an end (DĀ 1), hence for average human beings the absence of breath corresponds to the end of life (DĀ 7). However, the Buddha apparently let go of the breath even before passing away (DĀ 2), an ability related to the cessation of breathing associated with the attainment of the fourth absorption (DĀ 10).

---

another, it seems preferable to set aside the identification of individual steps with absorption attainment as the result of a literalist reading in later exegesis. Had absorption attainment been intended, it can safely be assumed it would have been mentioned explicitly.

19 Buddhadāsa 1988/1997: 67 comments that "we should not forget: in every step, in every stage and interval of the practice, we must note the breathing in and breathing out." As pointed out by Virtbauer 2016: 75: "in *ānāpāna-sati*, as the term implies, all the steps that are described in the canonical Buddhist discourses are connected to the in- and out-breaths. This means that all concentration and insight that may result from this practice is embodied in the present phenomenon of breathing."

VIII

TRANSLATIONS FROM THE *MADHYAMA-ĀGAMA*

THE WIND ELEMENT (MĀ 30)

The extracts surveyed in this chapter are from the *Madhyama-āgama* (T 26), a collection probably transmitted by Sarvāstivāda reciters.[1] The first passage to be taken up offers a description of each of the four elements. For internal manifestations of the wind element, the discourse lists the following:[2]

> Upward winds, downward winds, winds in the bowels, moving winds, pulling and contracting winds, cutting winds, mounting winds, irregular winds, winds in the joints, the winds of exhalations, and the winds of inhalations.

Although the Pāli parallel, the *Mahāhatthipadopama-sutta* (MN 28), gives a somewhat different listing of types of winds manifesting inside of the body, it ends similarly with the inhalations and exhalations.[3] Breathing also features as a manifestation of the wind element in a discourse in the *Ekottarika-āgama*.[4]

In all these passages, the wind element stands for the quality of motion. Besides the breath, this conception of wind as motion

1 On this topic see in more detail Anālayo 2017f.
2 MĀ 30 at T I 466b9 to 466b11 (already translated by Bingenheimer et al. 2013: 229).
3 MN 28 at MN I 188,30 (translated by Ñāṇamoli 1995/2005: 282); the same is the case for the **Śāriputrābhidharma*, T 1548 at T XXVIII 573a14 or else 578c19.
4 EĀ 28.4 at T II 652b1.

also seems to cover bodily energy that courses through the limbs, corresponding to some degree to the Chinese concept of *qì* (and to the *pneuma* of ancient Greek medicine).

From a practical viewpoint, breathing as a manifestation of motion qua the wind element points to its potential for offering a self-evident and palpable manifestation of impermanence. Although something that is motionless is of course also subject to the law of change, what moves is more easily experienced as changing. For this reason, mindfulness of breathing stands out among various meditation practices for providing easy access to a direct and tangible experience of impermanence. This might well be the reason why the scheme of sixteen steps involves a continuous awareness of the changing nature of the breath, evident in the constant alternation between inhalations and exhalations. It is hard to think of anything else, apart from breathing, that could provide such clear and unquestionable evidence for the reality of impermanence.

DISTRACTING THOUGHTS (MĀ 56)

The potential of mindfulness of breathing finds mention as part of an instruction that encourages the cultivation of several meditation practices and defines their chief purpose:[5]

> Cultivate [mindfulness] of inhalations and exhalations in order to abandon distracting thoughts.

The Pāli parallel similarly recommends the cultivation of mindfulness of breathing to cut off thoughts.[6] A passage found as part of an introduction to the Chinese translation of the *Ekottarika-āgama* collection also connects the sitting meditation practice of mindfulness of breathing to a stable mind that is free from distracting thoughts.[7]

This potential deserves to be highlighted, since the problem of how to deal with distraction is perhaps the most enduring challenge for many meditators. The ability to counter the mind's

---

5 MĀ 56 at T I 491c16 to 491c17 (already translated by Bingenheimer et al. 2013: 353); see also MĀ 57 at T I 492b6.
6 AN 9.3 at AN IV 358,16 (translated by Bodhi 2012: 1250).
7 T II 550a23.

tendency to distraction becomes particularly evident with the second and third tetrad of the sixteen-step scheme of mindfulness of breathing. It seems to be not just awareness of inhalations and exhalations as such that counters the mind's tendency to distraction, as one might assume if considering the above passage in isolation, but cultivating the meditative progression through the sixteen steps of mindfulness of breathing that can have such a remarkable effect on this tendency. I return to this topic below.

MINDFULNESS OF THE BODY (MĀ 81)

In what follows I examine a development that appears to have led to a reduction of mindfulness of breathing from the full scheme of sixteen steps down to just its first steps. This apparent reduction can be seen in two *Madhyama-āgama* discourses and in their parallels, the *Kāyagatāsati-sutta* (MN 119) and the *Satipaṭṭhāna-sutta* (MN 10) respectively. In what follows I translate and study these discourses in turn.

Both cases reflect a loss of the transition from the first steps of mindfulness of breathing towards arousing joy and happiness in the second tetrad, thereby missing out key aspects of the potential of the whole scheme of mindfulness of breathing for overcoming distracting thoughts and leading to concentration.

The *Kāyagatāsati-sutta* lists the first tetrad of mindfulness of breathing among its various modalities of mindfulness of the body, as does its *Madhyama-āgama* parallel (MĀ 81). Whereas in the *Kāyagatāsati-sutta* instructions on mindfulness of breathing constitute the first of its body contemplations, in the *Madhyama-āgama* discourse these occur at a later point. They are preceded by contemplation of postures and clear comprehension of bodily activities, as well as by two exercises not found in the Pāli version, which are abandoning unwholesome thoughts and forceful control of the mind. Neither fits the heading of mindfulness of the body, and both can safely be considered later additions.[8] Such additions are in line with an apparent

8 *Pace* Kuan 2008: 83, who envisions that exercises not related to the body and found in MĀ 81 would have been intentionally removed from the Pāli version.

tendency for the description of mindfulness of the body in the *Kāyagatāsati-sutta* and its *Madhyama-āgama* parallel to incorporate exercises found elsewhere among the discourses.

The instructions for mindfulness of breathing in the *Madhyama-āgama* discourse proceed as follows:[9]

> Being mindful of breathing in, one knows one is breathing in mindfully; being mindful of breathing out, one knows one is breathing out mindfully. Breathing in long, one knows one is breathing in long; breathing out long, one knows one is breathing out long. Breathing in short, one knows one is breathing in short; breathing out short, one knows one is breathing out short. One trains [in experiencing] the whole body when breathing in; one trains [in experiencing] the whole body when breathing out. One trains in calming bodily activity when breathing in; one trains in calming ⟨bodily⟩ activity when breathing out.[10]

Whereas the above *Madhyama-āgama* discourse only mentions the four steps of the first tetrad, the *Kāyagatāsati-sutta* also describes the preliminary withdrawing into seclusion, sitting down with body erect, and establishing mindfulness to the fore, after which it presents the same four steps.[11]

In the *Madhyama-āgama* parallel to the *Kāyagatāsati-sutta*, the extract translated above on mindfulness of breathing is then followed by descriptions of the bodily dimension of absorption experience. These absorption descriptions have a counterpart in the *Kāyagatāsati-sutta*, with the difference that the Pāli version also describes how the actual attainment of an absorption takes place. Given the overall concern with the body, the *Madhyama-āgama* discourse brings out more clearly that it is not the attainment of absorption as such but the bodily dimension of its experience that comes under the heading of mindfulness of the body in both discourses.

Both the *Kāyagatāsati-sutta* and its *Madhyama-āgama* parallel show an overall focus on the body and a clear emphasis on the cultivation of deeper levels of concentration leading to

---

9 MĀ 81 at T I 555b10 to 555b15 (already translated by Kuan 2008: 157f).

10 The original speaks of verbal activity when breathing out, which clearly is a textual error.

11 MN 119 at MN III 89,9 (translated by Ñāṇamoli 1995/2005: 950).

the attainment of the four absorptions. As part of an apparent tendency to assemble various practices that fit this overall thrust, an integration of the first tetrad of mindfulness of breathing is an obvious choice. One evident reason is that the *Ānāpānasati-sutta* (MN 118) explicitly reckons these four steps to correspond to contemplation of the body. Another contributing factor is the potential of mindfulness of breathing to lead to deeper levels of concentration. In combination, these two trajectories would have made it quite natural to add the part of mindfulness of breathing that is anyway equated with contemplation of the body to an exposition concerned with precisely this topic and with the potential of mindfulness of the body to lead to deep concentration.

It would also be quite understandable that only the first tetrad found such a placing and not any of the other three tetrads of mindfulness of breathing, which the *Ānāpānasati-sutta* reckons as instances of the other three *satipaṭṭhāna*s. Given that the *Kāyagatāsati-sutta* and its parallel only cover contemplation of the body and not the other *satipaṭṭhāna*s, there would have been no reason for including any of the other three tetrads, which correspond to contemplation of feeling tones, the mind, and dharmas.

As a net result of this apparent textual development, however, the first four steps of mindfulness of breathing are severed from their connection with the remainder of the sixteen-step scheme.

SATIPAṬṬHĀNA (MĀ 98)

The integration of the first tetrad in an exposition of different body contemplations in the *Kāyagatāsati-sutta* and its parallel could in turn have influenced the *Satipaṭṭhāna-sutta* (MN 10) and its *Madhyama-āgama* parallel (MĀ 98). Even though these two parallel discourses cover all four *satipaṭṭhāna*s, only the first tetrad of mindfulness of breathing features in their expositions of *satipaṭṭhāna* meditation. This makes it probable that the development under discussion would have originated in the *Kāyagatāsati-sutta* and its parallel. Given that each tetrad of mindfulness of breathing corresponds to one *satipaṭṭhāna*, had this development started in the *Satipaṭṭhāna-sutta* and its parallel, one would expect other tetrads to also become part of their exposition.

The *Kāyagatāsati-sutta* and the *Satipaṭṭhāna-sutta*, as well as their *Madhyama-āgama* parallels, are found in the same discourse collection. This makes an influence of one discourse on the other during oral transmission easily possible. Such influence can be seen particularly well in the case of the *Madhyama-āgama* collection, where an evident error in relation to the fourth step of mindfulness of breathing is found in both discourses, the parallel to the *Kāyagatāsati-sutta* and the parallel to the *Satipaṭṭhāna-sutta*.[12]

The *Satipaṭṭhāna-sutta* also has a parallel in a discourse in the *Ekottarika-āgama* (EĀ 12.1), which does not mention mindfulness of breathing at all in its survey of various body contemplations.[13] This supports the impression that at some point during the transmission of the texts the first tetrad of mindfulness of breathing was added to expositions of body contemplation.[14]

The relevant passage from the survey of body contemplations in the *Madhyama-āgama* parallel to the *Satipaṭṭhāna-sutta* proceeds in the same way as the passage translated above from the parallel to the *Kāyagatāsati-sutta*:[15]

> Being mindful of breathing in, one knows to be breathing in mindfully; being mindful of breathing out, one knows to be breathing out mindfully. Breathing in long, one knows to be breathing in long; breathing out long, one knows to be breathing out long. Breathing in short, one knows to be breathing in short; breathing out short, one knows to be breathing out short. One trains [in experiencing] the whole body when breathing in; one trains [in experiencing] the whole body when breathing out. One trains in calming bodily activity when breathing in; one trains in calming ⟨bodily⟩ activity when breathing out.[16]

---

12 The error is a shift from experiencing the "bodily activity" when breathing in to experiencing the "verbal activity" when breathing out; see above n. 10.
13 EĀ 12.1 at T II 568a16 to 568b27 (translated by Anālayo 2013b: 288–290).
14 Anālayo 2013b: 45–50.
15 MĀ 98 at T I 582c13 to 582c17 (translated by Anālayo 2013b: 271).
16 See above n. 10.

Whereas the two *Madhyama-āgama* discourses have the same text, their respective Pāli parallels differ from each other. The *Satipaṭṭhāna-sutta* additionally has a simile of a turner at his lathe to illustrate the practice of the first two steps, a simile not found in the *Kāyagatāsati-sutta* of the same *Majjhima-nikāya*.[17]

It is noteworthy that among Pāli discourses the turner simile is found only in the *Satipaṭṭhāna-sutta*. Since this simile could serve its purpose in the *Kāyagatāsati-sutta* just as well as it does in the *Satipaṭṭhāna-sutta*, there is no self-evident reason why it should be found in only one of the two discourses. Presumably this simile would have been added at a point in time during the transmission of the Pāli discourses when the exposition in the *Kāyagatāsati-sutta* had already reached a point of relative closure and for this reason the description of the turner was not added to this discourse.

The addition of this illustration is of additional interest, as the simile itself reflects a further degree of reduction. It only illustrates the first two steps, rather than the entire tetrad. Other similes employed to illustrate body contemplations in the *Satipaṭṭhāna-sutta* recur similarly in the *Kāyagatāsati-sutta* and illustrate the entire body contemplation described, not just its first half. For the turner simile to illustrate only half of the exercise does point to an emphasis on the first two steps only.

The final result of this trend towards reduction can then be seen in the **Śāriputrābhidharma*, representing the Dharmaguptaka tradition. In its exposition of the *satipaṭṭhāna* of contemplating the body, this work only mentions the first two steps of mindfulness of breathing, illustrated by the simile of the turner found also in the *Satipaṭṭhāna-sutta*.[18] In this version only the knowing of

17 MN 10 at MN I 56,22 (translated by Ñāṇamoli 1995/2005: 146); see also DN 22 at DN II 291,15 (translated by Walshe 1987: 336). Cousins 2015: 3 argues "that a deliberate process of making the breath long or short is envisaged is clear from the simile which compares the first two stages to a turner's knowing when he makes a long cut and knowing when he makes a short cut." Although this is a possible interpretation, alternatively it could also be argued that the comparison is between *understanding* the length of the breath and *understanding* the length of the turn on the lathe. Thus the simile need not be meant to imply an intentional changing of the length of the breath.

18 T 1548 at T XXVIII 613b7 or else 625b23 (translated by Anālayo 2020a); see also Anālayo 2019d.

long and short breaths has become a body contemplation in its own right, comparable to a turner at his lathe.

Another and unrelated discourse in the *Ekottarika-āgama* collection (EĀ 3.8), translated below (see p. 229), also reflects a tendency to reduce mindfulness of breathing to its first steps, here only the first three. In this case, too, it seems fairly clear that this is a later development. The same tendency to a reduction of the instructions on mindfulness of breathing to the first steps continues up to present times.[19]

Once the first few steps are considered a practice on their own, the connection between the groundwork laid in these steps and the dynamics of the remainder of the sixteen-step scheme is severed. In particular the arousing of joy and happiness in the ensuing tetrad is lost sight of. Such a loss divests mindfulness of breathing of a considerable part of its potential to overcome distracting thoughts and lead to concentration.

In this way, a development that would have had its origin in the wish to accord mindfulness of breathing a place among a survey of body contemplations conducive to deeper concentration appears to have had a rather unfortunate result. It seems to have led to losing sight of the meditative dynamics underlying the exposition of the sixteen steps and its potential to facilitate the deepening of concentration through the skilful cultivation of wholesome types of joy and happiness.

CONCENTRATION (MĀ 118)

The potential of mindfulness of breathing to lead to concentration finds mention in the context of a series of verses whose main

19 Some publications on the topic of mindfulness of breathing only cover the first tetrad or aspects of it; see, e.g., Gñānārāma 1989, Ariyadhamma 1995/2014, or Johnson 2012. Influenced by the commentarial understanding that the fourth step is an implicit reference to the fourth absorption, Pa-Auk (no date) instructs the meditator to proceed from the first tetrad of mindfulness of breathing to mastery of the four absorptions and the cultivation of insight into materiality (by way of the *kalāpas*) and mentality (by way of the cognitive process), as the starting point to progress through the insight knowledges. Only after covering all this does he take up the second tetrad of mindfulness of breathing. The underlying view can best be summarized with the help of a statement in Ledi 1999/2011: 40, according to which "the first tetrad is the main and essential stage."

purpose is to extol the Buddha:[20]

> Dwelling well in [mindfulness of] breathing in and out, the mind becomes well concentrated within.

The corresponding verse in the Pāli parallel also relates meditating on the inhalations to becoming well concentrated within.[21] It additionally specifies that such meditation involves the experience of delight (*rati*) in relation to the breath. This additional specification underlines the point made above regarding the apparent reduction of mindfulness of breathing to its first steps only and the resultant loss of a connection to the experience of joy and happiness with the second tetrad. Delight in the breath can serve as a tool to help keep the mind engaged in awareness of the inhalations and exhalations, rather than succumbing to distractions. As a result, the mind more easily becomes well concentrated.

This completes my survey of passages related to mindfulness of breathing from the *Madhyama-āgama*. In the next chapter I will turn to the *Saṃyukta-āgama*, a collection that has considerably more material on this topic than both the *Dīrgha-āgama* and the *Madhyama-āgama*, examined in the previous and the present chapter, taken together.

SUMMARY

An integration of the first tetrad of mindfulness of breathing among a survey of body contemplations conveys the impression that this first tetrad is a complete practice on its own, at the cost of the loss of the transition towards joy and happiness in the second tetrad (MĀ 81 and MĀ 98). Yet, it is the cultivation of the entire scheme of sixteen steps that activates the potential, mentioned in the discourses, of mindfulness of breathing to counter distraction (MĀ 56) and to lead to concentration (MĀ 118). Besides its potential to lead to mental tranquillity,

20 MĀ 118 at T I 608c13.

21 AN 6.43 at AN III 346,26 (the translation by Bodhi 2012: 909 follows the alternative sense of *assāsa* as "consolation", see Bodhi 2012: 1758n1324, which in view of the reading in MĀ 118 seems to be the less probable understanding. The circumstance that only inhalations are mentioned must be due to metrical reasons).

from an insight perspective the process of breathing, being a manifestation of the wind element as the principle of motion, is a particularly palpable manifestation of impermanence (MĀ 30).

IX

TRANSLATIONS FROM THE *SAṂYUKTA-ĀGAMA*

BODILY ACTIVITY (SĀ 568)

With the present chapter I turn to discourses found in the *Saṃyukta-āgama* (T 99), which for my present purposes is the collection with the largest amount of relevant material. The original text used for the translation of this collection into Chinese appears to stem from a Mūlasarvāstivāda transmission lineage. Discourses in this collection and in the *Ekottarika-āgama*, taken up in the next chapter, tend to be considerably shorter than those in the *Dīrgha-āgama* and *Madhyama-āgama*. Instead of providing just excerpts, as was the case in the preceding two chapters, in several instances I translate the whole discourse. In doing so, however, I do not translate the standard introduction and closing of the discourse, unless this is of particular relevance.

The first passage to be taken up explains why inhalations and exhalations are considered a bodily activity:[1]

> Inhalations and exhalations are of a bodily nature, they depend on the body, they belong to the body, and in dependence on the body they revolve. For this reason, inhalations and exhalations are called a bodily activity.

---

1 SĀ 568 at T II 150a27 to 150a28, parallel to SN 41.6 at SN IV 293,23 (translated by Bodhi 2000: 1322); the same definition occurs also in MN 44 at MN I 301,24 (translated by Ñāṇamoli 1995/2005: 399) and its Tibetan parallel Up 1005 at D 4094 *ju* 8a6 or Q 5595 *tu* 9a6 (translated by Anālayo 2012c: 46).

In the ancient Indian setting in general, a qualification of inhalations and exhalations as being merely bodily phenomena could have carried additional significance, beyond the specific context provided in this discourse. Rather than being a mere statement of an obvious fact, such a qualification might at times have served to set aside metaphysical speculations that viewed the breath as a manifestation of the self.[2]

The definition of bodily activity as corresponding to the inhalations and exhalations in the present discourse, found similarly in the *Saṃyutta-nikāya* parallel (SN 41.6), occurs in the context of a discussion on the attainment of the cessation of perceptions and feeling tones. The parallels agree that verbal activity ceases first and mental activity last.[3] In this way, the bodily activity of breathing stands between verbal activity, which is representative of the mental factors specific to the first absorption (*vitakka* and *vicāra*), and mental activity in the form of perception.[4] If the successive cessation of these three types of activity reflects their respective subtlety, then breathing would emerge as a more subtle phenomenon than the inclining and sustaining of the mind found in the first absorption. From the viewpoint of deepening concentration this is indeed the case, as according to passages surveyed above the breath would disappear with the fourth absorption (see above p. 160), whereas the activity of inclining and sustaining the mind is already left behind with the second absorption. Perception will in turn only

---

2 Radhakrishnan 1953/1992: 73 reports a traditional etymology according to which "the word 'ātman' is derived from *an* 'to breathe'. It is the breath of life", quoting *Ṛgveda* VII.87.2: *ātmā te vātaḥ*. In contrast, the *Vimuttimagga*, T 1648 at T XXXII 430c16 (translated by Ehara et al. 1961/1995: 160), comments, on the third step of experiencing the whole body, that the practitioner knows this is just a body, not a living being or a self. As noted by Pradhan 1986: 267 in his discussion of meditation related to the breath, "the reverence and devotion paid to it depends upon the degree of spirituality and divinity ascribed to it in different systems of philosophy and religion. In Buddhism it is nothing more than a mere tool in meditation." For a more detailed survey of the significance accorded to the breath in the ancient Indian setting see Ditrich 2018: 99–101.

3 SĀ 568 at T II 150b20 and SN 41.6 at SN IV 294,8. A different sequence can be found in MĀ 211 at T I 792a9; see also Anālayo 2011: 282f.

4 The parallels differ in so far as SĀ 568 at T II 150a25 defines mental activity as covering intentions and perceptions, whereas SN 41.6 at SN IV 293,17 speaks of perceptions and feelings; the same difference recurs between MN 44 and its Tibetan parallel, see Anālayo 2011: 281.

be subdued after progressing to the fourth of the immaterial attainments; in fact it only fully ends with the attainment of cessation itself.

Although the instructions in the fourth step of mindfulness of breathing speak of "calming" bodily activity, rather than of its cessation, with the conclusion of the first tetrad a considerable degree of subtlety can be achieved. Perhaps this helped fuel the trend towards a reduction of mindfulness of breathing to this single tetrad or its first steps, discussed above (see p. 165). In other words, although the potential of the whole scheme of sixteen steps is lost in this way, what remains can still lead to a considerable degree of subtlety in meditation practice.

The equation of bodily activity in the fourth step with inhalations and exhalations could also have contributed to the notion that the preceding step of experiencing the whole body is similarly concerned with the breath, in the sense of experiencing the whole body of the breath.[5] The problem remains that, on this interpretation, the third step would not offer anything distinctly new, as the entire length of the breath already needed to be discerned for the previous two steps when determining whether the breath was long or short.[6] This makes it more probable that the ensuing third step introduces something different, such as a shift to giving prominence to awareness of the whole physical body.

CENTRAL PURPOSE (SĀ 746)

The central purpose of mindfulness of breathing is to lead to the cultivation of the awakening factors:[7]

---

5 Vism 273,24 (translated by Ñāṇamoli 1991: 266): *sakalassa assāsakāyassa ādhimajjhapariyosānaṃ viditaṃ karonto ... sakalassa passāsakāyassa ādhimajjhapariyosānaṃ viditaṃ karonto.*

6 Nhat Hanh 1990: 43 notes that "the practice of being mindful of the whole 'breath body' was already dealt with in the ... exercise: 'breathing in a long breath, he knows, "I am breathing in a long breath." Breathing out a short breath, he knows, "I am breathing out a short breath."' Why then do we need to repeat this exercise?" Ṭhānissaro 2012: 117 comments that "the commentaries' interpretation of step 3 makes it redundant with steps 1 and 2. It's hard to understand how you could know whether the breath is long or short in those steps without being aware of the full length of the breath."

7 SĀ 746 at T II 198a5 to 198a10.

> Suppose a monastic cultivates mindfulness of breathing; having cultivated it much one gains great fruit and great benefit. How is great fruit and great benefit gained by cultivating mindfulness of breathing, having cultivated it much? Here a monastic, in a mind conjoined to mindfulness of breathing, cultivates the awakening factor of mindfulness supported by seclusion, supported by dispassion, and supported by cessation, conducing to letting go.
>
> *In a mind conjoined to mindfulness of breathing one cultivates the awakening factor of investigation-of-dharmas supported by seclusion, supported by dispassion, and supported by cessation, conducing to letting go.*
>
> *In a mind conjoined to mindfulness of breathing one cultivates the awakening factor of energy supported by seclusion, supported by dispassion, and supported by cessation, conducing to letting go.*
>
> *In a mind conjoined to mindfulness of breathing one cultivates the awakening factor of joy supported by seclusion, supported by dispassion, and supported by cessation, conducing to letting go.*
>
> *In a mind conjoined to mindfulness of breathing one cultivates the awakening factor of tranquillity supported by seclusion, supported by dispassion, and supported by cessation, conducing to letting go.*
>
> *In a mind conjoined to mindfulness of breathing one cultivates the awakening factor of concentration supported by seclusion, supported by dispassion, and supported by cessation, conducing to letting go.*
>
> *In a mind conjoined to mindfulness of breathing one* cultivates the awakening factor of equipoise supported by seclusion, supported by dispassion, and supported by cessation, conducing to letting go.

The Pāli parallel offers a similar presentation.[8] I will return below to the relationship between mindfulness of breathing and the awakening factors, which is a topic of such importance that it is taken up in several discourses. Suffice it for now to note that mindfulness of breathing is clearly seen as being invested with considerable potential to lead to their cultivation.

---

8 SN 46.66 at SN V 132,2 (translated by Bodhi 2000: 1620), which needs to be supplemented from SN V 129,5.

FOUNDATIONS (SĀ 801)

The next passage to be examined is the first of a set of fifteen discourses that comprise the section on mindfulness of breathing in the *Saṃyukta-āgama*. Together with its Pāli counterpart, the *Ānāpāna-saṃyutta*, this assembly of discourses is a chief source for instructions on mindfulness of breathing among the early discourses and therefore naturally occupies a central role in my survey. In what follows, I will take up each of these fifteen discourses in turn.

The first discourse in this part of the *Saṃyukta-āgama* has no Pāli parallel. However, its indications are well in line with the teachings in the Pāli discourses, in that a firm foundation in ethical conduct and related practices builds the groundwork for meditation practice:[9]

> Five states are of much benefit for cultivating mindfulness of breathing. What are the five? One dwells in pure morality, restrained by the code of rules. Endowed with deportment and conduct, one upholds the training in morality, being able to give rise to apprehension in relation to [even] a trifling offence. This is called the first [state] of much benefit for cultivating mindfulness of breathing.
>
> Again, monastics, one has few wishes, few affairs, and few tasks. This is called the second state of much benefit for cultivating mindfulness of breathing.
>
> Again, monastics, one knows one's measure with drink and food, being moderate in relation to their quantity and without giving rise to perceptions of urgent desires for drink and food, and one makes an effort in being attentive [in this respect]. This is called the third state of much benefit for cultivating mindfulness of breathing.
>
> Again, monastics, one is not attached to sleeping in the first and last watch of the night and makes an effort in being attentive [in this respect]. This is called the fourth state of much benefit for cultivating mindfulness of breathing.

---

9 SĀ 801 at T II 205c24 to 206a6.

> Again, monastics, one [dwells] in an empty place in the forest, secluded from din and bustle. This is called the fifth state of ⟨much⟩ benefit for cultivating mindfulness of breathing.[10]

The five states that provide the groundwork for mindfulness of breathing are:

- upholding morality,
- having few wishes and tasks,
- moderation with food,
- wakefulness,
- secluded dwelling.

The need to maintain good basics in ethical conduct is a recurrent theme in the early discourses and is as self-evident as the requirement to avoid having many wishes and consequently becoming overly busy with various affairs and tasks. Moderation with food and wakefulness are also standard topics in outlines of the gradual path.

A relationship between breathing and eating in particular emerges from a description in a discourse in the *Saṃyutta-nikāya* and its *Saṃyukta-āgama* parallels of King Pasenadi's condition due to having overeaten, which made breathing so difficult for him that he was found to be panting.[11] His predicament illustrates how moderation with food relates to the process of breathing.

The recommendation to find a secluded dwelling appears among the preliminaries for mindfulness of breathing in the standard instructions. The same is to some degree true for the need to lay a proper moral foundation, which can be seen as implicit in the fact that the instructions for mindfulness of breathing have a monastic as their protagonist and thus someone who, at least in theory, has dedicated the whole life to maintaining a high standard of ethical conduct.

---

10 The translation "much" in the last sentence is based on an emendation in line with the formulation found for the four earlier instances; the original text has an additional reference to "type" or "seed" that is clearly a textual error.

11 SN 3.13 at SN I 81,24 (translated by Bodhi 2000: 176) and SĀ 1150 at T II 306c4 describe him panting for breath and SĀ² 73 at T II 400a3 notes how breathing has become rather difficult for him; see also Anālayo 2018a, 2018b, and 2019a.

In this way, the present discourse fleshes out in what ways the proper groundwork can be laid for the cultivation of mindfulness of breathing.

TRANQUILLITY AND INSIGHT (SĀ 802)

The next discourse in the *Saṃyukta-āgama* is also without a parallel among Pāli discourses:[12]

> You should cultivate mindfulness of breathing. Suppose a monastic cultivates mindfulness of breathing, cultivating it much will lead to tranquillity of the body and tranquillity of the mind, to stilling [directed] awareness and [sustained] contemplation, and to fulfilment in the cultivation of the perceptions that wholly partake of knowledge.

The indication that mindfulness of breathing leads to tranquillity of body and mind mirrors steps four and eight in the standard instructions, which are precisely about calming bodily and mental activity. The passage translated above also mentions a stilling of [directed] awareness and [sustained] contemplation, corresponding to *vitakka* and *vicāra* in Pāli. These can function as factors of the first absorption, but here appear to carry a more general sense of initial and sustained mental activity.

The reference to the perceptions that wholly partake of knowledge points to the cultivation of liberating insight. This is in line with the correlation between mindfulness of breathing and the development of the awakening factors in a discourse already taken up in this chapter (SĀ 746). Judging from another discourse in the *Saṃyukta-āgama*, the reference in the present discourse to the perceptions that wholly partake of knowledge would be to the following six perceptions:[13]

- the perception of impermanence in all formations,
- the perception of *dukkha* in what is impermanent,
- the perception of not-self in what is *dukkha*,
- the perception of contemplating the nutriments,
- the perception of not delighting in the whole world,
- the perception of death.

12 SĀ 802 at T II 206a9 to 206a12.
13 SĀ 1034 at T II 270a29 (translated by Anālayo 2016b: 145).

The first of these relates particularly well to mindfulness of breathing, where impermanence is clearly a continuous theme. Insight into impermanence in turn builds the foundation for a deepening appreciation of the other two characteristics of *dukkha* and not-self.[14] The last perception, just as the first, has a direct relationship to the breath. The breath can serve as a tool for cultivating the perception of death, a topic to which I will return at the end of the next chapter (see below p. 242).

The present discourse throws into relief the potential of mindfulness of breathing to make a substantial contribution to both tranquillity and insight. It is important to keep this in mind, since with later traditions there is at times a tendency to see mindfulness of breathing as predominantly a tool for deepening concentration. It has an eminent potential in this respect, no doubt, but its ability to deepen insight is equally significant.

THE SIXTEEN STEPS (SĀ 803)

The third discourse in the section on mindfulness of breathing in the *Saṃyukta-āgama* presents the full scheme of sixteen steps, which in the Pāli *Saṃyutta-nikāya* collection on mindfulness of breathing occurs in the very first discourse.[15] In this way, from a structural viewpoint, the *Saṃyukta-āgama* discourse collection on mindfulness of breathing proceeds by first clarifying the groundwork to be covered through ethical conduct and related practices and by highlighting the potential of this practice in relation to both tranquillity and insight. In fact the present discourse begins by reiterating these benefits before embarking on a full exposition of the actual practice of the sixteen steps. This full exposition employs a considerable degree of abbreviation, which in what follows I will flesh out, marking

14 Regarding the perception of not-self, Buddhadāsa 1988/1997: 87 relates this in particular to the last step in the third tetrad: "the most direct way to practice step twelve is to examine the danger, the pain, and the suffering present in any moment that we cling to something as 'I' or 'mine'." Such practice can be summarized with an extract from Levine 1991: 45, to the effect that "when the breath breathes itself without self-consciousness ... the breather dies into the breath."

15 SN 54.1 at SN V 311,14 (translated by Bodhi 2000: 1765).

my supplementations by presenting them in italics.[16] Here is the main body of the discourse:[17]

> Cultivate mindfulness of breathing! Suppose a monastic cultivates mindfulness of breathing, cultivating it much will lead to tranquillity of body and mind, to the stilling of [directed] awareness and [sustained] contemplation, and to fulfilment in the cultivation of the perceptions that wholly partake of knowledge.[18]
>
> How does having cultivated mindfulness of breathing, cultivated it much, bring about tranquillity of body and mind, the stilling of [directed] awareness and [sustained] contemplation, and fulfilment in the cultivation of the perceptions that wholly partake of knowledge?
>
> Here suppose a monastic dwells in dependence on a ⟨hamlet⟩ or town.[19] In the morning, [having] put on the robes and taken the bowl, one enters the village to beg for food with the body guarded well, the doors of the faculties controlled, and keeping the mind well guarded. Having begged for food, one returns to one's lodgings. Having put away robes and bowl, and washed the feet, one enters a forest or an empty hut, or [goes to] the root of a tree or vacant open ground.[20]
>
> Seated properly with the body kept straight and keeping mindfulness to the fore, one abandons lustful cravings in the world and becomes purified by removing sensuality, ill-will, sloth-and-torpor, restlessness-and-worry, and doubt, crossing over all perplexity. The mind gains certainty in wholesome states and is far removed from the five hindrances that afflict the mind,

16 A rendering of the discourse without such supplementations can be found in Anālayo 2013b: 228f.

17 SĀ 803 at T II 206a15 to 206b13.

18 SN 54.1 at SN V 311,7 only indicates that mindfulness of breathing is of great fruit and great benefit.

19 The translation "hamlet" is based on an emendation of an obvious copyist's error.

20 SN 54.1 at SN V 311,10 does not describe going out to beg, etc.; it only mentions a forest, the root of a tree, and an empty hut as appropriate places for cultivating mindfulness of breathing. Namgyal 1992: 34f comments on the introductory phrase: "*gone to the forest, or to the root of a tree, or to an empty place, sits down* ... these are sitting exercises. There are other meditations that can be practised while working or doing service ... don't attempt to do *Ānāpānasati* while doing walking or in other activities. In those situations just have an overall loose awareness, particularly of the body and the body posture."

that cause a weakening of the power of wisdom, that partake of being obstructive, and that do not lead to Nirvāṇa.

One is mindful of the breath coming in, training well to keep being mindful of it, and one is mindful of the breath going out, training well to keep being mindful of it.

One trains well to keep being mindful of breathing *in* long, *and one trains well to keep being mindful of breathing out long. One trains well to keep being mindful of* breathing *in* short, *and one trains well to keep being mindful of breathing out short.* Experiencing the whole body when breathing in, one trains well *to experience* the whole body when breathing in; experiencing the whole body when breathing out, one trains well *to experience* the whole body when breathing out. Experiencing a calming of all bodily activity when breathing in, one trains well *to experience* a calming of all bodily activity when breathing in; experiencing a calming of all bodily activity when breathing out, one trains well *to experience* a calming of ⟨all⟩ bodily activity when breathing out.[21]

Experiencing joy *when breathing in, one trains well to experience joy when breathing in; experiencing joy when breathing out, one trains well to experience joy when breathing out.* Experiencing happiness *when breathing in, one trains well to experience happiness when breathing in; experiencing happiness when breathing out, one trains well to experience happiness when breathing out.* Experiencing ⟨mental⟩ activity *when breathing in,*[22] *one trains well to experience mental activity when breathing in; experiencing mental activity when breathing out, one trains well to experience mental activity when breathing out.* Experiencing a calming of mental activity when breathing in, one trains well to experience a calming of mental activity when breathing in; experiencing a calming of mental activity when breathing out, one trains well to experience a calming of mental activity when breathing out.

Experiencing the mind *when breathing in, one trains well to experience the mind when breathing in; experiencing the mind when breathing out, one trains well to experience the mind when breathing out.* Experiencing gladdening the mind *when breathing in, one trains*

21 The translation "all" in the last sentence is based on an emendation of what must be a copyist's error.

22 The translation "mental activity" is based on an emendation; the text erroneously here has "bodily activity".

well to experience gladdening the mind when breathing in; experiencing gladdening the mind when breathing out, one trains well to experience gladdening the mind when breathing out. Experiencing concentrating the mind *when breathing in, one trains well to experience concentrating the mind when breathing in; experiencing concentrating the mind when breathing out, one trains well to experience concentrating the mind when breathing out.* Experiencing liberating the mind when breathing in, one trains well to experience liberating the mind when breathing in; experiencing liberating the mind when breathing out, one trains well to experience liberating the mind when breathing out.

Contemplating impermanence *when breathing in, one trains well to contemplate impermanence when breathing in; contemplating impermanence when breathing out, one trains well to contemplate impermanence when breathing out.* Contemplating eradication *when breathing in, one trains well to contemplate eradication when breathing in; contemplating eradication when breathing out, one trains well to contemplate eradication when breathing out.* Contemplating dispassion *when breathing in, one trains well to contemplate dispassion when breathing in; contemplating dispassion when breathing out, one trains well to contemplate dispassion when breathing out;* contemplating cessation when breathing in, one trains well to contemplate cessation when breathing in; contemplating cessation when breathing out, one trains well to contemplate cessation when breathing out.[23]

This is called a cultivation of mindfulness of breathing that [leads to] tranquillity of the body and tranquillity of the mind, to stilling [directed] awareness and [sustained] contemplation, and to fulfilment in the cultivation of the perceptions that wholly partake of knowledge.

Before instructing in the sixteen steps, the discourse translated above explicitly mentions the removal of the five hindrances. The same is the case for expositions of mindfulness of breathing in the Mahāsāṅghika and Sarvāstivāda *Vinayas*.[24] Although overcoming the hindrances is not mentioned in the Pāli parallel, it seems to be

23 The last three steps in SN 54.1 at SN V 312,16 are rather dispassion (*virāga*), cessation (*nirodha*), and letting go (*paṭinissagga*).

24 T 1425 at T XXII 254c13 and T 1435 at T XXIII 8a20 (translated by Anālayo 2016b: 247). The same holds for an exposition of mindfulness of breathing in the **Śāriputrābhidharma*, T 1548 at T XXVIII 705b6 (translated by Anālayo 2020b).

implicit to some degree in the progression of practice delineated in the sixteen steps found in all versions.[25] These do not have any explicit reference to the five hindrances or their antidotes, yet they clearly lead up to concentrating and liberating the mind with the final steps of the third tetrad. Executing these steps would not be possible if the mind were still under the influence of the hindrances. This implies, as mentioned in previous chapters, that the scheme of sixteen steps takes for granted that the hindrances are at least temporarily kept at bay.

The situation is different in the case of the *Satipaṭṭhāna-sutta*, where the parallel versions mention the five hindrances explicitly, either at the outset of their description or else as one contemplation under the fourth *satipaṭṭhāna*.[26] It seems fair to conclude that the mode of practice presented in the *Satipaṭṭhāna-sutta* sets in at a more elementary level, whereas mindfulness of breathing in sixteen steps appears to be building on the kind of meditative expertise that can be gained through cultivating the four *satipaṭṭhāna*s in the way described in the *Satipaṭṭhāna-sutta*.

Another point of interest is that in the Pāli version the actual training only begins with the third step, whereas the *Saṃyukta-āgama* discourse seems to keep enjoining that one should "train" in the respective steps throughout. The description translated above clearly uses "training" for the preliminary practice of becoming aware of the breath, but its instructions for the first two steps of long and short breaths are abbreviated. I have supplemented a reference to training for these two, as the remaining fourteen steps keep explicitly mentioning training. Although this is what the context suggests, it needs to be kept in mind that this is only a supplementation on my part and not something explicitly indicated in the text.

The degree to which training is mentioned differs between expositions of the sixteen steps in general. No reference to training is found at all in descriptions of the sixteen steps in

25 Vimalaramsi 1995/2006: 68 argues that "the phrase 'establishing mindfulness in front of him' means that one puts aside all other worldly affairs and involvement with sensual pleasure."

26 See in more detail Anālayo 2013b: 174–176.

Vinaya texts of the Mahāsāṅghika and Sarvāstivāda traditions.[27] In the case of the *Madhyama-āgama* discourses translated in the previous chapter, however, the same pattern as in the Pāli version can be observed, in that the training starts with the third step (see above p. 166).[28]

Another discourse in the *Saṃyukta-āgama* does not mention any training, in agreement with its *Saṃyutta-nikāya* parallel (see below p. 192). In this case, this is because the discourse describes the Buddha's own practice.

Another recurrent difference concerns the last three steps in the scheme. Here the Pāli discourses and the Sarvāstivāda *Vinaya* proceed from impermanence to dispassion, cessation, and letting go.[29] Thus the different versions agree on impermanence as the foundation, leading onwards to the insight topics of dispassion and cessation.

BENEFITS (SĀ 804)

Cultivating the sixteen steps has additional benefits, not explicitly mentioned in the discourse above. The next discourse in the *Saṃyukta-āgama* makes this clear by presenting the

---

27 T 1425 at T XXII 254c14 (translated by Anālayo 2013b: 229f) and T 1435 at T XXIII 8a23 (translated by Anālayo 2016b: 247–249). The case of T 1448 at T XXIV 32c12 (translated by Anālayo 2016b: 245–247) is not directly relevant to the present point, as it describes the Buddha's own practice.

28 The same holds for the **Śāriputrābhidharma*, T 1548 at T XXVIII 705b14 (translated by Anālayo 2020a).

29 T 1435 at T XXIII 8b1; see Anālayo 2016b: 249n16 (the formulation in the first print run of Anālayo 2016b: 243,3 is due to an inadvertent error that occurred during revision and should be corrected to "namely dispassion, cessation, and letting go"). A correspondence to the sequence adopted in Pāli discourses can also be found in the case of the **Śāriputrābhidharma*, T 1548 at T XXVIII 705b21 (translated by Anālayo 2020a), the *Arthaviniścaya-sūtra*, Samtani 1971: 45,1 (translated by Samtani 2002: 32) and T 763 at T XVII 658a1, and the *Vimuttimagga*, T 1648 at T XXXII 430a5 (translated by Ehara et al. 1961/1995: 157); see also the survey in Dhammajoti 2008: 261–263. Rosenberg 1998: 58 brings out the thrust of the fourth tetrad, in the way described in these sources, by commenting that undertaking mindfulness of breathing in this way "is headed in the direction of letting go of everything you think you are", as a result of which "you gradually stop doing things for the sake of the image you have of yourself." Brahmavaṃso 2004/2006: 38 explains that here letting go "is not giving away what's 'out there' but giving away what's 'in here'. One should reflect on giving away, abandoning, all that is in here."

same exposition of mindfulness of breathing preceded by the indication that this practice serves in particular to abandon all thoughts:[30]

> You should cultivate mindfulness of breathing. Cultivating mindfulness of breathing, cultivating it much, one abandons all thoughts and [related] perceptions. How does one abandon all thoughts and [related] perceptions by cultivating mindfulness of breathing, cultivating it much?

The discourse continues with a full exposition of the sixteen steps, given in abbreviated form (beginning with the description of a monastic who dwells in dependence on a hamlet or town and then concluding with the final step of training to contemplate cessation when breathing out).

Going beyond thought activity already came up in a discourse from the *Madhyama-āgama* (see above p. 164) as one of several benefits of mindfulness of breathing, namely by way of countering the mind's tendency to distraction. The present case differs in so far as a whole discourse is dedicated to throwing into relief this particular benefit.

Following the present discourse, the *Saṃyukta-āgama* continues with an instruction to those who recite this part of the collection, indicating that they should also relate the same exposition of the sixteen steps to the following alternative benefits:[31]

> One [gains] imperturbability,
> one gains great fruit and great benefit,
> one gains the deathless,
> one [gains] the supreme deathless,
> one gains two fruits,
> one [gains] four fruits,
> one [gains] seven fruits.

The *Saṃyutta-nikāya* has three parallels to this survey of potential benefits of mindfulness of breathing. The first of these three *Saṃyutta-nikāya* discourses speaks of great fruit and great benefit, the second mentions two fruits, which are non-return and full awakening, and the third lists seven fruits, which are

30 SĀ 804 at T II 206b16 to 206b19.
31 T II 206b22 to 206b24.

full awakening and six types of non-return.[32] Although the *Saṃyukta-āgama* only lists these different fruits without spelling out their implications, it can safely be assumed that the mentions of two and seven fruits also refer to the highest two levels of awakening (the count of seven resulting from a subdivision of non-return into six types). On this understanding, the Chinese and Pāli versions can be seen to agree in throwing into relief the potential of mindfulness of breathing to lead to non-return and full awakening. This in turn confirms a point that already emerged earlier, namely that from the viewpoint of the early discourses mindfulness of breathing is clearly not a practice solely for cultivating concentration.

A DIFFERENT APPROACH (SĀ 805)

The potential of the sixteen steps finds a contrast in a different approach to mindfulness of breathing by the monastic Ariṭṭha. Both the *Saṃyukta-āgama* and the *Saṃyutta-nikāya* collections continue after their respective listing of benefits with a discourse in which Ariṭṭha describes his mode of practice. Here is the *Saṃyukta-āgama* version of his description:[33]

> At that time the Blessed One said to the monastics: "Do you cultivate mindfulness of breathing, as taught by me?"
>
> Then a monastic by the name of Ariṭṭha, who was seated in the gathering, rose from his seat, arranged his robes, and paid respect to the Buddha. With his right knee touching the ground and with his hands held together, he said to the Buddha:[34] "Blessed One, I have cultivated mindfulness of breathing, taught by the Blessed One."
>
> The Buddha said to the monastic Ariṭṭha: "How do you cultivate mindfulness of breathing, taught by me?"
>
> The monastic [Ariṭṭha] said to the Buddha: "Blessed One, I am not concerned with activities of the past, I do not give rise to enjoyment for activities of the future, and I do not give rise to

32 SN 54.3 at SN V 313,7, SN 54.4 at SN V 314,1, SN 54.5 at SN V 314,15 (translated by Bodhi 2000: 1767f).
33 SĀ 805 at T II 206b26 to 206c10.
34 The parallel SN 54.6 (translated by Bodhi 2000: 1768) does not describe Ariṭṭha's respectful behaviour.

> being defiled by attachment to activities of the present. Within and without I have well and properly dispelled perceptions of resistance.[35] In this way I have cultivated mindfulness of breathing, taught by the Blessed One."
>
> The Buddha said to the monastic Ariṭṭha: "You have truly cultivated mindfulness of breathing, taught by me. It is not that you have not cultivated it. Yet, monastic, there is another more excellent mindfulness of breathing that goes beyond and is superior to the one cultivated by you. What is this more excellent mindfulness of breathing that goes beyond the one cultivated by Ariṭṭha?"

This question then leads to an exposition of the sixteen steps of mindfulness of breathing as what is superior to the form of practice cultivated by Ariṭṭha.

In the Pāli parallel, Ariṭṭha's practice in regard to past and future is more specifically concerned with the abandoning of sensual desire (*kāmacchanda*).[36] Another difference is that the *Saṃyutta-nikāya* version explicitly mentions breathing in and out mindfully,[37] employing the same expression that, in other discourses, prefaces the sixteen steps (a part to which I refer as the "preliminaries"). Perhaps some such reference has been lost in the *Saṃyukta-āgama* discourse, as a result of which in this version Ariṭṭha only describes the type of mental attitude and results of his mode of practice, without relating this directly to mindfulness of breathing. Given the narrative setting, it is nevertheless clear that his description must be referring to mindfulness of breathing, which he in fact mentions in his concluding statement.

In both versions the Buddha acknowledges Ariṭṭha's way of practice as a viable approach. Instead of referring to the sixteen steps as more excellent, going beyond, and superior to what Ariṭṭha had described, in the Pāli parallel the Buddha introduces his exposition simply as a way of "fulfilling in detail" the cultivation of mindfulness of breathing.[38] Nevertheless, it

---

35 In SN 54.6 at SN V 315,6 he mentions that he breathes in and out mindfully.
36 SN 54.6 at SN V 315,3.
37 SN 54.6 at SN V 315,6.
38 SN 54.6 at SN V 315,9.

seems implicit that this way of fulfilling the practice in detail is superior to what Ariṭṭha had been practising.

Another difference occurs in relation to the Buddha's initial enquiry. In the *Saṃyutta-nikāya* discourse he simply asks the assembled monastics if they cultivate mindfulness of breathing.[39] The additional reference to mindfulness of breathing "as taught by me" in the *Saṃyukta-āgama* version is probably best understood as conveying the emphasis the Buddha gave to this practice in general, and not that he wanted to check if the monastics were doing it exactly as he had instructed. Otherwise Ariṭṭha would hardly have qualified his practice as something "taught by the Blessed One" and the Buddha would also not have acknowledged that he has "truly cultivated mindfulness of breathing, taught by me".

Both discourses testify to openness and flexibility in the way the practice was undertaken by the Buddha's disciples. The case of Ariṭṭha reflects a considerable degree of self-confidence in developing one's own individual approach. In his reply, the Buddha makes sure not to discourage such self-confidence by first acknowledging that what Ariṭṭha had been doing is indeed a viable approach. He only then adds that there is an alternative and more powerful mode of going about this practice, namely by way of the sixteen steps.

IMPERTURBABILITY (SĀ 806)

Following the case of Ariṭṭha, the *Saṃyutta-nikāya* and *Saṃyukta-āgama* collections continue with the practice of another monastic by the name of Kappina:[40]

> At that time, in the morning, the Blessed One put on his robes, took his bowl, and entered Sāvatthī to beg for food. Having [begged] for food, he returned to the monastery. Having put away his robes and bowl, and washed the feet, he took a sitting mat and entered Blind Man's Grove to sit under a tree for the day's meditation.[41]

39 SN 54.6 at SN V 314,29.
40 SĀ 806 at T II 206c15 to 207a1.
41 The parallel SN 54.7 (translated by Bodhi 2000: 1769) does not report what the Buddha did and begins by describing Mahākappina seated in meditation.

> Then, in the morning, the venerable Kappina also put on his robes, took his bowl, and entered Sāvatthī to beg for food. He returned and, having put away his robes and bowl, and washed the feet, he took a sitting mat and entered Blind Man's Grove. He sat for meditation under a tree not far from the Buddha, with straight body and immoveable, with his body and mind upright and with the most excellent attention.
>
> At that time a group of many monastics, rising from meditation in the afternoon, approached the Buddha, paid respect with their heads at the Buddha's feet, and withdrew to sit to one side. The Buddha said to the monastics: "Have you seen the venerable Kappina not far from me seated properly with the body kept straight, with immoveable body and mind, dwelling in the most excellent dwelling?"
>
> The monastics said to the Buddha: "Blessed One, we regularly see that venerable one seated properly with body kept straight, with body well controlled, without tilting and immoveable, single-mindedly [dwelling] in the most excellent [dwelling]."[42]
>
> The Buddha said to the monastics: "Suppose a monastic cultivates concentration with body and mind dwelling at ease, without tilting and immoveable, dwelling in the most excellent dwelling. This monastic has attained such concentration, with effortless means, attaining it according to his wishes."
>
> The monastics said to the Buddha: "What is the concentration that [this] monastic has attained, such a concentration that body and mind are immoveable and one dwells in the most excellent dwelling?"[43]

In reply to this enquiry, the Buddha expounds the sixteen steps of mindfulness of breathing. According to both versions, this was the type of practice that had enabled Kappina to reach such a superb degree of imperturbability.

His association with the practice of mindfulness of breathing has inspired a verse in the *Ekottarika-āgama*:[44]

---

42 In SN 54.7 at SN V 315,31 the monastics specify that they see him seated without trembling or shaking when he is among the community or when he is by himself.

43 In SN 54.7 the Buddha continues of his own accord, without a corresponding question by the monastics.

44 EĀ 30.3 at T II 662c15 to 662c16; a similar verse can be found in T 128b at T II 840b26.

Capable of practising [mindfulness] of exhalations and inhalations,
Encompassing the mind with wholesome practice,
His power of wisdom is utmost, fearless, and energetic:
He is called Kappina.

The *Saṃyukta-āgama* and *Saṃyutta-nikāya* discourses refer to mindfulness of breathing as a *samādhi*, literally "concentration",[45] although at times the same term can refer to "meditation" practices in general, a usage that goes beyond the implications of the term "concentration".[46]

Mindfulness of breathing has indeed an eminent potential to lead into deep states of mental unification. At the same time, however, its practice is not confined to this purpose. In fact the overall purpose of cultivating the sixteen steps is to fulfil the cultivation of the four *satipaṭṭhāna*s and the seven awakening factors so as to lead to liberation, a topic to which I will return in more detail below.

THE DWELLING OF A TATHĀGATA (SĀ 807)

The next discourse in the *Saṃyukta-āgama* reports the Buddha

---

45 The significance of the term *samādhi* in the present case is especially evident in the usage in SN 54.7 at SN V 316,10 of the compound "concentration by mindfulness of breathing", *ānāpānasati-samādhi*; see also Anālayo 2020a. This compound recurs in the *Saṃyutta-nikāya* only after the present discourse and is not found at all in the *Saṃyukta-āgama*. An occurrence in SN 54.9 has a counterpart in a version of the same tale in Vin III 70,19. A similar expression can be found in the corresponding part of the Dharmaguptaka *Vinaya*, T 1428 at T XXII 576b7. Parallels in the Mahāsānghika *Vinaya*, T 1425 at T XXII 254c7, the Mahīśāsaka *Vinaya*, T 1421 at T XXII 7c6, and the Sarvāstivāda *Vinaya*, T 1435 at T XXIII 8a13, however, do not combine the term "mindfulness of breathing" with "concentration" (the Mūlasarvāstivāda *Vinaya* does not relate this episode to mindfulness of breathing). This suggests that the presentation in SN 54.7 would have given rise to this compound during oral transmission, which then influenced the wording of subsequent discourses in this part of the *Saṃyutta-nikāya*; an influence that would have happened early enough to be reflected also in the Dharmaguptaka tradition. From a comparative perspective, it seems clear that early Buddhist meditation on the breath was predominantly a cultivation of mindfulness rather than being just a matter of focusing on the breath.

46 For a survey of different usages of *samādhi* in Pāli discourses see Anālayo 2006a.

undertaking mindfulness of breathing during a long retreat:[47]

At that time the Blessed One said to the monastics: "I wish to sit in meditation for two months.[48] All monastics should no longer come to contact me, except only for the monastic who brings me food and for the time of the observance day."[49]

At that time, having said this, the Blessed One sat in meditation for two months. Not a single monastic dared to come to contact him, except only to bring him food and for the time of the observance day.

At that time, having completed the two months of sitting in meditation and coming out of meditation, the Blessed One sat in front of the community of monastics and said to the monastics:

"If outside wanderers come and ask you: 'In what meditation has the recluse Gotama been sitting during these two months?', you should reply: 'The Tathāgata has been dwelling by giving attention to mindfulness of breathing during the two months of sitting in meditation.' Why is that?

"In these two months I dwelled giving much attention to mindfulness of breathing. When breathing in I was mindfully breathing in, understanding it as it really is;[50] when breathing out I was mindfully breathing out, understanding it as it really is.

"When *breathing in* long, *I was mindfully breathing in long, understanding it as it really is; when breathing out long, I was mindfully breathing out long, understanding it as it really is*. When *breathing in* short, *I was mindfully breathing in short, understanding it as it really is; when breathing out short, I was mindfully breathing out short, understanding it as it really is*.

"I was mindfully experiencing the whole body when breathing in, understanding it as it really is; I was mindfully experiencing the whole body when breathing out, understanding it as it really

47 SĀ 807 at T II 207a9 to 207b3 (partially translated by Anālayo 2017e: 64–65).

48 The parallel SN 54.11 at SN V 326,1 (translated by Bodhi 2000: 1778) speaks instead of a retreat of three months.

49 SN 54.11 does not refer to the *uposatha*, the fortnightly meeting of monastics to recite the code of rules.

50 The recurrent reference to being "mindful" and to "understanding as it really is" is without a counterpart in SN 54.11, although the same can safely be assumed to be implicit in the case of a meditation practice undertaken by the Buddha himself.

is. I was mindfully calming bodily activity when breathing in, understanding it as it really is; *I was mindfully calming bodily activity when breathing out, understanding it as it really is.*

"I was mindfully experiencing joy when breathing in, understanding it as it really is; I was mindfully experiencing joy when breathing out, understanding it as it really is. I was mindfully experiencing happiness when breathing in, understanding it as it really is; I was mindfully experiencing happiness when breathing out, understanding it as it really is.

"I was mindfully experiencing mental activity when breathing in, understanding it as it really is; I was mindfully experiencing mental activity when breathing out, understanding it as it really is. I was mindfully calming mental activity when breathing in, understanding it as it really is; I was mindfully calming mental activity when breathing out, understanding it as it really is.

"I was mindfully experiencing the mind when breathing in, understanding it as it really is; I was mindfully experiencing the mind when breathing out, understanding it as it really is. I was mindfully gladdening the mind when breathing in, understanding it as it really is; I was mindfully gladdening the mind when breathing out, understanding it as it really is.

"I was mindfully concentrating the mind when breathing in, understanding it as it really is; I was mindfully concentrating the mind when breathing out, understanding it as it really is. I was mindfully liberating the mind when breathing in, understanding it as it really is; I was mindfully liberating the mind when breathing out, understanding it as it really is.

"I was mindfully contemplating impermanence when breathing in, understanding it as it really is; I was mindfully contemplating impermanence when breathing out, understanding it as it really is. I was mindfully contemplating eradication when breathing in, understanding it as it really is; I was mindfully contemplating eradication when breathing out, understanding it as it really is.

"I was mindfully contemplating dispassion when breathing in, understanding it as it really is; I was mindfully contemplating dispassion when breathing out, understanding it as it really is. I was mindfully contemplating cessation when breathing in, understanding it as it really is; I was mindfully *contemplating* cessation when breathing out, understanding it as it really is.

"Having understood it all, at that time I thought: 'This dwelling with attention thus is coarse. Having stilled this attention now, by cultivating a very subtle [attention], I could in turn dwell cultivating another dwelling.'

"At that time, having stopped coarse attention,[51] I in turn entered a dwelling with very subtle attention, dwelling much in it.

"Then, when the night was over, three deities of superb appearance approached me. One deity said: 'The recluse Gotama has reached his time.'[52] Another deity said: 'He has not reached his time, he is about to reach his time.' The third deity said: 'He has not reached his time and he is not about to reach his time. He is thus cultivating an abiding. This is just the tranquillity of arahants.'"

The Buddha said to the monastics: "If one were to speak rightly of a noble dwelling, a celestial dwelling, a divine dwelling, the dwelling of a trainee, the dwelling of a non-trainee, the dwelling of a Tathāgata, by which those in training will gain what has not [yet] been gained, will reach what has not [yet] been reached, will realize what has not [yet] been realized, and which for non-trainees is a pleasant abiding in the present, it is reckoned to be mindfulness of breathing of which this can rightly be thus said."

The final part of the text translated above, found after the exposition of the sixteen steps, has no counterpart in the Pāli parallel.[53] A similar description of deities (*deva*s) who perceive the Buddha's condition to be close to death occurs in other

51 My rendering "stopped" reflects two Chinese characters that in combination carry this meaning. However, the first of these two can, on its own, mean "breath" and the second, on its own, still convey the sense "to stop". This makes it possible that the idea of stopping applies not only to the coarse form of attention but also to the breath. This seems less probable to me given the syntax, as the single character meaning "to stop" occurs between the one that could alternatively mean "breath" and those that render "coarse attention". Moreover, a parallel in the Mūlasarvāstivāda *Vinaya*, T 1448 at T XXIV 32c21, refers to coarse formations but not to the breath.

52 The reference to reaching one's time appears to correspond to the Pāli phrase *kālaṃ āgacchati*, literally "going towards the time", which is a way of referring to passing away. In the parallel in the Mūlasarvāstivāda *Vinaya*, T 1448 at T XXIV 32c25, the first *deva* thinks the Buddha has reached complete extinction.

53 A similar description can be found in the Mūlasarvāstivāda *Vinaya*; see the discussion in Anālayo 2017e: 66.

discourses, which report his pre-awakening ascetic practices.[54] The description of the Buddha's meditative dwelling such that others mistake him for dead resembles descriptions of entry into the attainment of cessation, apparently a condition easily mistaken for death by observers.[55]

Whatever may be the final word on the implications of the attainment reached through more subtle attention than that employed during the sixteen steps, the description as such does point to a progression from being aware of the breath to being aware of something subtler. In an attempt to relate this to ordinary cultivation of mindfulness of breathing, this could perhaps be seen as relevant to occasions when practice has led up to a point where even just being aware of the breath appears coarse. For such a juncture of practice, the above passage could be taken to suggest the option of trying to find some way of deploying attention in a subtler way.

Although the passage does not offer further details on how this could be implemented, from a practical viewpoint a subtler mode of attention could be related to tranquillity or insight. As already mentioned in previous chapters (see above pp. 87 and 116), a tranquillity approach could take place through entry into absorption with the step of "liberating the mind" that forms the conclusion of the third tetrad. An insight approach could be related to contemplating letting go as the final step of the sixteen-step scheme, cultivated in such a way that it occupies the entire field of perception. In this way, the mind would completely incline towards Nirvāṇa, which would indeed be subtler than attending to anything that is still within the realm of what is conditioned.

Be that as it may, the *Saṃyukta-āgama* discourse and its Pāli parallel agree in reckoning the sixteen steps of mindfulness of breathing as a noble and divine dwelling, as well as a dwelling

54 MN 36 at MN I 245,1 (translated by Ñāṇamoli 1995/2005: 339), EĀ 31.8 at T II 671a7, the *Mahāvastu*, Senart 1890: 208,4 (Jones 1952/1976: 198), and an *Udāna* collection, T 212 at T IV 644b13.

55 An example is MN 50 at MN I 333,25 (Ñāṇamoli 1995/2005: 432) and its parallels MĀ 131 at T I 620c24 and T 67 at T I 867a29. Another relevant passage is EĀ 28.1 at T II 648c20, which reports that a monastic, who has entered the attainment of cessation, is perceived by an onlooker as dead since breathing is no longer discernible.

of the Tathāgata.[56] This goes to show that the reference to a coarse form of attention is relative, pointing to something that is superior even to this extraordinary mode of practice. After all, even mindfulness of breathing is only a raft for the purpose of crossing over.

Another point to be taken from this discourse would be the Buddha's predilection for mindfulness of breathing. The specific quality of the Buddha's own practice of the sixteen steps is that this requires no "training" on his part. The lack of any need to train comes up again in the next discourse in the *Saṃyukta-āgama* and the *Saṃyutta-nikāya* collections.

THE DWELLING OF A TRAINEE (SĀ 808)

The next discourse in the *Saṃyukta-āgama* (whose Pāli parallel is also the next discourse in the *Saṃyutta-nikāya*) quotes the above report of the Buddha's retreat practice as an illustration of the dwelling of a Tathāgata. This stands in contrast to the dwelling of a trainee (one who has reached one of the three lower levels of awakening):[57]

> At that time the Sakyan Mahānāma approached a monastic, the venerable Kāmabhū.[58] Having paid respects at the feet of the monastic Kāmabhū, he withdrew to sit to one side and said to the monastic Kāmabhū: "How is it, venerable Kāmabhū, does the dwelling of a trainee serve as the dwelling of the Tathāgata, or does the dwelling of a trainee differ from the dwelling of the Tathāgata?"
>
> The monastic Kāmabhū replied: "Mahānāma, the dwelling of a trainee differs from the dwelling of the Tathāgata. Mahānāma, a trainee dwells abandoning the five hindrances, much dwelling in it. The Tathāgata dwells having known that the five hindrances have already been abandoned, abandoned at their root, like cutting off the crown of a Palmyra tree so that it will no more grow, being of a nature not to arise in the future."

56 SN 54.11 at SN V 326,27.
57 SĀ 808 at T II 207b7 to 207b14.
58 In the parallel SN 54.12 at SN V 327,4 (translated by Bodhi 2000: 1779) the name of the monastic whom Mahānāma approaches is Lomasavaṅgīsa.

Following this clarification, Kāmabhū repeats the previous discourse concerning the Buddha's retreat practice. The point of bringing in this illustration seems to be that the Buddha's own practice of mindfulness of breathing comes without any reference to "training". This differs from the standard instructions on the sixteen steps, where training is required for fourteen of the steps according to the *Saṃyutta-nikāya* and apparently for all sixteen steps according to the *Saṃyukta-āgama*.

The discourse above explicitly notes that, whereas a Tathāgata has forever abandoned the hindrances, a trainee has done so only temporarily. Once the hindrances have been forever left behind through full awakening, a progression through the sixteen steps would no longer require any more training because the hindrances stand no chance of emerging again. As long as this much has not been achieved, however, some degree of training when progressing through the sixteen steps is required to prevent the re-arising of any of the hindrances.

Such training need not be a forceful matter, but can simply take the form of remaining continuously aware of the alternation between inhalations and exhalations alongside whichever of the sixteen steps is being executed. Due to the liveliness of practice that can be cultivated with the scheme of sixteen steps, the mind is so engaged that the hindrances have little room to arise. If they should manifest, they are quickly noted and therefore more easily abandoned. This mode of training eventually leads up to such purification of the mind that a progression through the sixteen steps can take place with the natural ease and effortlessness of knowing that the hindrances have simply no chance at all of disturbing the meditation.

STILLING UNWHOLESOME STATES (SĀ 809)

Following on the topic of the hindrances, the next discourse in the *Saṃyukta-āgama*, which has a counterpart in the *Saṃyutta-nikāya* and also parallels in several *Vinaya*s, turns to mindfulness of breathing as a remedy for a serious mental imbalance caused by unskilful meditation practice:[59]

> At that time the Blessed One spoke to the monastics on contemplating the absence of beauty; he praised contemplating the absence of beauty, saying: "Monastics, one who cultivates contemplating the absence of beauty, cultivates it much, attains great fruit and great benefit."[60]
>
> Then, having cultivated contemplating the absence of beauty, the monastics exceedingly loathed their bodies. Some killed themselves with a knife, some took poison, some hanged themselves with a rope or committed suicide by throwing themselves down from a crag, some got another monastic to kill them.[61]
>
> A certain monastic, who had given rise to the [perception] of impurity and absence of beauty with excessive loathing, approached the son of a brahmin [called] Deer Forest.[62] He said to Deer Forest, the son of a brahmin: "Venerable, if you can kill me, my robes and bowl will belong to you."[63]
>
> Then Deer Forest, the son of a brahmin, killed that monastic. Carrying the knife, he went to the bank of the river Vaggumudā. When he was washing the knife, a Māra deity stood in mid-air and praised Deer Forest, the son of a brahmin: "It is well, it is well, venerable one. You are attaining innumerable merits by being able to get recluses, sons of the Sakyan, upholders of morality and endowed with virtue, who have not yet crossed over to cross over, who have not yet been liberated to be liberated, getting

59 SĀ 809 at T II 207b22 to 207c21, which has parallels in SN 54.9 at SN V 320,7 (translated by Bodhi 2000: 1773), Vin III 68,1 (translated by Horner 1938/1982: 116), and in the Dharmaguptaka *Vinaya*, T 1428 at T XXII 575c11, the Mahāsāṅghika *Vinaya*, T 1425 at T XXII 254a17, the Mahīśāsaka *Vinaya*, T 1421 at T XXII 7a27, the Mūlasarvāstivāda *Vinaya*, T 1442 at T XXIII 659c21 (or else T 1443 at T XXIII 923b14) and D 3 *ca* 133a3 or Q 1032 *che* 119a7 (or else D 5 *ta* 51b7 or Q 1034 *the* 50b2), and the Sarvāstivāda *Vinaya*, T 1435 at T XXIII 7b21; for a comparative study see Anālayo 2014.

60 SN 54.9 does not report any direct speech and therefore only has a counterpart to the preceding sentence, according to which the Buddha spoke in praise of cultivating *asubha*, the absence of beauty (in the body).

61 SN 54.9 at SN V 320,23 reports that on a single day ten, twenty, or thirty monastics committed suicide.

62 A more detailed discussion of this name, which I here just translate literally, can be found in Anālayo 2014: 13n5.

63 Such a tale is not found in SN 54.9, although it does occur in the Theravāda *Vinaya*, Vin III 68,21.

those who have not yet been stilled to attain stillness, getting those who have not yet [attained] Nirvāṇa to attain Nirvāṇa; and all their monastic possessions, robes, bowls, and various things, they all belong to you."

Then, having heard this praise, Deer Forest, the son of a brahmin, further increased his evil and wrong view, thinking: 'I am truly creating great merit now by getting recluses, sons of the Sakyan, upholders of morality and [endowed] with virtue, who have not yet crossed over to cross over, who have not yet been liberated to be liberated, getting those who have not yet been stilled to attain stillness, getting those who have not yet [attained] Nirvāṇa to attain Nirvāṇa; and their robes, bowls, and various things all belong to me.'

Thereupon he went around the living quarters, the areas for walking meditation, the individual huts, and the meditation huts, holding in his hand a sharp knife. On seeing monastics he spoke in this way: "Which recluses, upholders of morality and endowed with virtue, who have not yet crossed over can I get to cross over, who have not yet been liberated can I get to be liberated, who have not yet been stilled can I get to attain stillness, who have not yet [attained] Nirvāṇa can I get to attain Nirvāṇa?"

Then all monastics who loathed their bodies came out of their monastic living quarters and said to Deer Forest, the son of a brahmin: "I have not yet attained the crossing over, you should [make] me cross over, I have not yet attained liberation, you should liberate me, I have not yet attained stillness, you should get me to attain stillness, I have not yet attained Nirvāṇa, you should get me to attain Nirvāṇa."

Then Deer Forest, the son of a brahmin, killed the monastics one after another with his sharp knife until he had killed sixty men.

At that time, on the fifteenth day, at the time for reciting the rules, the Blessed One sat in front of the community and said to the venerable Ānanda: "What is the reason, what is the cause that the monastics have come to be few, have come to decrease, have come to disappear?"

In reply to this question, Ānanda informs the Buddha of the suicides.

A comparative study of this narrative in a range of parallels, found mostly in *Vinaya* texts, gives the overall impression that the story acquired different additions and elaborations in various transmission lineages.[64] Hence some of its more extreme features are best taken as reflections of narrative embellishment. For example, the description in the Pāli versions that, while the suicides were happening, the Buddha had been on retreat is not found in any of the other versions and thus probably is a later addition.[65]

The basic storyline that forms the common heritage of the different versions is that the Buddha had given a recommendation to the monastics to cultivate the perception of non-beauty. Presumably because they engaged in this practice without first receiving proper guidance and instructions, and also apparently being unaware of the importance of mental balance in early Buddhist meditation (in contrast to other more ascetically inclined traditions in ancient India), several monastics committed suicide. When informed of what had happened, the Buddha delivered instructions on mindfulness of breathing.

The *Saṃyukta-āgama* discourse reports that, after being informed by Ānanda of the suicides, the Buddha introduced his instructions as follows:[66]

> Therefore I will now teach you step by step [how] to dwell in a subtle dwelling that inclines to awakening and that quickly brings about the stilling of already arisen and not yet arisen evil and unwholesome states. It is just as a heavy rain from the sky can bring about the stilling of arisen and not yet arisen dust. In the same way, monastics, cultivating this subtle dwelling can bring about the stilling of all arisen and not yet arisen evil and unwholesome states.
>
> Ānanda, what is the subtle dwelling which, being much cultivated, inclines to awakening, and which can bring about the stilling of already arisen and not yet arisen evil and unwholesome states? It is dwelling in mindfulness of breathing.

Next comes an exposition of the sixteen steps (given in abbreviated form), beginning with the description of a monastic who goes begging. The simile of the rain in the *Saṃyutta-*

64 Anālayo 2014.
65 SN 54.9 at SN V 320,13 and Vin III 68,7.
66 SĀ 809 at T II 207c27 to 208a3.

nikāya parallel differs in so far as it only mentions dust that has already arisen, not dust that has not yet arisen.[67] Another minor difference is that the Pāli version qualifies mindfulness of breathing as peaceful and sublime; it does not mention explicitly that its practice inclines to awakening.[68]

The two discourse parallels agree that mindfulness of breathing in sixteen steps will bring about the stilling of unwholesome states. An appreciation of this indication requires keeping in mind that the instructions given by the Buddha in the above *Saṃyukta-āgama* discourse cover the removal of the hindrances prior to the practice of mindfulness of breathing. It is based on such removal that the scheme of sixteen steps unfolds.

In fact the audience of these instructions are those monastics who had not become prey to loathing their own bodies to the extent of committing suicide. It is to them that the instructions on the sixteen steps, based on having overcome any hindrance (including aversion as a modality of the second hindrance), are addressed. Building on the absence of excessive self-loathing and the temporary removal of the hindrances, mindfulness of breathing then serves to inculcate a balanced and healthy attitude towards the body. This stands in stark contrast to the unbalanced attitude of the monastics who came to abhor their own bodies to such an extent that they wanted to commit suicide.

Lack of clarity regarding the proper approach to emerging from sensuality, which requires getting rid of certain mental tendencies rather than of the body itself, could be compared to dust that has arisen, due to being swirled up by wind. During the hot season in India, when everything becomes extremely dry and parched, such swirling up of dust would have been a familiar experience to the Buddha's audience. Here mindfulness of breathing provides the timely rain that settles the dust and leads to clarity. It shows that a gradual training of the mind is the way out of sensuality and any other unwholesome condition. This training relies on the body rather than requiring a wholesale rejection of it.

Besides providing an example of the potential pitfalls of unbalanced forms of meditative practice, the present episode

67 SN 54.9 at SN V 321,26.
68 SN 54.9 at SN V 321,22.

throws into relief the intrinsically peaceful and calming nature of mindfulness of breathing. The degree to which this can manifest is well exemplified in the description of the imperturbability of Kappina (see above p. 189). His depiction contrasts starkly with the monastics who became so agitated by negativity towards their own body that they wished to commit suicide. A central implication to be taken away from this alarming episode is the need for balance, and that such balance can conveniently be cultivated through mindfulness of breathing.

THE FACTORS OF AWAKENING (SĀ 810 TO 812)

The *Saṃyukta-āgama* proceeds at this juncture with a set of three discourses that show how mindfulness of breathing leads to the arousing of the awakening factors; these three are parallels to four *Saṃyutta-nikāya* discourses. The shift from the above episode to the topic of the awakening factors to some degree mirrors a recurrent contrast in the early discourses between the hindrances and the awakening factors. The first of the discourses to take up the theme of the awakening factors proceeds as follows:[69]

> At that time the venerable Ānanda, while reflecting and meditating in a secluded and quiet place, had the following thought: 'Is there one dharma that, on being cultivated, much cultivated, brings to fulfilment four dharmas; these four dharmas being fulfilled, they fulfil seven dharmas; these seven dharmas being fulfilled, they fulfil two dharmas?'[70]
>
> Then, having risen from his meditation, the venerable Ānanda approached the Buddha, paid homage with his head at [the Buddha's] feet, withdrew to sit to one side and said to the Buddha:
>
> "Blessed One, while reflecting and meditating in a secluded and quiet place, I had the following thought: 'Is there one dharma that, on having been cultivated much, brings four dharmas to fulfilment, *these four dharmas being fulfilled, they fulfil seven dharmas; these seven dharmas being fulfilled,* they fulfil two dharmas?' I now ask the Blessed One, could there be one dharma that, on having

69 SĀ 810 at T II 208a10 to 208a23 (translated by Anālayo 2007).
70 The parallel SN 54.13 at SN V 328,24 (translated by Bodhi 2000: 1780) sets in only once Ānanda approaches the Buddha, who is staying at Sāvatthī.

been cultivated much, can bring *four dharmas to fulfilment, these four dharmas being fulfilled, they fulfil seven dharmas; these seven dharmas being fulfilled*, they fulfil two dharmas?"

The Buddha said to Ānanda: "There is one dharma that, on having been cultivated much *can bring four dharmas to fulfilment, these four dharmas being fulfilled, they can fulfil seven dharmas; these seven dharmas being fulfilled*, they can bring two dharmas to fulfilment. What is that one dharma? It is mindfulness of breathing which, on having been cultivated much, can bring to fulfilment the four establishments of mindfulness. The four establishments of mindfulness being fulfilled, they will fulfil the seven awakening factors. The seven awakening factors being fulfilled, they will fulfil knowledge and liberation.

"How does cultivating mindfulness of breathing fulfil the four establishments of mindfulness?"

At this juncture the discourse gives an abbreviated reference to the full account of the practice of mindfulness of breathing, beginning with the first part of the description of a monastic who dwells in dependence on a village and concluding with the final step of contemplating cessation when breathing out. Then each tetrad is taken up separately in order to show its relationship to the respective *satipaṭṭhāna* in the following way:[71]

Ānanda, in this way a noble disciple when breathing in mindfully thus trains to breathe in mindfully, when breathing out mindfully thus trains to breathe out mindfully.[72] *One trains to keep being mindful of breathing in* long, *and one trains to keep being mindful of breathing out long. One trains to keep being mindful of breathing in* short, *and one trains to keep being mindful of breathing out short.* Experiencing the whole ⟨body⟩ when breathing in mindfully,[73] one

71 SĀ 810 at T II 208a23 to 208b13.

72 SN 54.13 consistently refers to a monastic, whereas SĀ 810 begins by mentioning a monastic, but here changes to a noble disciple, and later reverts again to a monastic.

73 My translation is based on an emendation; the original speaks of the "whole bodily activity" in relation to the third step. That the present instance in SĀ 810 must be the result of a textual error finds confirmation in SĀ 803 and SĀ 807, where the third step is just about the "whole body". It is also noteworthy that SĀ 810 keeps mentioning mindfulness in its description of each step of the first three tetrads. This could be another textual error, influenced by the precedent set by the description of the Buddha's own

thus trains *to experience the whole body when* breathing in mindfully, *experiencing the whole body when* breathing out mindfully, one thus trains to *experience the whole body when* breathing out mindfully. Calming bodily activity when breathing in mindfully, one thus trains to calm bodily activity when breathing in mindfully; calming bodily activity when breathing out mindfully, one thus trains to calm bodily activity when breathing out mindfully.

At such a time a noble disciple dwells contemplating the body as a body, being mindful of some [aspect of] the body.[74] That is also how a monastic gives attention in accordance with the body.[75]

Suppose there is a time when a noble disciple, experiencing joy *when breathing in mindfully, thus trains to experience joy when breathing in mindfully; experiencing joy when breathing out mindfully, thus trains to experience joy when breathing out mindfully.* Experiencing happiness *when breathing in mindfully, one thus trains to experience happiness when breathing in mindfully; experiencing happiness when breathing out mindfully, one thus trains to experience happiness when breathing out mindfully.* Experiencing mental activity *when breathing in mindfully, one thus trains to experience mental activity when breathing in mindfully; experiencing mental activity when breathing out mindfully, one thus trains to experience mental activity when breathing out mindfully.* Experiencing a calming of mental activity when breathing in mindfully, one thus trains to calm mental activity when breathing in mindfully; *experiencing a* calming of mental activity when breathing out mindfully, one thus trains to calm mental activity when breathing out mindfully.

---

practice in SĀ 807, where mindfulness indeed features explicitly in each step. In the case of SĀ 810 this mode of presentation creates an internal inconsistency, as mindfulness is not mentioned in relation to any of the steps of the fourth tetrad, yet an earlier abbreviated reference to the complete scheme of sixteen steps in SĀ 810 at T II 208a23 does mention mindfulness for the last step of the fourth tetrad. This inconsistency makes it safe to conclude that the explicit references to mindfulness would be the result of a copying error influenced by SĀ 807.

74 The translation "some" is based on the assumption that the Chinese original, which literally means "different", renders an Indic original corresponding to Pāli *aññatara* rather than *añña*. SN 54.13 at SN V 329,28, which reckons the breath to be a certain kind of body, adds here and in relation to the other three *satipaṭṭhāna*s that practice is undertaken diligently, clearly knowing and mindful, free from desire and discontent in regard to the world.

75 Here and below, the reference to the monastic is truncated in the original and only given in full as a variant.

At such a time a noble disciple dwells contemplating feeling tones as feeling tones, again, being thus mindful of some feeling tone. That is also how a monastic gives attention in accordance with feeling tones.[76]

[Suppose] there is a time when a noble disciple, experiencing the mind *when breathing in mindfully, thus trains to experience the mind when breathing in mindfully; experiencing the mind when breathing out mindfully, thus trains to experience the mind when breathing out mindfully. Experiencing* gladdening the mind *when breathing in mindfully, one thus trains to experience gladdening the mind when breathing in mindfully; experiencing gladdening the mind when breathing out mindfully, one thus trains to experience gladdening the mind when breathing out mindfully. Experiencing* concentrating the mind *when breathing in mindfully, one thus trains to experience concentrating the mind when breathing in mindfully; experiencing concentrating the mind when breathing out mindfully, one thus trains to experience concentrating the mind when breathing out mindfully.* Experiencing liberating the mind when breathing in mindfully, one thus trains *to experience liberating the mind when* breathing in mindfully; *experiencing* liberating the mind when breathing out mindfully, one thus trains *to experience* liberating the mind when breathing out mindfully.

At such a time a noble disciple dwells contemplating the mind as mind, being thus mindful of there being some state of mind. That is also how a monastic gives attention in accordance with the mind.

Suppose there is a time when a noble disciple, contemplating impermanence *when breathing in, thus trains to contemplate impermanence when breathing in; contemplating* impermanence *when breathing out, thus trains to contemplate impermanence when breathing out. Contemplating* eradication *when breathing in, one thus trains to contemplate eradication when breathing in; contemplating* eradication *when breathing out, one thus trains to contemplate eradication when breathing out. Contemplating* dispassion *when breathing in, one thus trains to contemplate dispassion when breathing in; contemplating* dispassion *when breathing out, one thus trains to contemplate dispassion when breathing out. Contemplating* cessation *when breathing in, one thus trains to contemplate cessation when*

76 Adopting a variant in accordance with the formulation found in the case of the contemplations of the mind and of dharmas.

breathing in; contemplating cessation when breathing out, one thus trains to dwell contemplating cessation *when breathing out.*

At such a time a noble disciple dwells contemplating dharmas as dharmas, being mindful of some dharma. [That] is also how a monastic gives attention in accordance with dharmas.

This is called fulfilling the four establishments of mindfulness by cultivating mindfulness of breathing.

A minor but noteworthy difference emerges in relation to the scope of the first *satipaṭṭhāna*. In the Pāli account this corresponds to understanding long breath, understanding short breath, experiencing the whole body, and calming bodily activity. In the *Saṃyukta-āgama* discourse translated above, however, the preliminary step of mindfully breathing in and out is also included in what corresponds to contemplation of the body.

Otherwise the basic correlations are the same, although in the Pāli parallel these come with further specifications. In the case of the second tetrad on contemplation of feeling tones, the *Saṃyutta-nikāya* version explains that close attention to breathing in and breathing out is a certain kind of feeling tone.[77] This explanation is unexpected, since elsewhere in the discourses attention (*manasikāra*) is not reckoned a type of feeling tone. The Pāli commentary on the same explanation given in the *Ānāpānasati-sutta* recognizes this difficulty and explains that this is just a figure of speech and does not refer to attention itself.[78]

The rationale given in the *Saṃyutta-nikāya* discourse for correlating the third tetrad to contemplation of the mind is that there is no development of concentration through mindfulness of breathing for one who is of muddled mindfulness and without clear comprehension.[79] Although this is indeed the case, mindfulness and clear comprehension would be required for all tetrads of mindfulness of breathing. It is not entirely clear why this requirement should provide a link specifically between the third tetrad and contemplation of the mind.

According to the *Saṃyutta-nikāya* discourse, the fourth tetrad relates to contemplation of dharmas because by this stage of

77 SN 54.13 at SN V 330,11.
78 Ps IV 140,14 (translated by Ñāṇamoli 1952/1982: 50).
79 SN 54.13 at SN V 330,23.

practice one has seen with wisdom the abandoning of desire and discontent and one looks on with equanimity.[80] Now a progression through the first three tetrads can indeed be expected to lead to a high level of equanimity, aloof from desire and discontent (see below p. 214). At the same time, however, the *Ānāpānasati-sutta* relates each tetrad of mindfulness of breathing to dwelling "diligent, clearly comprehending, and mindful, free from desire and discontent with regard to the world".[81] From this viewpoint, then, the absence of desire and discontent is something relevant to the practice of each tetrad and not only contemplation of dharmas.

The commentary on the *Ānāpānasati-sutta* in fact explains that the relationship between the fourth tetrad and contemplation of dharmas can be found in the reference to having seen the absence of desire and discontent "with wisdom", since the wisdom referred to here should be understood to reflect the insight arisen through the contemplations described in the last tetrad of mindfulness of breathing.[82]

In sum, although the points made in the *Saṃyutta-nikāya* discourse are of considerable interest, the simple explanations offered in the *Saṃyukta-āgama* version for correlating the second to fourth tetrads of mindfulness of breathing with the second to fourth *satipaṭṭhāna* seem sufficient to make the main point. Understood in this way, the correspondence between the four tetrads and the four *satipaṭṭhāna*s simply reflects that with the first tetrad one contemplates bodily phenomena, with the second tetrad there is an emphasis on feeling tone, the third tetrad has as its chief object the mind, and the fourth tetrad directs mindfulness to aspects of the teachings.

The *Saṃyukta-āgama* discourse then continues as follows:[83]

> Ānanda said to the Buddha: "In this way cultivating mindfulness of breathing will [indeed] bring to fulfilment the four establishments of mindfulness. How does cultivating the four establishments of

80 SN 54.13 at SN V 330,32.
81 MN 118 at MN III 83,30, 84,8, 84,22, and 85,3.
82 Ps IV 142,13.
83 SĀ 810 at T II 208b13 to 208c1.

mindfulness bring to fulfilment the seven awakening factors?"[84]

The Buddha said to Ānanda: "Suppose a monastic dwells contemplating the body as a body with mindfulness; having dwelled with mindfulness, dwelled indeed with mindfulness that is collected and being without forgetfulness, at that time one diligently cultivates the awakening factor of mindfulness. Having cultivated the awakening factor of mindfulness, the awakening factor of mindfulness becomes fulfilled.

"The awakening factor of mindfulness being fulfilled, one investigates and examines the Dharma.[85] At that time one diligently cultivates the awakening factor of investigation-of-dharmas. Having cultivated the awakening factor of investigation-of-dharmas, the awakening factor of investigation-of-dharmas becomes fulfilled.

"Having investigated, discerned, and examined the Dharma, one gains diligent energy. At that time one diligently cultivates the awakening factor of energy. Having cultivated the awakening factor of energy, the awakening factor of energy becomes fulfilled.

"Having been diligent and energetic, the mind becomes joyful. At that time one diligently cultivates the awakening factor of joy. Having cultivated the awakening factor of joy, the awakening factor of joy becomes fulfilled.

"Having become glad and joyful, body and mind become tranquil and calm. At that time one diligently cultivates the awakening factor of tranquillity. Having cultivated the awakening factor of tranquillity, the awakening factor of tranquillity becomes fulfilled.

"Body and mind having become happy, one gains concentration. At that time one diligently cultivates the awakening factor of concentration. Having cultivated the awakening factor of concentration, the awakening factor of concentration becomes fulfilled.

"The awakening factor of concentration having been fulfilled, desire and discontent cease and one attains balance and equipoise.

84 In SN 54.13 at SN V 331,6 the Buddha continues straightaway with his exposition, without an enquiry by Ānanda about the relationship between the four *satipaṭṭhāna*s and the seven awakening factors.

85 In SN 54.13 at SN V 331,18 the object of such investigation is in the singular, *taṃ dhammaṃ paññāya pavicinati*; the same appears to be the case in SĀ 810. Both singular and plural forms would fall within the scope of this awakening factor; see the discussion in Gethin 1992: 147–154.

> At that time one diligently cultivates the awakening factor of equipoise. Having cultivated the awakening factor of equipoise, the awakening factor of equipoise becomes fulfilled."

After an indication that the same mode of presentation should also be applied to the other three *satipaṭṭhāna*s, the concluding statement is as follows:

> This is called cultivating the four establishments of mindfulness to bring to fulfilment the seven awakening factors.

The description of how to arouse the awakening factors is similar in the Pāli version. An additional specification in the *Saṃyutta-nikāya* discourse clarifies that the joy arisen at this stage is of a non-worldly type.[86]

Regarding the last of the seven awakening factors, the Pāli parallel indicates instead that at this stage one oversees without interfering the state of mind that has been concentrated in this way.[87] The *Saṃyukta-āgama* version's reference to the removal of desire and discontent confirms that freedom from desire and discontent is relevant to all four tetrads, as the above description applies not only to the case of contemplating the body, but also to contemplating feeling tones, the mind, and dharmas.

Regarding the role of equipoise as an awakening factor, whereas the *Saṃyukta-āgama* version emphasizes that a mental condition of balance and equipoise is the result of completely leaving behind any desire and discontent, the corresponding description in the *Saṃyutta-nikāya* offers the helpful indication that the inner balance of equipoise takes as its object the concentrated condition of the mind reached at this juncture of practice (which of course also requires leaving behind desire and discontent).

The final part of the *Saṃyukta-āgama* discourse proceeds in this way:[88]

> Ānanda said to the Buddha: "This is [indeed] called cultivating the four establishments of mindfulness to bring to fulfilment

86 SN 54.13 at SN V 332,7.
87 SN 54.13 at SN V 332,26.
88 SĀ 810 at T II 208b29 to 208c8.

the seven awakening factors. How does cultivating the seven awakening factors fulfil knowledge and liberation?"[89]

The Buddha said to Ānanda: "Suppose a monastic cultivates the awakening factor of mindfulness supported by seclusion, supported by dispassion, and supported by cessation, conducing to letting go. Having cultivated the awakening factor of mindfulness [in this way] fulfils knowledge and liberation.

"One cultivates the awakening factor of investigation-of-dharmas supported by seclusion, supported by dispassion, and supported by cessation, conducing to letting go. Having cultivated the awakening factor of investigation-of-dharmas in this way fulfils knowledge and liberation.

"One cultivates the awakening factor of energy supported by seclusion, supported by dispassion, and supported by cessation, conducing to letting go. Having cultivated the awakening factor of energy in this way fulfils knowledge and liberation.

"One cultivates the awakening factor of joy supported by seclusion, supported by dispassion, and supported by cessation, conducing to letting go. Having cultivated the awakening factor of joy in this way fulfils knowledge and liberation.

"One cultivates the awakening factor of tranquillity supported by seclusion, supported by dispassion, and supported by cessation, conducing to letting go. Having cultivated the awakening factor of tranquillity in this way fulfils knowledge and liberation.

"One cultivates the awakening factor of concentration supported by seclusion, supported by dispassion, and supported by cessation, conducing to letting go. Having cultivated the awakening factor of concentration in this way fulfils knowledge and liberation.

"One cultivates the awakening factor of equipoise supported by seclusion, supported by dispassion, and supported by cessation, conducing to letting go. Having cultivated the awakening factor of equipoise in this way fulfils knowledge and liberation.

"Ānanda, these are called dharmas that are related to one another, dharmas that enrich each other. In this way with these thirteen dharmas, as each dharma becomes predominant, that dharma becomes the way to proceed forward in sequence, by being cultivated and fulfilled."

89 In SN 54.13 at SN V 333,16 the Buddha continues on his own with his exposition, without an enquiry by Ānanda prompting him to do so.

The reference to thirteen dharmas must be an allusion to the four *satipaṭṭhāna*s, the seven awakening factors, and knowledge and liberation. This last paragraph has no counterpart in the Pāli parallel. Apart from this difference, however, the two versions are in close agreement regarding the all-important teaching on how the awakening factors should be cultivated in order to actualize their awakening potential. This takes place "in dependence on" or "supported by" seclusion, dispassion, and cessation, "culminating in" or "conducing to" letting go.

The importance of this correlation between mindfulness of breathing and the four *satipaṭṭhāna*s, the seven awakening factors, and knowledge and liberation is evident from the fact that the *Saṃyukta-āgama* and the *Saṃyutta-nikāya* continue with further discourses that repeat the same exposition and differ only in their respective audience. In the case of the *Saṃyukta-āgama*, instead of Ānanda, an enquiry by an unnamed male monastic motivates the Buddha to offer this exposition, and on yet another occasion he does the same to an audience of monastics without being prompted by a corresponding enquiry.[90]

THE CHARIOT SIMILE (SĀ 813)

The correlation between mindfulness of breathing and the four *satipaṭṭhāna*s recurs again in the next discourse in the *Saṃyukta-āgama*, whose introductory narration features a monastic apparently not too interested in this topic:[91]

> At that time the Blessed One said to the venerable Kimbila: "I will now teach you the energetic cultivation of the four establishments of mindfulness. Listen carefully and pay proper attention to what

90 SĀ 811 and SĀ 812 at T II 208c10, paralleling SN 54.15 and SN 54.16 at SN V 334,19 (translated by Bodhi 2000: 1786). The *Saṃyutta-nikāya* has still another discourse of the same type, addressed by the Buddha to Ānanda without being prompted by a corresponding enquiry, namely SN 54.14 at SN V 333,23 (translated by Bodhi 2000: 1785). Given Ānanda's proverbial memory, it seems improbable that he needed to receive the same instruction twice (SN 54.13 and SN 54.14). The absence of a counterpart in Chinese makes it quite possible that SN 54.14 is the result of a transmission error.

91 SĀ 813 at T II 208c13 to 208c21; a similar presentation can be found in the Mūlasarvāstivāda *Vinaya*, D 1 *kha* 97a6 or Q 1030 *ge* 90a1 (the Chinese counterpart, 1448 at T XXIV 37a6, abbreviates).

I will teach you." At that time the venerable Kimbila remained silent. It went like this three times.

At that time the venerable Ānanda said to the venerable Kimbila: "The great teacher is now talking to you." He said it three times. The venerable Kimbila said to the venerable Ānanda: "I know it already, venerable Ānanda, I know it already, venerable one [from the] Gotama [clan]."

At that time the venerable Ānanda said to the Buddha: "Blessed One, this is the time, Blessed One, this is the time; may the Well-gone One teach to the monastics the energetic cultivation of the four establishments of mindfulness. Having heard it, the monastics will receive it respectfully."

In reply to this invitation by Ānanda, the Buddha expounds the sixteen steps of mindfulness of breathing.

According to the introductory narration in the *Saṃyutta-nikāya* parallel, instead of announcing a teaching on the four *satipaṭṭhāna*s, the Buddha had asked Kimbila how the cultivation of concentration on mindfulness of breathing can be very fruitful.[92] Being asked up to three times, Kimbila remained silent. This then motivated Ānanda (who in this version does not speak to Kimbila directly) to invite the Buddha to expound on the topic.

In this way, in the Pāli version mindfulness of breathing was the topic from the outset, its detailed exposition being motivated by Kimbila's apparent lack of acquaintance with this form of practice. In the *Saṃyukta-āgama* discourse, however, the four *satipaṭṭhāna*s are the topic mentioned at the outset. The exposition of the sixteen steps of mindfulness of breathing then serves to show how the four *satipaṭṭhāna*s can be cultivated "energetically".

The remainder of the discourse in both versions relates the sixteen steps to the four *satipaṭṭhāna*s. For the practice from the preliminary awareness of the breath to the final step of the first tetrad, this correlation is as follows in the *Saṃyukta-āgama* version:[93]

"At that time a noble disciple dwells contemplating the body as a body with mindfulness. At that time, having dwelled

92 SN 54.10 at SN V 322,18 (translated by Bodhi 2000: 1775).
93 SĀ 813 at T II 208c26 to 208c30.

contemplating the body as a body with mindfulness, a noble disciple knows to be paying attention well in this way within."[94]

The Buddha said to Ānanda: "It is just like a person who drives a chariot that comes from the east over bumpy terrain. At that time, will it flatten all mounds of earth?"

[The venerable] Ānanda said to the Buddha: "It is like this, Blessed One."

The specification that the practitioner "knows to be paying attention well in this way within" is not found in the Pāli parallel. The same specification occurs with subsequent tetrads and might be related to the idea of an "energetic cultivation" of the four *satipaṭṭhāna*s, mentioned at the outset of the discourse.

Another difference is that the *Saṃyutta-nikāya* discourse has the simile of the chariot at the end of the whole exposition, instead of after each tetrad. The Pāli version of this simile specifies that, just as the chariot flattens a mound of soil at a crossroads, contemplating body, feeling tones, mind, and dharmas flattens unwholesome states.[95] The same sense can safely be assumed to be implicit in the *Saṃyukta-āgama* simile of the chariot, in that the issue at stake is the potential of mindfulness of breathing to "flatten" unwholesome states. The simile recurs in relation to the second tetrad with the only difference that the chariot comes from another direction:[96]

"*At that time* a noble disciple dwells contemplating feeling tones as feeling tones with mindfulness. Having [dwelled] contemplating feeling tones as feeling tones with mindfulness, a noble disciple knows to be paying attention well in this way within.[97]

"It is just like a person who drives a chariot that comes from the south over bumpy terrain. How is it, Ānanda, will it flatten a mound of earth?"

[The venerable] Ānanda said to the Buddha: "It is like this, Blessed One."

---

94 SN 54.10 at SN V 323,28 has the same explanation as SN 54.13, discussed above p. 206, for relating the first tetrad to contemplation of the body, namely that the breath is a certain kind of body.

95 SN 54.10 at SN V 325,1.

96 SĀ 813 at T II 209a2 to 209a6.

97 SN 54.10 at SN V 324,7 explains, in line with SN 54.13, that close attention to breathing in and breathing out is a certain kind of feeling.

The same pattern continues with the third tetrad:[98]

> "At that time a noble disciple dwells contemplating mind as mind with mindfulness. Having in this way dwelled contemplating mind as mind with mindfulness, *a noble disciple* knows to be paying attention well *in this way* within.[99]
>
> "It is just like a person who drives a chariot that comes from the west [over bumpy terrain]. Will it flatten a mound of earth?"
>
> [The venerable] Ānanda said to the Buddha: "It is like this, Blessed One."

The exposition of the fourth tetrad proceeds in the same vein:[100]

> "Having well relinquished and extinguished desire and dejection in relation to body, feeling tones, and mind, at that time a noble disciple dwells contemplating dharmas as dharmas with mindfulness. Having in this way dwelled contemplating dharmas as dharmas with mindfulness, a noble disciple knows to be paying attention well [in this way] within.
>
> "Ānanda, it is just like a mound of soil on a crossroads and a person drives a chariot that comes from the north over bumpy terrain. Will it flatten the mound of earth?"
>
> [The venerable] Ānanda said to the Buddha: "It is like this, Blessed One."

The *Saṃyutta-nikāya* parallel explains that by this stage of practice one has seen with wisdom the abandoning of desire and discontent and one looks on with equanimity.[101] As mentioned above, the need to stay aloof from desire and discontent is to some degree a requirement for all four *satipaṭṭhāna*s. In fact the *Saṃyukta-āgama* discourse also refers to overcoming desire and discontent, which here are precisely related to the previous three *satipaṭṭhāna*s. What the passage conveys is that, by the time of reaching the thirteenth step of contemplating impermanence, desire and dejection in relation to body, feeling tones, and the mind have been left well behind. This confirms that a gradual

---

98 SĀ 813 at T II 209a9 to 209a12.

99 Similar to SN 54.13, SN 54.10 at SN V 324,18 notes that there is no development of concentration through mindfulness of breathing for one who is of muddled mindfulness and without clear comprehension.

100 SĀ 813 at T II 209a15 to 209a19.

101 SN 54.10 at SN V 324,27.

build-up takes place when progressing through the sixteen steps, with the last tetrad setting in at a level of mental balance that provides an ideal foundation for the cultivation of liberating insight.

As a context for appreciating the idea of flattening unwholesome states, it is helpful to keep in mind that, according to the standard instruction in the *Saṃyukta-āgama*, the removal of the hindrances is a precondition for embarking on the sixteen steps of mindfulness of breathing, similar to sitting down in a secluded place. Once the hindrances have already been abandoned, at least temporarily, the unwholesome states to be flattened would have to be of a subtler nature. This concords with a general characteristic of the sixteen-step scheme of taking the absence of gross unwholesome states for granted. Building on such absence, the practice then leads to a further flattening of whatever subtle unwholesomeness might still be present.

The simile of the chariot driving over or through the mound of earth, rather than trying to drive around it, can then be taken to convey nuances of a willingness to confront directly whatever traces of unwholesomeness are still left, until they have been completely flattened out. At the same time, the main purpose of driving the chariot is to lead to a particular destination and the flattening of the mound of earth is only a by-product of progressing straight towards the journey's end. In the same vein, even though the instructions for mindfulness of breathing do not explicitly describe how to remove unwholesome conditions, progressing straight through the sixteen steps towards the culmination of the practice in letting go will result in flattening them.

ATTAINMENTS (SĀ 814)

From the simile of the chariot as an illustration of the potential of mindfulness of breathing to "flatten" unwholesome states, the *Saṃyukta-āgama* proceeds to an exposition of a range of attainments that can be realized with this practice. The relevant discourse begins with a brief statement of some benefits of the practice. Next it presents the sixteen steps, then it reiterates the earlier brief statement, before proceeding to a range of attainments. The translation below sets in after the sixteen steps and thus begins with the reiteration of the earlier introductory statement:[102]

> This is called a cultivation of mindfulness of breathing that does not fatigue the body, does not trouble the eyes, and one dwells contemplating happiness accordingly, experiencing happiness without being defiled by attachment to the happiness. One who cultivates mindfulness of breathing in this way gains great fruit and great benefit.
>
> A monastic who wishes to be secluded from sensual pleasures, secluded from evil and unwholesome states and, with [directed] awareness and [sustained] contemplation, with joy and ⟨happiness⟩ born of seclusion,[103] to dwell fully in the first absorption, that monastic should cultivate mindfulness of breathing.
>
> In this way by cultivating mindfulness of breathing one gains great fruit and great benefit.
>
> A monastic who wishes *to dwell fully* in the second absorption, *that monastic should cultivate mindfulness of breathing.*
>
> *A monastic who wishes to dwell fully* in the third absorption, *that monastic should cultivate mindfulness of breathing.*
>
> *A monastic who wishes to dwell fully* in the fourth absorption, *that monastic should cultivate mindfulness of breathing.*
>
> *A monastic who wishes to dwell fully* in benevolence (mettā), *that monastic should cultivate mindfulness of breathing.*[104]
>
> *A monastic who wishes to dwell fully* in compassion, *that monastic should cultivate mindfulness of breathing.*
>
> *A monastic who wishes to dwell fully* in sympathetic joy, *that monastic should cultivate mindfulness of breathing.*
>
> *A monastic who wishes to dwell fully* in equanimity, *that monastic should cultivate mindfulness of breathing.*
>
> *A monastic who wishes to dwell fully* in the sphere of [boundless] space, *that monastic should cultivate mindfulness of breathing.*
>
> *A monastic who wishes to dwell fully* in the sphere of [boundless]

---

102 SĀ 814 at T II 209a29 to 209b13.

103 The translation "happiness" is based on an emendation; the original instead refers to being "wholesome" (a Chinese character that in handwriting can be confused with the one for "happiness").

104 The *brahmavihāra*s are not mentioned in the parallel SN 54.8.

consciousness, *that monastic should cultivate mindfulness of breathing.*

A monastic who wishes to dwell fully in the sphere of nothingness, *that monastic should cultivate mindfulness of breathing.*

A monastic who wishes to dwell fully in the sphere of neither-perception-nor-non-perception, *that monastic should cultivate mindfulness of breathing.*[105]

A monastic who wishes to eradicate three fetters completely and gain the fruit of stream-entry, *that monastic should cultivate mindfulness of breathing.*

A monastic who wishes to eradicate three fetters, weaken lust, aversion, and delusion, and gain the fruit of once-return, *that monastic should cultivate mindfulness of breathing.*

A monastic who wishes to eradicate the five lower fetters and gain the fruit of non-return, *that monastic should cultivate mindfulness of breathing.*

A monastic who wishes to gain innumerable types of supernormal powers, *that monastic should cultivate mindfulness of breathing.*

A monastic who wishes to gain the divine ear, *that monastic should cultivate mindfulness of breathing.*

A monastic who wishes to gain knowledge of the minds of others, *that monastic should cultivate mindfulness of breathing.*

A monastic who wishes to gain recollection of past lives, *that monastic should cultivate mindfulness of breathing.*

A monastic who wishes to gain knowledge of the passing away and being reborn [of beings], *that monastic should cultivate mindfulness of breathing.*

A monastic who wishes to gain the knowledge of the destruction of the influxes, *that monastic should cultivate mindfulness of breathing.*

In this way, monastics, you should cultivate mindfulness of breathing. Cultivating mindfulness of breathing in this way one gains great fruit and great benefit.

The *Saṃyutta-nikāya* parallel similarly speaks of the body and eyes not being fatigued, although it differs in so far as it relates these benefits to the Buddha's own pre-awakening experience,

105 At this juncture, the parallel SN 54.8 at SN V 319,12 (translated by Bodhi 2000: 1772) continues instead with the attainment of the cessation of perception and feeling tone, and then describes insight into and non-attachment towards feeling tones, illustrated with the example of an oil lamp that is extinguished.

followed by stating that this meditative abiding led to his liberating the mind from the influxes.[106] This last statement is without a counterpart in the *Saṃyukta-āgama* version.

According to the standard accounts in other discourses, the Buddha's awakening took place by way of the three higher knowledges.[107] The Pāli commentarial tradition suggests that he used mindfulness of breathing to build up the concentration required for being able to cultivate recollection of past lives, the divine eye, and eventually the destruction of the influxes.[108] The fact that this relation between the Buddha's awakening and mindfulness of breathing is not mentioned in the above *Saṃyukta-āgama* discourse leaves open the possibility that it could reflect a later development.

Regarding the indication that the body and eyes can become fatigued, the Pāli commentary mentions meditating on the four elements as an example of what can fatigue the body and meditating on a *kasiṇa* device as an example of what can fatigue the eyes.[109] Neither of these two meditation exercises has a direct relationship to the standard descriptions of the Buddha's progress to awakening. It is also not entirely clear in what way contemplation of the four elements could be physically tiring. The same holds for the development of the inner vision of a *kasiṇa*, be it based on one of these elements or on a colour experienced as all-pervasive. The eyes could of course become fatigued during the preparatory work when one might be staring at some object to arouse the vision that then is to be cultivated internally. But the internal vision used for the actual meditation would not require the physical eyes any longer and therefore should not fatigue them.

At least as far as bodily fatigue is concerned, it seems fair to assume that this could be a reference to the Buddha's ascetic practice

106 SN 54.8 at SN V 317,10.
107 MN 4 at MN I 22,9 (translated by Ñāṇamoli 1995/2005: 105) and its parallel EĀ 31.1 at T II 666b22; see also Anālayo 2017e: 96–124.
108 Ps I 124,28 explains that he used mindfulness of breathing to cultivate the four absorptions. In fact, according to Ps II 291,2 already in his early youth he had entered the first absorption through mindfulness of breathing; on this absorption experience see also Anālayo 2017e: 78–83.
109 Spk III 264,7.

of breath control.[110] Fatigue of the eyes could then perhaps be a result of lack of sleep combined with dryness of the eyes due to insufficient hydration, both of which might have been conditions also caused by his ascetic practice, in particular the period of fasting.

Be that as it may, the next benefit in the introductory statement in the *Saṃyukta-āgama* discourse concerns "realizing happiness without being defiled by attachment to the happiness". Although this fits the practice of mindfulness of breathing very well, the first additional benefit mentioned in the Pāli version is instead the abandoning of memories of the household.[111] Perhaps the two indications could be read in conjunction in the sense that, for a monastic, the practice of mindfulness of breathing can become a source of happiness free of attachment and thereby serve to abandon any (fond) memories of former lay life.

The *Saṃyutta-nikāya* list of benefits continues with the ability to gain control over perceptions of repulsiveness and its opposite, which are not mentioned in the *Saṃyukta-āgama* discourse. The two versions agree in mentioning the four absorptions and the four immaterial attainments; a difference is that the *Saṃyutta-nikāya* list does not bring in the *brahmavihāra*s. The Pāli version continues with the attainment of cessation and then relates mindfulness of breathing to a contemplation of feeling tones that leads to insight into their impermanent nature and to the absence of any attachment to them. This culminates in a description of the freedom of a fully awakened one in regard to feeling tones, whose becoming cool after death finds illustration in an oil lamp that becomes extinguished through lack of fuel.

In this way, the benefits mentioned in both versions are:

- body and eyes are not fatigued,
- attainment of four absorptions,
- attainment of four immaterial spheres,
- full awakening.

110 Woodward 1930/1979: 281n1 comments on the present reference in SN 54.8 that this might "refer to the usual exercises of *hatha-yoga*, such as, unnatural postures, staring at a bright object or retaining the breath, etc."

111 SN 54.8 at SN V 317,17.

ACCOMPLISHED PRACTITIONERS (SĀ 815)

The next discourse, which is the final one in the section on mindfulness of breathing in the *Saṃyukta-āgama*, parallels the *Ānāpānasati-sutta* of the *Majjhima-nikāya*. It begins with an extended introductory narration that depicts senior monastics teaching their students:[112]

> At that time many senior disciples were in the vicinity of the Blessed One, dwelling under tree roots and in caves for the rains retreat.[113] Then many junior monastics approached the Buddha, paid respect with the heads at the Buddha's feet, and sat back to one side. The Buddha spoke to the junior monastics in many ways about the Dharma, instructing, teaching, illuminating, and delighting them. Having instructed, taught, illuminated, and delighted them, he remained silent. Hearing what the Buddha had said, the junior monastics rejoiced in it and were delighted. They rose from their seats, paid respect, and left.
>
> The junior monastics approached the senior monastics and, having paid respect at the feet of the seniors, sat [back] to one side. Then the senior monastics thought: 'We should take in these junior monastics, either one person accepting one person or one person accepting two, three, or many persons.' Having thought that, they in turn took them up, one person accepting either one person or accepting two, three, or many persons, or else some elders accepted up to sixty persons.[114]
>
> At that time, it being the fifteenth of the month, the time of the observance day (uposatha), the Blessed One was seated on a seat prepared in front of the great community. At that time the Blessed One, having surveyed the [assembly of] monastics, said to the monastics: "It is well, it is well, I am pleased now with the monastics practising in proper ways. For this reason, monastics,

112 SĀ 815 at T II 209b16 to 210a2.

113 The parallel MN 118 at MN III 78,23 (translated by Ñāṇamoli 1995/2005: 941) mentions by name Sāriputta, Mahāmoggallāna, Mahākassapa, Mahākaccāna, Mahākoṭṭhita, Mahākappina, Mahācunda, Anuruddha, Revata, and Ānanda. As already noted in Anālayo 2011: 664n120, the suggestion by Akanuma 1929/1990: 169 that T 96 might be another parallel to SĀ 815 and MN 118 is not borne out by closer examination.

114 MN 118 at MN III 79,4 does not envisage that a senior might be teaching just one, two, or three students; it only speaks of teaching groups of ten, twenty, thirty, or forty.

you should be diligent and energetic. [I will stay] here in Sāvatthī for the Kattika full moon."

Monastics from the countryside heard that the Blessed One was spending the rains retreat at Sāvatthī [until] the Kattika full moon becomes full. Their robes having been made up completely, they took their robes and bowl to travel through the countryside of Sāvatthī. They gradually approached Sāvatthī.

Having put away their robes and bowls and washed their feet, they approached the Blessed One.[115] Having paid respect with the heads at his feet, they sat back to one side. At that time the Blessed One spoke to the monastics from the countryside in many ways about the Dharma. Having instructed, taught, illuminated, and delighted them, he remained silent. At that time, hearing what the Buddha had said, the monastics from the countryside rejoiced in it and were delighted. They rose from their seats, paid respect, and left.

They approached the senior monastics and, having paid respect with the heads at their feet, they sat back to one side. Then the seniors thought: "We should accept these monastics from the countryside, one person accepting either one person or two, three, or many persons." They in turn accepted them, one person accepting either one person or accepting two, three, [or many persons], accepting up to sixty persons. Those senior monastics accepted the monastics from the countryside, instructing them and guiding them to proper understanding in successive order.

At that time, it being the fifteenth of the month, the time of the observance day, the Blessed One was seated on a seat prepared in front of the great community. Surveying the assembly of monastics, he said to the monastics: "It is well, it is well, monastics, I am pleased with your practising in proper ways, I delight in your practising in proper ways. Monastics, Buddhas of the past also had assemblies of monastics practising properly, like this assembly now. Buddhas of the future will also have assemblies of monastics who will practise properly in this way, like this assembly now.[116] Why is that?

---

115 MN 118 does not report that the monastics from the countryside went to see the Buddha and received teachings from him.

116 Instead of bringing in Buddhas of past and future times, in MN 118 at MN III 80,6 the Buddha praises the monastics for being worthy of receiving gifts and respect.

"Now in this assembly there are elder monastics who have attained the first absorption, the second absorption, the third absorption, the fourth absorption; who dwell fully in benevolence, compassion, sympathetic joy, equanimity, the sphere of [boundless] space, the sphere of [boundless] consciousness, the sphere of nothingness, and the sphere of neither-perception-nor-non-perception.

"There are monastics who have eradicated the three fetters and attained stream-entry, being of a nature not to fall into bad realms and being certain of rightly progressing to awakening, within seven lives among deities and humans making a complete end of dukkha. There are monastics who have eradicated the three fetters, weakened lust, aversion, and delusion, and attained once-return. There are monastics who have eradicated the five lower fetters and attained non-return, who on being reborn will attain Nirvāṇa without being born again in this world.

"There are monastics who have attained innumerable bases of supernormal powers, the divine ear, knowledge of the minds of others, recollection of past lives, knowledge of the passing away and being reborn [of beings], and knowledge of the destruction of the influxes.

"There are monastics who cultivate contemplation of the absence of beauty (asubha) to abandon sensual lust, who cultivate a mind of benevolence to abandon anger, who cultivate the perception of impermanence to abandon the conceit 'I am', and who cultivate mindfulness of breathing to abandon thoughts and [related] perceptions.

"How is it, monastics, that cultivating mindfulness of breathing one abandons thoughts and [related] perceptions?"

This query then leads on to an exposition of mindfulness of breathing. The *Ānāpānasati-sutta* instead states that mindfulness of breathing is of great fruit and benefit; it fulfils the four *satipaṭṭhāna*s, which in turn fulfil the seven awakening factors, and these in turn fulfil knowledge and liberation.[117]

When describing the attainments reached by some monastics, the *Ānāpānasati-sutta* only lists the four levels of awakening.[118]

117 MN 118 at MN III 82,17.
118 MN 118 at MN III 80,20.

It thus does not mention the four absorptions or the four immaterial attainments, etc. The survey of practices undertaken by members of the monastic assembly in the *Ānāpānasati-sutta* lists all of the thirty-seven qualities and practices pertinent to awakening, the *bodhipakkhiyā dhammā*,[119] as well as the four divine abodes (*brahmavihāra*s). It agrees with the *Saṃyukta-āgama* in listing contemplation of the absence of beauty, perception of impermanence, and mindfulness of breathing, although without specifying their respective purpose (and without mentioning benevolence in this particular context).[120]

Alongside such differences, the *Ānāpānasati-sutta* and its *Saṃyukta-āgama* parallel agree in reporting that the Buddha delivered a teaching on the sixteen steps of mindfulness of breathing to an assembly of accomplished and seriously practising monastics. This throws into relief the eminency of this particular meditation practice.[121] Not only is the Buddha reported to have engaged in its practice when going on a retreat, but, when having in front of him a large assembly of seasoned meditators wholeheartedly dedicated to practice, he decides to instruct them in the sixteen steps of mindfulness of breathing.

From a practical perspective, the narrative setting of the present discourse gives the impression that mindfulness of breathing is relevant even for those who are cultivating other meditation practices. Although some of the monastics present already engaged in mindfulness of breathing, it seems rather improbable that the Buddha is depicted as addressing only them. Instead, it seems more probable that in some way the sixteen steps of mindfulness of breathing should be reckoned as relevant also for those who cultivate the *brahmavihāra*s or contemplation of the absence of beauty, etc.

---

119 This reference could well be a later addition; see Anālayo 2011: 666.

120 MN 118 at MN III 82,10.

121 Vajirañāṇa 1962/1975: 237 sums up that mindfulness of breathing "is extremely peaceful, quiet, calm and happy in its intrinsic nature. The aspirant will feel continually refreshed and serene through its aid, and will never be satiated, owing to its sublime state of peace and intellectual profundity ... from the very beginning it calms both mind and body; every taint of mind will disappear, full knowledge of Vipassanā will be attained, and finally the disciple will realize the ultimate result, the happiness of Nirvāṇa."

Here it may well be of relevance that mindfulness of breathing is recurrently commended as a practice that helps to calm distracting thoughts. Such a potential would indeed be useful to any meditation practice. The stabilizing potential of being aware of breathing could serve the same role in other meditation practices as it does for most of the sixteen steps, namely by way of keeping the alternation between inhalations and exhalations in awareness. In other words, instead of training oneself to execute steps three to sixteen while remaining aware of breathing in and out, one might instead train oneself to dwell in a *brahmavihāra* or contemplate the absence of beauty while remaining aware of breathing in and out. Although the *Ānāpānasati-sutta* does not offer any explicit indication that would support this suggestion, from a practical perspective this would be a way of putting to good use the potential of mindfulness of breathing to overcome the mind's tendency to distraction.

With this discourse the *Saṃyukta-āgama* collection of discourses on the topic of mindfulness of breathing comes to its conclusion. Before turning to passages of relevance from the *Ekottarika-āgama*, it is perhaps worthy of note that the sequence of discourses on mindfulness of breathing in the *Saṃyukta-āgama* reflects a meaningful progression: SĀ 801 presents preliminaries to the practice. SĀ 802 broaches the topic of tranquillity and insight. SĀ 803 then presents the actual practice in sixteen steps, followed by a list of its benefits in SĀ 804.

SĀ 805 reports a different approach to being mindful of the breath by a particular monastic and SĀ 806 takes up another monastic's imperturbability due to mindfulness of breathing. These examples naturally lead over to the Buddha's own practice when on retreat, reported in SĀ 807, an advanced mode of practice superior to that of a trainee, as shown in SĀ 808. This in turn serves to establish the balance that some monastics had lost through unskilful practice of another meditation leading them to commit suicide, as reported in SĀ 809.

With these various dimensions clarified, the *Saṃyukta-āgama* proceeds to the all-important relationship of the sixteen steps to the four *satipaṭṭhāna*s and the seven *bojjhaṅga*s, shown in SĀ 810 to SĀ 812 and illustrated with a simile in SĀ 813. A range of possible attainments to be reached in this way are the topic of SĀ 814, followed by the present discourse, SĀ 815, as the final discourse in the collection that gives this practice pride of place in front of an assembly of seasoned practitioners. In this way, the reciters of the *Saṃyukta-āgama* arranged the discourses in this section in a meaningful sequence, comparable to the similarly meaningful sequence adopted by the reciters of the *Saṃyutta-nikāya*.

In the next and final chapter of this book, I turn to relevant material found in the *Ekottarika-āgama* preserved in Chinese translation. Although this collection does not have as many relevant discourses as the *Saṃyukta-āgama* (and the *Saṃyutta-nikāya*), it still provides several significant perspectives.

SUMMARY

Mindfulness of inhalations and exhalations, which are a bodily activity (SĀ 568), appears to have been open to developing one's own individual approach (SĀ 805), leaving room for flexibility. Its cultivation in sixteen steps was the form of practice undertaken by the Buddha himself during self-retreat (SĀ 807) and taught by him even to a large assembly of accomplished practitioners (SĀ 815). Proper groundwork for mindfulness of breathing is laid through moral conduct, fewness of wishes, knowing one's measure with food, wakefulness, and living in seclusion (SĀ 801). Its cultivation in sixteen steps is based on having overcome the hindrances (SĀ 803); keeping these at bay requires training while progressing through the sixteen steps (SĀ 808). Mindfulness of breathing leads to bodily and mental tranquillity (SĀ 802), even to the absence of any bodily fidgeting (SĀ 806). The same practice can counter an unbalanced attitude towards the body by way of excessive repugnance (SĀ 809) and lead to overcoming unwholesome states comparable to a chariot that drives over and thereby flattens a mound of earth (SĀ 813). Mindfulness of breathing serves to abandon thoughts and can lead to a whole range of attainments in the realm of tranquillity and insight (SĀ 814) and the highest two levels of awakening (SĀ 804). The most prominent purpose of the sixteen steps is to issue in a cultivation of the awakening factors (SĀ 746), which can take place in relation to each of the four tetrads (SĀ 810).

X

TRANSLATIONS FROM THE *EKOTTARIKA-ĀGAMA*

ONE THING TO CULTIVATE (EĀ 2.8)

In this last chapter of my survey I examine extracts from the *Ekottarika-āgama*. Material from this collection needs to be considered with some caution, as there is clear evidence that the extant Chinese text combines translation of an Indic original with some degree of reworking of the collection and addition of extraneous material in China.[1] Although the collection does contain much material that is of relevance for reconstructing early Buddhist thought, at times it reflects ideas and notions that are considerably later.[2] The first discourse to be taken up, however, seems unproblematic:[3]

> You should cultivate one thing, you should make much of one thing, and in turn you will accomplish supernormal powers, discard all distracting perceptions, gain the fruits of recluse-ship, and reach Nirvāṇa yourselves. What is that one thing?
>
> It is reckoned to be mindfulness of breathing, which you should cultivate well, you should make much of, and in turn

---

1 For the addition of a whole discourse that must have happened in China see Anālayo 2013c; on several cases testifying to an apparent tendency to rework early discourse material see Anālayo 2014/2015 and 2015b.

2 On Mahāyāna thought in the *Ekottarika-āgama* (of which some instances, but not all, could already have become part of the collection before it reached China) see Anālayo 2013a.

3 EĀ 2.8 at T II 553b8 to 553b13 (already translated in an abbreviated manner by Huyên-Vi 1986: 31).

> you will accomplish supernormal powers, discard all distracting perceptions, gain the fruits of recluse-ship, and reach Nirvāṇa yourselves.
>
> For this reason, monastics, you should cultivate [this] one thing, you should make much of [this] one thing. In this way, monastics, you should undertake this training.

The present discourse is one in a series of short discourses, found in the second chapter of the *Ekottarika-āgama*, that consecutively take up ten meditative recollections.[4] The Pāli parallel to the discourse translated above instead serves as the first in the collection of discourses on mindfulness of breathing in the *Saṃyutta-nikāya*. The Pāli version similarly reckons mindfulness of breathing to be the one thing to be cultivated, differing in that it does not spell out its benefits but merely states that this practice is of great fruit and benefit.[5] Another difference is that the *Saṃyutta-nikāya* discourse follows this initial indication by describing the sixteen steps.

THREE STEPS ONLY (EĀ 3.8)

Whereas the second chapter of the *Ekottarika-āgama* recommends each of the ten recollections as one thing to be cultivated, the third chapter of this collection proceeds through the same ten recollections by way of providing additional instructions and details. The *Ekottarika-āgama* discourse that provides further detail on the topic of mindfulness of breathing (as the one thing to be cultivated) does not have a Pāli parallel. The discourse proceeds as follows:[6]

---

4 A reference to mindfulness of breathing as one of the recollections recurs elsewhere in this collection, such as in the introduction, T II 550b19, or else in, e.g., EĀ 40.5 at T II 740a4, EĀ 46.5 at T II 780c11 (supplemented text), EĀ 46.8 at T II 779c27, and EĀ 47.1 at T II 781a3.

5 SN 54.1 at SN V 311,7 (translated by Bodhi 2000: 1765). Another discourse on mindfulness of breathing as the one thing to be practised is SĀ[3] 15 at T II 497a2. Similar to the case of EĀ 2.8, this discourse only highlights potential benefits of mindfulness of breathing, without getting into a description of the actual practice.

6 EĀ 3.8 at T II 556a16 to 556b13 (already translated in an abbreviated manner by Huyên-Vi 1986: 35).

At that time the Blessed One said to the monastics: "You should cultivate one thing, you should make much of one thing. Having cultivated one thing, you will in turn become esteemed, accomplish great fruit, become endowed throughout with all that is wholesome, attain the taste of the deathless, reach the sphere of the unconditioned, accomplish in turn supernormal powers, discard all distracting perceptions, gain the fruits of recluse-ship, and reach Nirvāṇa yourselves. What is that one thing? It is reckoned to be mindfulness of breathing."

The Buddha said to the monastics: "How does one cultivate mindfulness of breathing and in turn become esteemed, accomplish great fruit, become endowed throughout with the assembly of what is wholesome, attain the taste of the deathless, reach the sphere of the unconditioned, accomplish in turn supernormal powers, discard all distracting perceptions, gain the fruits of recluse-ship, and reach Nirvāṇa oneself?"

At that time the monastics said to the Blessed One: "The foundation of all teachings is in what the Tathāgata declares. May the Blessed One teach the monastics its sublime meaning. Having heard it from the Tathāgata, the monastics will in turn remember it."

At that time the Blessed One said to the monastics: "Listen, listen and pay proper attention to what I will widely teach and analyse for you."

The monastics replied: "So be it, Blessed One." The monastics came forward to receive the teaching.

The Blessed One said: "Suppose a monastic sits down cross-legged with straight body and straight intention, with collected mindfulness to the fore and, without having other perceptions, focuses mindfulness on the breathing, namely on the breath:

"If the breath is long, then one should also contemplate and know: 'I now have a long breath'; again, if the breath is short, one should also contemplate and know: 'I now have a short breath.'

"If the breath is quite cold, one should also contemplate and know: 'I now have a cold breath.' Again, if the breath is warm, one should also contemplate and know: 'I now have a warm breath.'

"One fully contemplates the physical body, from the head to the feet; one should contemplate and know it all. Again, if the breath is long or short, one should also contemplate the breath as being long or being short. Using the mind to hold the body [in awareness], one knows the breath to be long or short, knowing it completely. One investigates the breath going out and coming in, discerning and understanding it. If the mind holds the body [in awareness] to know the breath to be long or short, one also further knows it. Repeatedly breathing in long or short, one discerns and understands it.

"In this way, monastics, this is called mindfulness of breathing. When one in turn gains mastery of it, one accomplishes great fruit, reaches all that is wholesome throughout, attains the taste of the deathless, reaches the sphere of the unconditioned, accomplishes in turn supernormal powers, discards all distracting perceptions, gains the fruits of recluse-ship, and reaches Nirvāṇa oneself.

"For this reason, monastics, you should constantly pay attention to and not be separated from mindfulness of breathing and you will in turn gain all these wholesome qualities. In this way, monastics, you should undertake this training."

The above instruction appears to be based on an extract from the first tetrad of mindfulness of breathing. The first two steps are clearly discernible and the reference to "completely contemplating the physical body from the head to the feet" seems to reflect the third step. I will return to this issue below when studying the next *Ekottarika-āgama* discourse.

The remainder of the exposition brings in new elements. One of these is the temperature of the breath. A meditation manual compiled by Kumārajīva at the beginning of the fifth century, the "Scripture on Sitting Absorbed in Concentration", notes that exhalations are warmer and inhalations are cooler.[7] A commentary on the *Ekottarika-āgama*, preserved in Chinese, offers the same explanation, in that the distinction made between cool and warm breaths refers to recognizing the difference in temperature between inhalations and exhalations.[8]

Particularly in a cold climate, there can indeed be a distinct difference between the colder inhalations and the warmer exhalations. This difference in temperature could then be

7 T 614 at T XV 275a11 (translated by Yamabe and Sueki 2009: 28).

8 T 1507 at T XXV 49c2 (commenting on the instruction to Rāhula in EĀ 17.1): "The inhalation is cool; the exhalation is warm"; on the nature of this work see Palumbo 2013.

employed as an aid, in addition to sensing the direction of the flow of air, for clearly distinguishing between inhalations and exhalations.[9]

The significance of the somewhat cryptic reference to "using the mind to hold the body [in awareness]" perhaps refers to a rooting of mindfulness in the body as a support for observing the breathing. If that should be the implication, it would point to combining whole-body awareness with noting the length of the breath. On this understanding, the above instructions would proceed from noting the difference in temperature between inhalations and exhalations to being aware of the whole body when one "completely contemplates the physical body, from the head to the feet". Then attention returns to noting whether the breath is long or short. Based on having alternated between these two modes of paying attention, with the present injunction one would then combine the two when "the mind holds the body [in awareness] to know the breath to be long or short."

Be that as it may, another noteworthy aspect in the passage translated above is a reference in the original Chinese that might imply counting the breaths, an idea otherwise not found among the early discourses.[10] However, the same Chinese character occurs also in a description of the Buddha's pre-awakening practice of breath retention, to which I turn below (see p. 239). As it is hardly possible to count the breaths when they have been stopped, it seems to me preferable here as well to understand this character in its alternative sense of "repeatedly" rather than "counting".[11]

9 Another aid for such distinction has been suggested by Sucitto 2011: 47: "if you focus on the experience of energy, it's obvious that the inhalation is different from the exhalation: breathing in brightens and arouses bodily energy; breathing out softens and diffuses bodily energy. The body senses the difference."

10 Dhammadīpa 2009: 574 notes that, although not attested even in early Abhidharma texts, a range of different traditions refer to counting (and other stages of practice related to it). This suggests that, although not reflecting the earliest stages of the practice of mindfulness of breathing, this mode of practice still arose at a sufficiently early time to be able to achieve widespread recognition. On probable reasons for its gradual emergence see Anālayo 2020a.

11 Deleanu 2003: 92n66 points out possible nuances of the Chinese character in question and concludes that "without an Indic parallel, it is hard to determine the precise meaning of the word here." He refers to another occurrence of the same character in relation to mindfulness of breathing

The idea of counting as such becomes prominent in later meditation manuals. The *Visuddhimagga*, for example, recommends counting between five and ten breaths. Practice proceeds from at first counting the completed breaths and then, with more expertise, one shifts to counting the breaths as soon as they start.[12] The meditation manual by Kumārajīva recommends counting for practitioners who tend to have many thoughts. Beginners should count from one to ten, whether the breath is long or short.[13] Advanced practitioners still employ counting, making sure to count exactly at the time when the corresponding breath is over and to start all over again if they should miscount.[14]

Counting the breaths can serve as a tool when the mind is distracted and just does not stay with the breath. However, comparable to the general need to use concepts judiciously and only to the extent to which they help rather than hinder the practice,[15] counting similarly needs to be employed with caution. Its proper use requires mindful monitoring to ensure that this additional technique does not result in shifting attention from the actual experience of the breath to the concepts required for counting. The *Yogācārabhūmi* in fact considers counting to be relevant mainly for those with dull faculties and not for those who have sharp faculties.[16] It seems indeed advisable not to regard counting as the default mode for approaching

---

in EĀ 28.6 at T II 653b15, according to which [mindfulness] of breathing in and out is one of four things that are at first unpleasant but later become pleasant. Here the sense of "counting" would work for the character in question, as would the sense of "repeatedly" being aware of inhalations and exhalations.

12 Vism 278,21 (translated by Ñāṇamoli 1991: 272).

13 T 614 at T XV 273a14 (translated by Yamabe and Sueki 2009: 18). A different approach has been described by Shaw 2018: 12f, where "the practitioner counts up to a given number during the inbreath, and counts back down from it during the outbreath", and the count then relates to discerning the length of the breath, with the correspondence of "the 'longest' breath, to the meditator's own count of nine, the 'longer', to the count of six, the 'shorter', to the count of three, and the 'shortest', to the count of one."

14 T 614 at T XV 273a19; for a survey of various texts that expound stages of practice that begin with counting the breaths see Dhammajoti 2009.

15 See Anālayo 2018d: 7f.

16 Shukla 1973: 225,12 and T 1579 at T XXX 431c4; counting can in fact at times stimulate conceptual activity: see Anālayo 2003b: 133n68.

mindfulness of breathing and rather see it as a skilful means that can at times be helpful, if employed with circumspection.

The absence of any reference to such counting in the early discourses (leaving aside the present somewhat ambivalent case) could well be reflecting that such additional tools gained prominence only once actual practice came to focus only on the first steps of the first tetrad. In particular the loss of the progression to joy and happiness with the second tetrad results in a pressing need for such props in order to keep the mind with the breath. From a practical perspective, it therefore seems meaningful to combine any counting, if one wishes to employ this technique, with an intentional cultivation of the joy of being in the present moment while contemplating the breath.[17] In this way the mind's tendency to chase after something more entertaining than the bland experience of the breath is naturally diminished. The resulting reduced need for counting as a support makes it easier to use this technique judiciously, just to the extent necessary for aiding the stabilization of the mind.

INSTRUCTIONS TO RĀHULA (EĀ 17.1)

The next discourse from the *Ekottarika-āgama* does have a Pāli parallel in the *Mahārāhulovāda-sutta* (MN 62). Unfortunately, however, this appears to be one of the cases where a discourse has suffered from reworking in China, in that a section of the original appears to have been taken out and added to another discourse.[18]

The instructions given by the Buddha to his son Rāhula on mindfulness of breathing proceed as follows in this *Ekottarika-āgama* discourse:[19]

> In this way, Rāhula, suppose a monastic delights in secluded places without people and in turn sits down cross-legged with

17 Such joy can at times be of a rather subtle type and therefore not immediately evident. Brahmavaṃso 2004/2006: 17 explains that "feelings of joy and happiness are there in the [experience of] the breath. You may not have recognized them because they are not the happiness and joy of excitement. They are the happiness and joy of peace."

18 Anālayo 2014/2015: 76f.

19 EĀ 17.1 at T II 582a13 to 582a23 (already translated by Huyên-Vi 1993: 216).

straight body and straight mind, collecting the mind at the tip of the nose without thinking of anything else.

Breathing out long, one knows the breath to be long; breathing in long, one also knows the breath to be long. Breathing out short, one also knows the breath to be short; breathing in short, one also knows the breath to be short.

Breathing out cool, one also knows the breath to be cool; breathing in cool, one also knows the breath to be cool. Breathing out warm, one also knows the breath to be warm; breathing in warm, one also knows the breath to be warm.

Completely contemplating the physical body one breathes in and breathes out; one comes to know it all.

At a time when there is breath, one also further knows it to be there; at a time when there is no breath, one also further knows it to be absent. If one is breathing out from the heart, one also further knows to be breathing out from the heart; if one is breathing in from the heart, one also further knows to be breathing in from the heart.[20]

Rāhula, one who is able to cultivate mindfulness of breathing in this way will be without worrisome and disturbing perceptions and gain great fruit, attaining the taste of the deathless.

Similar to the previous discourse, this instruction also reflects only the first three steps of the scheme of sixteen steps for mindfulness of breathing. The full scheme is found in the parallel, the *Mahārāhulovāda-sutta*.[21]

The instructions in the *Mahārāhulovāda-sutta* lead up to the proclamation that cultivating mindfulness of breathing in sixteen steps will ensure that one will be aware even of one's last breaths.[22] This proclamation bridges two uses of the breath as an object of meditation in the early discourses. The main mode involves the sixteen steps, in addition to which there is the employment of the breath as a way to cultivate recollection of death. I will return to the latter topic at the end of this chapter.

---

20 Huyên-Vi 1993: 217 understands the present passage in EĀ 17.1 to imply "breathing out conditioned by the mind" and "breathing in conditioned by the mind". This makes less sense from a practical perspective and is also a less accurate rendering of the original, in particular of the character *cóng*, which can mean "from" or "since", but not "conditioned by"; see Anālayo 2011: 352n63.

21 MN 62 at MN I 425,6 (translated by Ñāṇamoli 1995/2005: 531).

22 MN 62 at MN I 426,1.

The sixteen steps of mindfulness of breathing are not found at all in the *Ekottarika-āgama*. In evaluating this finding, the chequered history of this collection needs to be borne in mind. This is also responsible for the difficulty of determining its school affiliation, in the sense of a monastic lineage of textual transmission, which has been a topic of continuous discussion among scholars. In the case of two school affiliations that have been proposed,[23] the (in my view more probable) Mahāsāṅghika tradition and the (in my view improbable) Sarvāstivāda tradition, the corresponding *Vinaya*s do have the sixteen steps.[24] In the case of a third (and in my view also improbable) proposition that this *Ekottarika-āgama* could have been transmitted by Dharmaguptaka reciters,[25] we have evidence that the sixteen steps of mindfulness of breathing were known in this tradition from the **Śāriputrābhidharma*, an early canonical Abhidharma text.[26]

It follows that, regardless of which monastic transmission lineage one might prefer to associate with this collection, there is clear evidence for the sixteen steps in other canonical texts of the same school. In other words, the sixteen-step scheme (with a bit of variation in the last tetrad) can safely be considered to be an ancient formulation of instructions on mindfulness of breathing.[27]

Although this in turn makes it fair to conclude that the above two *Ekottarika-āgama* discourses must be reflecting later developments, a reduction of mindfulness of breathing to the first steps from the scheme of sixteen is in line with what is evident from the *Kāyagatāsati-sutta* and the *Satipaṭṭhāna-sutta* together with their *Madhyama-āgama* parallels (see above p. 165). A difference is that in these versions mindfulness of breathing

23 For a survey of relevant evidence and findings by other scholars see Anālayo 2016a: 172–178 and 211–214. According to the review by Kuan 2017: 446f, an argument by Palumbo 2013 in favour of a Sarvāstivāda affiliation is based on a misunderstanding of a Chinese idiom.
24 See Anālayo 2013b: 229f and 2016b: 247–249.
25 Mayeda 1985: 103 notes that this had been proposed by some Japanese scholars.
26 T 1548 at T XXVIII 705a28 to 710c29 (translated by Anālayo 2020a).
27 Deleanu 1992: 49 comments that "I think we can agree that the sixteen bases of the mindfulness of breathing are a practice peculiar to Buddhism and that they belong to the earliest Buddhist stratum."

is reduced to the first four steps rather than the first three steps. As already mentioned when discussing this reduction, the **Śāriputrābhidharma* includes only the first two steps of mindfulness of breathing in its exposition of the *satipaṭṭhāna* of contemplating the body. Thus the tendency to reduction as such is found in canonical texts of a number of early Buddhist schools. In all of these versions the importance of an integral practice of the sixteen steps has been replaced by a focus on its first four or just three or even just two steps. However, in the case of the two discourses from the *Ekottarika-āgama* it is difficult to determine how far their presentation reflects the Indic original or the influence of the Chinese translators responsible for reworking the collection.

Another noteworthy aspect in the discourse translated above is the injunction to collect the mind at the tip of the nose. Counterparts to the Pāli expression "having established mindfulness to the fore", *parimukhaṃ satiṃ upaṭṭhapetvā*, found elsewhere in *Ekottarika-āgama* discourses speak similarly of having "mindfulness to the fore".[28] In the case of an occurrence of this phrase at an earlier junction in the same *Mahārāhulovāda-sutta*, the present *Ekottarika-āgama* discourse just refers to "unification of the mind".[29] This makes it fair to conclude that the reference to the nose at the present juncture is a later element.

The instructions in the *Ekottarika-āgama* discourse also mention knowing when there is no breath. A commentary on the *Ekottarika-āgama*, preserved in Chinese, explains:[30]

> At the time of breathing in, one does not know from where it comes; at the time of breathing out, one does not know where it goes to. One understands that it does not come and go.

From a practical perspective, this could be applied to the gaps between breaths. On this understanding, it could be noticed clearly that the inhalation ends completely before the exhalation starts, and similarly the exhalation ends completely before the inhalation starts. Noting in this way can throw into relief the

28 Anālayo 2011: 350n51; an example is EĀ 37.3 at T II 711c19, parallel to MN 32 at MN I 219,30.
29 EĀ 17.1 at T II 581c12, paralleling MN 62 at MN I 421,14.
30 T 1507 at T XXV 49c4.

impermanent nature of breathing and in particular drive home the truth of its recurrent cessation. The resultant understanding that the breath "does not come and go" would underscore the fact that it is not the same breath that goes in and out.

Another reference in the *Ekottarika-āgama* discourse that invites further comment is the instruction to know that breathing comes from the heart. Here, again, the commentary on this discourse collection offers additional information:[31]

> Short breaths return from the heart; long breaths are reckoned to come from within the heels.

On this understanding, the reference to breathing in and out "from the heart" would refer to comparatively shorter breaths that affect the body only as far as the lung area. With longer breaths, the effects created in the body reach further down. This is particularly evident in the abdominal area. However, the commentarial gloss goes further than that, as it brings in the idea that long breaths come from the heels. This reflects a tendency also evident in other texts, in that breathing is in some way to be experienced in the whole body.[32]

This tendency can be exemplified with the help of the meditation manual by Kumārajīva. The manual clearly recognizes that the actual experience of the breath can reach from the mouth or nose to the navel.[33] Nevertheless, the same work instructs to perceive the breath as pervading the whole body and filling all of its pores down to the toes, an experience illustrated with the example of water soaking into sand.[34] Perhaps such notions have

31 T 1507 at T XXV 49c1 to 49c2.

32 E.g. the **Mahāvibhāṣā*, T 1545 at T XXVII 136a29, in a discussion on the significance of the third step of mindfulness of breathing, speaks of experiencing the breath through the pores of the body.

33 T 614 at T XV 275b3 (translated by Yamabe and Sueki 2009: 29).

34 T 614 at T XV 275b26. An example for a comparable approach from the Theravāda tradition would be the instruction in Dhammadharo 1979/2010: 17f to let the "breath sensation spread to the different parts of the body. To begin with, inhale the breath sensation at the base of the skull and let it flow all the way down the spine. Then, if you are male, let it spread down your right leg to the sole of your foot, to the ends of your toes, and out into the air. Inhale the breath sensation at the base of the skull again and let it spread down your spine, down your left leg to the ends of your toes, and out into the air. (If you are female, begin with the left side first) ... Then let the breath from the base of the skull spread down over both shoulders, past your elbows and wrists,

their origin in an attempt to execute the third step of experiencing the whole body in an extended manner.[35] Such a mode of practice, where alongside the inhalations and exhalations one tries to sense various parts of the body distinctly, could in the course of time have resulted in relating these two aspects of the practice more closely to each other.

From a subjective viewpoint, it is indeed possible to experience an extension of the motion of the in-breath, for example, beyond those regions of the body that are directly affected by the incoming air. Such subjective experience of some degree of continuation could be related to the vital energy in the bodies of living beings. Inasmuch as the conception of the wind element in early Buddhist thought comprises such bodily energy, coursing through the limbs (see above p. 163), it would not be surprising if observation of the breath should in the course of time have led to a directing of awareness to such energy processes related to the breath and subjectively experienced as being an extension of one's breathing.

At times Chinese translations of the third step of mindfulness of breathing are formulated in such a manner as to give the

---

to the tips of your fingers, and out into the air." Another example is the following instruction by Culadasa 2015/2017: 220f: "you first direct your attention to the breath at the abdomen. Then ... you shift your attention to a particular body part, such as your hand. Define your scope of attention to include *that area only*. Then further refine your scope to include *only the breath sensations in the hand*. Ignore all other sensations by excluding them completely from attention, but let them remain in peripheral awareness. Next, move to another body part, perhaps the forearm, and do the same thing. Each moment of attention should include a very strong *intention* to focus clearly on breath-related sensations and to exclude everything else. As your skill improves, keep increasing the scope of your attention to include larger and larger areas. Also, keep shifting between larger and smaller areas. For example, you might move between one finger and the entire arm. Your intention should be to observe all breath-related sensations as clearly in the whole arm as in that one finger."

35 An example would be the instructions given in Nhat Hanh 1988: 46: "you begin by breathing out and you observe, 'I am breathing out and am aware of the hair on my head.' 'I am breathing in and am aware of the contents of my skull.' You can continue like this until you reach the tips of your toes." Such instructions are simply a detailed approach to achieve an experience of the whole body while breathing in and out. Nevertheless, at the same time these instructions could easily lead on to a mode of practice similar to those described in the previous note or in Kumārajīva's manual, whereby the breath itself is experienced as pervading the whole body.

impression that one is to breathe with the whole body.[36] In the same vein, Kumārajīva's manual specifically instructs that one should contemplate the breath coming in and going out through all pores and the nine apertures of the body, understanding that the breath pervades the whole body.[37] Similar notions can be found in the *Ekottarika-āgama* account of the Buddha's practice of breath control during his quest for awakening, to which I turn next.

BREATH CONTROL (EĀ 31.8)

A report of the Buddha's pre-awakening ascetic practice of breath control in an *Ekottarika-āgama* parallel to the *Mahāsaccaka-sutta* (MN 36) proceeds in this way:[38]

> At that time I thought again: 'I could now enter breathless meditation.' I in turn entered breathless meditation repeatedly on breathing in or out.[39] Now on employing that repeatedly on breathing in or out, I realized that there was air coming out of my ears. Then the sound of the winds [within] was like the rumble of thundering. At that time I thought again: 'I will now close my mouth and block my ears, making sure the breath does not go out.'
>
> Then, the breath being without outlet, the air within went in turn out from the hands and feet, just as I was making sure that the air did not get out from the ears, the nose, and the mouth.

---

36 An example is MĀ 81 at T I 555b13, translated above p. 165: "one trains [in experiencing] the whole body when breathing in." The Chinese passage has no counterpart to the Pāli expression *paṭisaṃvedī*, "experiencing", and thus can easily be read to convey the idea that one should train to breathe in (and out) with the whole body. On the probable reason for this apparent loss of a reference to experiencing see Kuan 2008: 213n9 (and 209n18).

37 T 614 at T XV 275c1 (translated by Yamabe and Sueki 2009: 31).

38 EĀ 31.8 at T II 671a12 to 671a29 (already translated by Bronkhorst 1993/2000: 13); for a comparative study of this episode see Anālayo 2017e: 60–68.

39 This is the passage discussed above p. 232, where the Chinese character could refer to counting rather than conveying the sense of "repeatedly". Although a verb would work well from the viewpoint of the grammar of the sentence, the idea of counting the breaths fails to make sense in the context. Once the Buddha had entered "breathless" meditation, there would no longer be any breaths coming in or going out that he could have counted.

> At that time the sound within was like roaring thunder. Again, at that time it was for me also like this: I was then alive and conscious, following the body's winds.[40]
>
> Then I thought again: 'It is proper for me to enter breathless meditation further.' Then I completely blocked all apertures for the breath. Then, all my [apertures] for breathing in or out being blocked, I was in turn afflicted by pain in the forehead. It was similar to a person who uses a drill to drill into one's head, in the same way I also had extremely painful headaches. As formerly, I was alive and conscious at that time.
>
> At that time I thought again: 'I could now further sit in meditation and not let the air of the breath go out or come in.' At that time I in turn blocked breathing in or out. Then all the breaths completely collected in the belly. The appearance of the breath, which at that time was extremely whirling around, was being decreased. It was just like a cow being killed with a knife at a cow butcher's residence;[41] I was afflicted by extreme pains just like that. It was also just like two strong men who together grab one weak man and roast him over a fire.[42] He would be extremely afflicted by unbearable pain. I was also like that, with such pains as cannot be described completely. At that time I still kept being alive and conscious.

The report in the above passage that the air went out by the hands and feet is not found in the parallel versions. This notion is nevertheless in line with Kumārajīva's manual, taken up above, where the idea is similarly that the breath can exit through all pores and the nine apertures of the body.

Whereas the passage translated above mentions three forms of "breathless meditation", its parallels in the *Mahāsaccaka-sutta* as well as in a Sanskrit fragment describe altogether five different modalities of breath retention.[43] In the case of other

40 Such an indication is not found in the parallels.

41 A comparison with a butcher carving up the belly of an ox occurs in the parallels MN 36 at MN I 244,14 (translated by Ñāṇamoli 1995/2005: 338) and fragment 334r2, Liu 2010: 183, illustrating the fourth modality of breath retention.

42 A similar illustration can be found in the parallels MN 36 at MN I 244,28 and fragment 334r6, Liu 2010: 186, in relation to the fifth modality of breath retention.

43 MN 36 at MN I 243,4 and fragment 333r2, Liu 2010: 171.

ascetic practices undertaken by the future Buddha, the parallels mention only a single modality of forceful mind control and a single modality of fasting. Thus the Buddha-to-be appears to have had a special interest in the practice of breath control, to the extent of trying out three or even five modalities of it.

An emphasis on breath control might have been in line with a belief in ancient India that control of the breath enables control of the unconscious activities of the mind.[44] Once the earlier attempt to force unwholesomeness out of the mind had not worked, the future Buddha might have tried to achieve the same with breath control. This could have seemed to him so promising an avenue that he pursued it in different ways before moving on to try to reach his goal instead by fasting.

From this viewpoint, then, a backdrop to the Buddha's instructions on the sixteen steps might have been a prevalent interest in the breath in the ancient Indian setting as a tool for progress to realization. The decisive difference from other such approaches would then be that, rather than attempting to control the breath, its natural occurrence is used as a basis for cultivating mindfulness.[45] As an expression of the Buddha's realization of awakening, the practice of mindfulness of breathing is based on a chief feature of mindfulness in early Buddhist thought: non-interfering and balanced observation rather than trying to enforce control.[46]

This can be related to the story of the mass suicide of monastics, discussed above (see p. 200). Rather than fostering ascetic disgust, progression on the middle path requires mindful balance in combination with wholesome types of joy. Such can indeed be cultivated with the sixteen steps of mindfulness of breathing.

---

44 According to Radhakrishnan 1953/1992: 90f, the individual self "*jīva* is literally 'that which breathes', from *jīv* 'to breathe' ... the *jīva* consists of a material body, the principle of breath (*prāṇa*), regulating the unconscious activities of the individual, and the principle of conscious activities (*manas*)."

45 As Solé-Leris 1986/1992: 79 explains, "it is essential *not* to attempt any kind of breath control (unlike in certain Yoga exercises), but simply to let the breath come naturally."

46 See in more detail Anālayo 2019b.

RECOLLECTION OF DEATH (EĀ 40.8)

Complementing the survey of mindfulness of breathing in this chapter, the last passage to be taken up is an *Ekottarika-āgama* discourse that presents a different but related use of paying attention to the breath, namely as a reminder of one's own mortality.[47] The entire discourse and its two Pāli parallels (AN 6.19 and AN 8.73) are concerned with proper practice of mindfulness of death.[48] For this purpose, the breath commends itself as a way of bringing awareness of one's mortality right into the present moment. The task is to avoid pretending that death will only occur at some rather distant time in the future and instead allow the realization to sink into the mind that it could happen any time, even right now. Here are the relevant instructions:[49]

> If a monastic gives attention to the perception of death, with mindfulness collected to the fore,[50] with a mind that is unshaken, being mindful of an exhalation or an inhalation for the time it takes for them to go out and return, and during that period he gives attention to the seven awakening factors, that would indeed be of much benefit [to him] in the Tathāgata's teaching.[51]
>
> This is because all formations are entirely empty, they all become appeased, they rise and cease, they are all [like] a magical illusion that is without any true essence.[52]
>
> Therefore, monastics, you should give attention to the perception of death in the interval between an exhalation and an inhalation, so that you will be liberated from birth, old age, disease, death, grief, worry, pain, and vexation.[53] In this way,

47 This shows that Cousins 2015: 3 is not correct in stating that, "significantly, there does not appear to be anywhere in the canonical literature where meditation on the normal breath is recommended. Rather, it should always be made long or short in the practice of mindfulness with in and out breathing."
48 See in more detail Anālayo 2016b: 200–207.
49 EĀ 40.8 at T II 742a25 to 742b2 (translated by Anālayo 2016b: 202).
50 The translation "mindfulness" is based on a variant reading.
51 The parallels AN 6.19 and AN 8.73 (translated by Bodhi 2012: 878 and 1221) do not mention the awakening factors.
52 AN 6.19 and AN 8.73 do not make such a statement.
53 AN 6.19 at AN III 306,15 and AN 8.73 at AN IV 319,32 conclude by highlighting that training in the recollection of death can lead to the destruction of the influxes.

monastics, should you train yourselves.[54]

These instructions in a way bring out the central underlying theme of mindfulness of breathing from an insight perspective. The breath, just as all formations, is of a nature to rise and cease again. Its impermanent nature implies its empty nature, the lack of any truly enduring essence. In this way, key aspects of liberating insight fall into place.

To breathe is to be alive and the ending of life is the ending of the process of breathing. Therefore the breath can serve as a tool to learn to face the fearful prospect of one's own death. With sustained practice, death loses its sting and the final breath can be taken without a trace of fear. This is what a passage taken up in an earlier chapter confirms with its depiction of the Buddha's last breath (see above p. 157). His mind was imperturbable to such an extent that he was able to exercise complete meditative mastery by proceeding through all four absorptions and immaterial attainments in forward and backward order. His superb mastery of the mind was such that he remained totally unaffected by the onset of death, to the extent that he was able to let go of the breathing process even before passing away.

Combining this impressive feat with the Buddha's evident predilection for mindfulness of breathing as a regular practice once again throws into relief the outstanding potential of the scheme of sixteen steps and its manifold benefits.

SUMMARY

Mindfulness of breathing is the one thing to be cultivated to gain freedom from distraction, supernormal powers, and the different levels of awakening (EĀ 2.8). An apparent tendency to reduce the sixteen steps has found its expression in descriptions of mindfulness of breathing that only reflect the first three steps of the full scheme, adding to these a discernment of the temperature of the breath (EĀ 3.8) or clearly noting when there is no breath (EĀ 17.1). The breath as an object of meditation appears to have been of interest to the Buddha already during his quest for awakening, when he engaged in breath control (EĀ

54 The translation is based on a variant reading.

31.8). In addition to the scheme of sixteen steps, the breath can also serve as a meditation object for the purpose of recollection of death (EĀ 40.8).

CONCLUSION

In the present conclusion I summarize what emerged in the previous chapters, beginning with various perspectives on the breath that have become apparent from passages translated in the last four chapters.

From the *Dīrgha-āgama* it emerges that the coming to an end of the process of breathing corresponds to the end of life. An exception to this rule appears to have been the Buddha himself, as he seems to have let his breathing come to an end even before passing away. Such ability relates to the cessation of breathing associated in the discourses with the attainment of the fourth absorption.

The *Madhyama-āgama* presents the process of breathing as a manifestation of the wind element, in the sense of the principle of motion. Awareness of the breath thus offers an easily accessible manifestation of impermanence. In addition to the insight perspective that emerges in this way, the potential of mindfulness of breathing to counter distraction and to lead to concentration is explicitly highlighted. The meditative dynamic responsible for this potential is no longer evident when the first tetrad of mindfulness of breathing occurs on its own in a survey of body contemplations. The resultant impression that this first tetrad is a complete practice by itself involves a loss of the transition towards joy and happiness in the second tetrad.

The *Saṃyukta-āgama* shows that mindfulness of inhalations and exhalations, which are a bodily activity, was open to developing one's own individual approach, leaving room for flexibility. The Buddha's own preferred practice during self-retreat involved the sixteen steps and this scheme was also taught by him regularly to his disciples, even to a large assembly of accomplished practitioners. Laying the groundwork for mindfulness of breathing requires moral conduct, fewness of wishes, knowing one's measure with food, wakefulness, and living in seclusion. A progression through the sixteen steps keeps the hindrances at bay through training, based on their removal previous to embarking on mindfulness of breathing. Such training leads to bodily and mental tranquillity, even to the absence of any bodily fidgeting. It can counter excessive repugnance towards the body and overcome unwholesome states, comparable to a chariot that drives over a mound of earth. The benefits of mindfulness of breathing range from abandoning thoughts to the highest levels of awakening, thereby covering a range of attainments in the realm of tranquillity and insight. The most prominent purpose of the sixteen steps, however, is to issue in a cultivation of the awakening factors, which can be undertaken based on each of the four tetrads.

The *Ekottarika-āgama* relates mindfulness of breathing to the gaining of freedom from distraction, supernormal powers, and the different levels of awakening. Some descriptions of mindfulness of breathing only reflect the first three steps of the full scheme, adding to these a discernment of the temperature of the breath or clearly noting when there is no breath. Already during his quest for awakening the Buddha appears to have been interested in the breath, evident in his practice of breath control. Besides the sixteen steps, the breath can also be employed for the purpose of recollection of death.

Based on the background to mindfulness of breathing that emerges in this way from a survey of relevant textual passages, the actual practice of mindfulness of breathing has its starting point in withdrawing into seclusion (ideally bodily and mentally), sitting down with body kept straight and bringing mindfulness mentally to the fore. Turning to the process of breathing with mindfulness, in particular the distinction between inhalations and exhalations is to be noted. Already at this juncture the subtle joy of being in the present moment can manifest, representative of the tranquillity potential of mindfulness of breathing, which can be combined with noting the changing nature of the breath, representing its insight potential.

Arousing an attitude of investigation, the length of the breath can be discerned as long or short, either after having taken an intentionally long breath or else just by turning to the breath as it naturally manifests. The first option can be helpful to provide grounding and counter a tendency to distraction; the second option commends itself when the mind is well settled. The more focused mode of attention required to distinguish clearly the length of the breath leads over to emphasis on awareness of the whole body. This progression enables experimenting with modalities of attention, as from this junction onwards the alternation between inhalations and exhalations is to be kept in peripheral awareness rather than being focused on. Next, breath and body can be allowed to become increasingly calm, such that a sense of deep relaxation pervades the whole of bodily experience.

Joining the breath to the pleasant feeling tone of being in the present moment can lead to the spontaneous arising of joy. As the mind becomes increasingly calm, the experience of joy turns into the happiness of a mind inwardly contented and tranquil. Next, mental activity in general can be discerned, with a particular emphasis on noting what could lead to its increase. Learning to maintain uninvolved awareness of mental activity leads to its calming down and the mind eventually becomes naturally still.

Mental activity having been stilled, mind as such can be experienced in its bare condition. As this experience comes conjoined to mindfulness of the alternation between inhalations and exhalations, the changing nature of the mind is apparent throughout. This enables a profound experience of the mind as such without leaving room for reifying it as a permanent entity. Practice proceeds to the experiences of gladness and concentration, which are to some extent already dimensions of the experience of the mind as such. Turning attention to them deepens their manifestation. Moving on to liberating the mind could lead to entry into absorption. Giving emphasis to the cultivation of insight instead could find its expression in liberating the mind from all conceit and sense of self-reference, by "breathing without a breather".

Practice proceeds to contemplation of impermanence, bringing to the forefront of attention a theme that has been present throughout, evident in the alternation between inhalations and exhalations kept in peripheral awareness. Letting the implications of impermanence sink into the mind and transform its affective disposition leads to becoming dispassionate and to giving full recognition to cessation. A culmination point can be reached with letting go and inclining the mind towards the supreme freedom possible with the realization of Nirvāṇa.

Proceeding through the sixteen steps can implicitly touch on each of the seven awakening factors during the first three tetrads and with the last tetrad lead to a cultivation of the awakening themes, with the final aim of letting go as completely as possible. Based on having once gone through the entire scheme, any of the tetrads can be taken up individually, with the respective last step serving as a launching pad for cultivating and balancing the awakening factors. Here lack of energy can be countered by more emphasis on investigation–energy–joy and excess of energy by instead giving attention to tranquillity–concentration–equipoise.

This completes my study of mindfulness of breathing in six chapters dedicated to its practice and another four chapters examining relevant material from the Chinese *Āgama*s. At this point, what remains to be said is simply to repeat the injunction given in the last discourse taken up in the preceding chapter, which combines the experience of the breath with the perception of death. Regret will arise if, at the time of breathing our last, it becomes clear that we have not dedicated ourselves sufficiently to meditation practice. Hence the injunction:

You should train yourselves!

QUOTATIONS

In what follows I provide references to the standard English translations of the passages quoted in the course of my exploration (except for quotes from MN 118, for which I offer my own translation), in order to enable the reader to follow up any of these and consider them in their original context. References to discourses are by number; those to *Vinaya* and other works by volume and page of the PTS edition.

EPIGRAPH

SN 54.9 (p. xvi)	Bodhi 2000: 1774

INTRODUCTION

MN 36 (p. 1)	Ñāṇamoli 1995/2005: 337
SN 54.11 (p. 1)	Bodhi 2000: 1778

CHAPTER I	**MINDFULNESS AND THE BREATH**
MN 4 (p. 7)	Ñāṇamoli 1995/2005: 102
Vism 269 (p. 8)	Ñāṇamoli 1991: 263
AN 10.72 (p. 8)	Bodhi 2012: 1428
MN 77 (p. 8)	Ñāṇamoli 1995/2005: 629
DN 25 (p. 8)	Walshe 1987: 386
Vin II 158 (p. 8)	Horner 1952/1975: 222

MN 152 (p. 9)	Ñāṇamoli 1995/2005: 1147
SN 35.97 (p. 10)	Bodhi 2000: 1180
SN 35.206 (p. 11)	Bodhi 2000: 1256 (given as number 247)
SN 47.20 (p. 11)	Bodhi 2000: 1649
DN 17 (p. 12)	Walshe 1987: 286
MN 20 (p. 14)	Ñāṇamoli 1995/2005: 211
Vism 278 (p. 15)	Ñāṇamoli 1991: 271
Vism 271 (p. 15)	Ñāṇamoli 1991: 264
Vibh 252 (p. 16)	Thiṭṭila 1969: 328
Vism 271 (p. 17)	Ñāṇamoli 1991: 264
MN 107 (p. 17)	Ñāṇamoli 1995/2005: 876
SN 54.6 (p. 17)	Bodhi 2000: 1768
MN 10 (p. 18)	Ñāṇamoli 1995/2005: 145
Vism 283 (p. 21)	Ñāṇamoli 1991: 276
AN 3.47 (p. 22)	Bodhi 2012: 246
MN 44 (p. 23)	Ñāṇamoli 1995/2005: 401
SN 54.6 (p. 24)	Bodhi 2000: 1768
AN 10.60 (p. 24)	Bodhi 2012: 1411

CHAPTER II **CONTEMPLATION OF THE BODY**

AN 10.60 (p. 30)	Bodhi 2012: 1411
MN 10 (p. 31)	Ñāṇamoli 1995/2005: 146
MN 36 (p. 34)	Ñāṇamoli 1995/2005: 337
Vism 273 (p. 37)	Ñāṇamoli 1991: 266
SN 54.12 (p. 43)	Bodhi 2000: 1779
MN 44 (p. 45)	Ñāṇamoli 1995/2005: 399
SN 41.6 (p. 45)	Bodhi 2000: 1322
Paṭis I 184 (p. 45)	Ñāṇamoli 1982: 185
AN 4.38 (p. 46)	Bodhi 2012: 428
SN 54.7 (p. 48)	Bodhi 2000: 1769

CHAPTER III **CONTEMPLATION OF FEELING TONES**

Vism 287 (p. 56)	Ñāṇamoli 1991: 280
MN 51 (p. 57)	Ñāṇamoli 1995/2005: 450
SN 35.97 (p. 57)	Bodhi 2000: 1180

MN 51 (p. 60)	Ñāṇamoli 1995/2005: 450
MN 44 (p. 64)	Ñāṇamoli 1995/2005: 399
Paṭis I 188 (p. 64)	Ñāṇamoli 1982: 190
MN 20 (p. 68)	Ñāṇamoli 1995/2005: 212

CHAPTER IV	CONTEMPLATION OF THE MIND
Paṭis I 190 (p. 77)	Ñāṇamoli 1982: 193
Paṭis I 190 (p. 83)	Ñāṇamoli 1982: 194
MN 128 (p. 88)	Ñāṇamoli 1995/2005: 1012
SN 48.9 (p. 90)	Bodhi 2000: 1671
SN 48.10 (p. 90)	Bodhi 2000: 1672
SN 48.11 (p. 90)	Bodhi 2000: 1673
SN 48.50 (p. 90)	Bodhi 2000: 1694
MN 43 (p. 91)	Ñāṇamoli 1995/2005: 391
Vism 289 (p. 92)	Ñāṇamoli 1991: 282
Paṭis I 191 (p. 92)	Ñāṇamoli 1982: 196
SN 28.1–9 (p. 93)	Bodhi 2000: 1015

CHAPTER V	CONTEMPLATION OF DHARMAS
SN 22.102 (p. 101)	Bodhi 2000: 961
AN 9.1 (p. 101)	Bodhi 2012: 1247
Paṭis I 191 (p. 102)	Ñāṇamoli 1982: 197
AN 10.60 (p. 102)	Bodhi 2012: 1412
SN 23.1 (p. 107)	Bodhi 2000: 984
AN 10.60 (p. 108)	Bodhi 2012: 1413
MN 64 (p. 108)	Ñāṇamoli 1995/2005: 540
AN 10.60 (p. 109)	Bodhi 2012: 1413
AN 10.94 (p. 110)	Bodhi 2012: 1469
MN 37 (p. 111)	Ñāṇamoli 1995/2005: 344
AN 7.58 (p. 111)	Bodhi 2012: 1061 (given as number 61)
SN 36.7 (p. 112)	Bodhi 2000: 1266
SN 36.8 (p. 112)	Bodhi 2000: 1268

CHAPTER VI	AWAKENING
MN 10 (p. 123)	Ñāṇamoli 1995/2005: 145
SN 54.10 (p. 123)	Bodhi 2000: 1777
AN 10.60 (p. 124)	Bodhi 2012: 1414
SN 46.14–16 (p. 124)	Bodhi 2000: 1580
SN 46.42 (p. 124)	Bodhi 2000: 1595
SN 46.51 (p. 130)	Bodhi 2000: 1598
SN 46.4 (p. 138)	Bodhi 2000: 1573

INSTRUCTIONS ON MINDFULNESS OF BREATHING

In what follows I bring together the different translated excerpts of the instructions in the *Ānāpānasati-sutta* on mindfulness of breathing, for ease of reference, followed by a survey in chart form.

THE SIXTEEN STEPS

Here gone to a forest or to the root of a tree or to an empty hut, one sits down; having folded the legs crosswise, keeping the body erect, and having established mindfulness to the fore, mindful one breathes in and mindful one breathes out.

Breathing in long, one understands: 'I breathe in long'; breathing out long, one understands: 'I breathe out long.' Breathing in short, one understands: 'I breathe in short'; breathing out short, one understands: 'I breathe out short.' One trains: 'experiencing the whole body I shall breathe in'; one trains: 'experiencing the whole body I shall breathe out.' One trains: 'calming bodily activity I shall breathe in'; one trains: 'calming bodily activity I shall breathe out.'

One trains: 'experiencing joy I shall breathe in'; one trains: 'experiencing joy I shall breathe out.' One trains: 'experiencing happiness I shall breathe in'; one trains: 'experiencing happiness I shall breathe out.' One trains: 'experiencing mental activity I shall breathe in'; one trains: 'experiencing mental activity I shall breathe out.' One trains: 'calming mental activity I shall breathe in'; one trains: 'calming mental activity I shall breathe out.'

One trains: 'experiencing the mind I shall breathe in'; one trains: 'experiencing the mind I shall breathe out.' One trains: 'gladdening the mind I shall breathe in'; one trains: 'gladdening the mind I shall breathe out.' One trains: 'concentrating the mind I shall breathe in'; one trains: 'concentrating the mind I shall breathe out.' One trains: 'liberating the mind I shall breathe in'; one trains: 'liberating the mind I shall breathe out.'

One trains: 'contemplating impermanence I shall breathe in'; one trains: 'contemplating impermanence I shall breathe out.' One trains: 'contemplating dispassion I shall breathe in'; one trains: 'contemplating dispassion I shall breathe out.' One trains: 'contemplating cessation I shall breathe in'; one trains: 'contemplating cessation I shall breathe out.' One trains: 'contemplating letting go I shall breathe in'; one trains: 'contemplating letting go I shall breathe out.'

THE AWAKENING FACTORS

One dwells contemplating diligent, clearly comprehending, and mindful, free from desire and discontent with regard to the world. At that time mindfulness is established continuously. At a time when mindfulness is established in one continuously, at that time the awakening factor of mindfulness is aroused in one, at that time one cultivates the awakening factor of mindfulness, at that time the awakening factor of mindfulness comes to be accomplished in one by cultivation.

Dwelling mindfully in this way, one discerns, investigates, and makes an examination of that state with wisdom. At a time when, dwelling mindfully in this way, one discerns, investigates, and makes an examination of that state with wisdom, at that time the awakening factor of investigation-of-dharmas is aroused in one, at that time one cultivates the awakening factor of investigation-of-dharmas, at that time the awakening factor of investigation-of-dharmas comes to be accomplished in one by cultivation.

In one who discerns, investigates, and makes an examination of that state with wisdom, unwavering energy is aroused. At a time when unwavering energy is aroused in one who discerns, investigates, and makes an examination of that state with wisdom, at that time the awakening factor of energy is aroused in one, at that time one cultivates the awakening factor of energy, at that time the awakening factor of energy comes to be accomplished in one by cultivation.

In one who has aroused energy, unworldly joy arises. At a time when unworldly joy arises in one who has aroused energy, at that time the awakening factor of joy is aroused in one, at that time one cultivates the awakening factor of joy, at that time the awakening factor of joy comes to be accomplished in one by cultivation.

In one who is joyous, the body becomes tranquil and the mind becomes tranquil. At a time when, in one who is joyous, the body becomes tranquil and the mind becomes tranquil, at that time the awakening factor of tranquillity is aroused in one, at that time one cultivates the awakening factor of tranquillity, at that time the awakening factor of tranquillity comes to be accomplished in one by cultivation.

In one whose body is tranquil and who is happy, the mind becomes concentrated. At a time when, in one whose body is tranquil and who is happy, the mind becomes concentrated, at that time the awakening factor of concentration is aroused in one, at that time one cultivates the awakening factor of concentration, at that time the awakening factor of concentration comes to be accomplished in one by cultivation.

One carefully oversees, without interfering, the mind that has become concentrated in this way. At a time when one carefully oversees, without interfering, the mind that has become concentrated in this way, at that time the awakening factor of equipoise is aroused in one, at that time one cultivates the awakening factor of equipoise, at that time the awakening factor of equipoise comes to be accomplished in one by cultivation.

THE AWAKENING THEMES

One develops the mindfulness awakening factor in dependence on seclusion, in dependence on dispassion, and in dependence on cessation, culminating in letting go.

One develops the investigation-of-dharmas awakening factor *in dependence on seclusion, in dependence on dispassion, and in dependence on cessation, culminating in letting go.*

One develops the energy awakening factor *in dependence on seclusion, in dependence on dispassion, and in dependence on cessation, culminating in letting go.*

One develops the joy awakening factor *in dependence on seclusion, in dependence on dispassion, and in dependence on cessation, culminating in letting go.*

One develops the tranquillity awakening factor *in dependence on seclusion, in dependence on dispassion, and in dependence on cessation, culminating in letting go.*

One develops the concentration awakening factor *in dependence on seclusion, in dependence on dispassion, and in dependence on cessation, culminating in letting go.*

One develops the equipoise awakening factor in dependence on seclusion, in dependence on dispassion, and in dependence on cessation, culminating in letting go.

CHART

The chart below is meant to reflect the salient points of the practice of mindfulness of breathing at one glance. Proceeding from left to right, first are the objects of the four establishments of mindfulness that correspond to the four tetrads. Next come the sixteen steps, which are numbered. To their right are the seven awakening factors, placed at the level of those steps of the first three tetrads that can be used to stimulate them (see above p. 128), and the four awakening themes, with the last three placed at the level of the corresponding last three steps.

0.	mindfulness to the fore; mindful breathing in/out	mindfulness
1.	breathing in/out long	investigation-of-dharmas
2.	breathing in/out short	
3.	experiencing the whole body & breathing in/out	energy
4.	calming bodily activity & breathing in/out	
5.	experiencing joy & breathing in/out	joy
6.	experiencing happiness & breathing in/out	
7.	experiencing mental activity & breathing in/out	
8.	calming mental activity & breathing in/out	tranquillity
9.	experiencing the mind & breathing in/out	
10.	gladdening the mind & breathing in/out	
11.	concentrating the mind & breathing in/out	concentration
12.	liberating the mind & breathing in/out	equipoise
13.	contemplating impermanence & breathing in/out	in dependence on seclusion
14.	contemplating dispassion & breathing in/out	in dependence on dispassion
15.	contemplating cessation & breathing in/out	in dependence on cessation
16.	contemplating letting go & breathing in/out	culminating in letting go

ABBREVIATIONS

AN	*Aṅguttara-nikāya*
D	Derge edition
DĀ	*Dīrgha-āgama* (T 1)
DN	*Dīgha-nikāya*
EĀ	*Ekottarika-āgama* (T 125)
Kv	*Kathāvatthu*
MĀ	*Madhyama-āgama* (T 26)
MN	*Majjhima-nikāya*
Ps	*Papañcasūdanī*
PTS	Pali Text Society edition
Q	Peking edition
SĀ	*Saṃyukta-āgama* (T 99)
SĀ²	*Saṃyukta-āgama* (T 100)
SĀ³	*Saṃyukta-āgama* (T 101)
SN	*Saṃyutta-nikāya*
Spk	*Sāratthappakāsinī*
T	Taishō edition
Up	*Abhidharmakośopāyikā-ṭīkā*
Vibh	*Vibhaṅga*
Vin	*Vinaya*
Vism	*Visuddhimagga*
⟨⟩	emendation
[]	supplementation

REFERENCES

Akanuma Chizen 1929/1990: *The Comparative Catalogue of Chinese Āgamas & Pāli Nikāyas*, Delhi: Sri Satguru.

Anālayo 2003a: "Nimitta", in *Encyclopaedia of Buddhism*, W.G. Weeraratne (ed.), 7.4: 177–179, Sri Lanka: Department of Buddhist Affairs.

— 2003b: *Satipaṭṭhāna, The Direct Path to Realization*, Birmingham: Windhorse Publications.

— 2006a: "Samādhi", in *Encyclopaedia of Buddhism*, W.G. Weeraratne (ed.), 7.4: 650–655, Sri Lanka: Department of Buddhist Affairs (reprinted in Anālayo 2012b).

— 2006b: "Saṅkhāra", in *Encyclopaedia of Buddhism*, W.G. Weeraratne (ed.), 7.4: 732–737, Sri Lanka: Department of Buddhist Affairs (reprinted in Anālayo 2012b).

— 2007: "Mindfulness of Breathing in the Saṃyukta-āgama", *Buddhist Studies Review*, 24.2: 137–150 (reprinted in Anālayo 2015c).

— 2009a: "Vimutti", in *Encyclopaedia of Buddhism*, W.G. Weeraratne (ed.), 8.3: 615–622, Sri Lanka: Department of Buddhist Affairs (reprinted in Anālayo 2012b).

— 2009b: "Virāga", in *Encyclopaedia of Buddhism*, W.G. Weeraratne (ed.), 8.3: 688–690, Sri Lanka: Department of Buddhist Affairs (reprinted in Anālayo 2012b).

— 2009c: "Vossagga", in *Encyclopaedia of Buddhism*, W.G. Weeraratne (ed.), 8.3: 725–728, Sri Lanka: Department of Buddhist Affairs (reprinted in Anālayo 2012b).

— 2011: *A Comparative Study of the Majjhima-nikāya*, Taipei: Dharma Drum Publishing Corporation.

— 2012a: "The Dynamics of Theravāda Insight Meditation", in *Buddhist Meditation Traditions: An International Symposium*, Kuo-pin Chuang (ed.), 23–56, Taiwan: Dharma Drum Publishing Corporation.

— 2012b: *Excursions into the Thought-world of the Pāli Discourses*, Washington: Pariyatti.
— 2012c: *Madhyama-āgama Studies*, Taipei: Dharma Drum Publishing Corporation.
— 2013a: "Mahāyāna in the Ekottarika-āgama", *Singaporean Journal of Buddhist Studies*, 1: 5–43 (reprinted in Anālayo 2016a).
— 2013b: *Perspectives on Satipaṭṭhāna*, Cambridge: Windhorse Publications.
— 2013c: "Two Versions of the Mahādeva Tale in the Ekottarika-āgama, A Study in the Development of Taishō No. 125", in *Research on the Ekottarika-āgama (Taishō 125)*, Dhammadinnā (ed.), 1–70, Taipei: Dharma Drum Publishing Corporation (reprinted in Anālayo 2016a).
— 2014: "The Mass Suicide of Monks in Discourse and Vinaya Literature", *Journal of the Oxford Centre for Buddhist Studies*, 7: 11–55 (reprinted in Anālayo 2017g).
— 2014/2015: "Discourse Merger in the Ekottarika-āgama (2), The Parallels to the Kakacūpama-sutta and the Alagaddūpama-sutta", *Journal of the Centre for Buddhist Studies, Sri Lanka*, 12: 63–90 (reprinted in Anālayo 2016a).
— 2015a: *Compassion and Emptiness in Early Buddhist Meditation*, Cambridge: Windhorse Publications.
— 2015b: "Discourse Merger in the Ekottarika-āgama (1), The Parallel to the Bhaddāli-sutta and the Latukikopama-sutta, Together with Notes on the Chinese Translation of the Collection", *Singaporean Journal of Buddhist Studies*, 2: 5–35 (reprinted in Anālayo 2016a).
— 2015c: *Saṃyukta-āgama Studies*, Taipei: Dharma Drum Publishing Corporation.
— 2016a: *Ekottarika-āgama Studies*, Taipei: Dharma Drum Publishing Corporation.
— 2016b: *Mindfully Facing Disease and Death, Compassionate Advice from Early Buddhist Texts*, Cambridge: Windhorse Publications.
— 2017a: *Dīrgha-āgama Studies*, Taipei: Dharma Drum Publishing Corporation.
— 2017b: *Early Buddhist Meditation Studies*, Barre: Barre Center for Buddhist Studies.
— 2017c: "How Compassion Became Painful", *Journal of the Centre for Buddhist Studies, Sri Lanka*, 14: 85–113.
— 2017d: "The Luminous Mind in Theravāda and Dharmaguptaka Discourses", *Journal of the Oxford Centre for Buddhist Studies*, 13: 10–51.
— 2017e: *A Meditator's Life of the Buddha, Based on the Early Discourses*, Cambridge: Windhorse Publications.
— 2017f: "The 'School Affiliation' of the Madhyama-āgama", in *Research on the Madhyama-āgama*, Dhammadinnā (ed.), 55–76, Taipei: Dharma Drum Publishing Corporation.
— 2017g: *Vinaya Studies*, Taipei: Dharma Drum Publishing Corporation.
— 2017h: "What About Neutral Feelings?", *Insight Journal*, 43: 1–10.

— 2018a: "The Influxes and Mindful Eating", *Insight Journal*, 44: 31–42.
— 2018b: "Overeating and Mindfulness in Ancient India", *Mindfulness*, 9.5: 1648–1654.
— 2018c: *Rebirth in Early Buddhism and Current Research*, Somerville: Wisdom Publications.
— 2018d: *Satipaṭṭhāna Meditation, A Practice Guide*, Cambridge: Windhorse Publications.
— 2019a: "Food and Insight", *Insight Journal*, 45: 1–10.
— 2019b: "How Mindfulness Came to Plunge into Its Objects", *Mindfulness*, 10: 1181-1185.
— 2019c: "The Insight Knowledge of Fear and Adverse Effects of Mindfulness Practices", *Mindfulness*, 10.
— 2019d: "Meditation on the Breath: Mindfulness and Focused Attention", *Mindfulness*, 10: 1684–1691.
— 2020a: "How the Steps of Mindfulness of Breathing Decreased from Sixteen to Two", in *Buddhist Studies in Honour of Venerable Professor K.L. Dhammajoti*, T. Endo (ed.), Hong Kong: Centre of Buddhist Studies, University of Hong Kong.
— 2020b: *Mindfulness in Early Buddhism, Characteristics and Functions*, Cambridge: Windhorse Publications.
Ariyadhamma, Nauyane 1995/2014: *Ānāpānasati, Meditation on Breathing*, Kandy: Buddhist Publication Society (online PDF version).
Bingenheimer, Marcus, Bh. Anālayo, and R. Bucknell 2013 (vol. 1): *The Madhyama Āgama (Middle Length Discourses)*, Berkeley: Numata Center for Buddhist Translation and Research.
Bodhi, Bhikkhu 2000: *The Connected Discourses of the Buddha, A New Translation of the Saṃyutta Nikāya*, Somerville: Wisdom Publications.
— 2012: *The Numerical Discourses of the Buddha, A Translation of the Aṅguttara Nikāya*, Somerville: Wisdom Publications.
Brahmavaṃso, Ajahn 2004/2006: *Ānāpānasati Sutta & Satipaṭṭhāna Sutta*, Carmel: The Buddhist Association of the United States.
Bronkhorst, Johannes 1993/2000: *The Two Traditions of Meditation in Ancient India*, Delhi: Motilal Banarsidass.
Buddhadāsa Bhikkhu 1988/1997: *Mindfulness with Breathing, A Manual for Serious Beginners*, Santikaro (trsl.), Somerville: Wisdom Publications.
Cousins, L.S. 2015: "The Sutta on Mindfulness with In and Out Breathing", in *Buddhist Meditative Praxis, Traditional Teachings & Modern Applications*, K.L. Dhammajoti (ed.), 1–24, Hong Kong: Centre of Buddhist Studies, University of Hong Kong.
Culadasa (John Yates) 2015/2017: *The Mind Illuminated, A Complete Meditation Guide Integrating Buddhist Wisdom and Brain Science for Greater Mindfulness*, New York: Touchstone.
Deleanu, Florin 1992: "Mindfulness of Breathing in the Dhyāna Sūtras", in *Transactions of the International Conference of Orientalists in Japan*, 37: 42–57.

— 2003: "The Newly Found Text of the Anban shou yi jing Translated by An Shigao", *Journal of the International College for Advanced Buddhist Studies*, 6: 63–100.

Dhammadharo, Ajahn Lee 1979/2010: *Keeping the Breath in Mind and Lessons in Samadhi*, Bhikkhu Ṭhānissaro (trsl.), Valley Center: Metta Forest Monastery.

Dhammadīpa, Bhikkhu 2009: "Two Divisions of Ānāpānasati/smṛti in Their Chronological Development", in *Buddhist and Pāli Studies in Honour of the Venerable Professor Kakkapalliye Anuruddha*, K.L. Dhammajoti and Y. Karunadasa (ed.), 567–582, Hong Kong: University of Hong Kong.

Dhammajoti, Bhikkhu K.L. 2008: "The Sixteen-mode Mindfulness of Breathing", *Journal of the Centre for Buddhist Studies, Sri Lanka*, 6: 251–288.

— 2009: "The Doctrine of the Six-stage Mindfulness of Breathing", in *Buddhist and Pāli Studies in Honour of the Venerable Professor Kakkapalliye Anuruddha*, K.L. Dhammajoti and Y. Karunadasa (ed.), 639–650, Hong Kong: University of Hong Kong.

Ditrich, Tamara 2018: "Mindfulness of Breathing in Early Buddhism", in *Atmospheres of Breathing*, L. Škof and P. Berndtson (ed.), 99–113, Albany: State University of New York Press.

Ehara, N.R.M., Soma Thera, and Kheminda Thera 1961/1995: *The Path of Freedom (Vimuttimagga), By the Arahant Upatissa*, Kandy: Buddhist Publication Society.

Gethin, Rupert 1992: *The Buddhist Path to Awakening: A Study of the Bodhi-pakkhiyā Dhammā*, Leiden: E.J. Brill.

Gñānārāma, Mātara Sri 1989: *Ānāpānasatibhāvanā (Mindfulness of In and Out Breathing)*, Mitra Wettimuny (trsl.), Mitirigala: Nissarana Vanaya.

Horner, I.B. 1938/1982 (vol. 1) and 1952/1975 (vol. 5): *The Book of the Discipline (Vinaya-Piṭaka)*, London: Pali Text Society.

Huyên-Vi, Thích 1986: "Ekottarāgama III", *Buddhist Studies Review*, 3.1: 31–38.

— 1993: "Ekottarāgama XV", *Buddhist Studies Review*, 10.2: 213–222.

Ichimura Shohei 2015: *The Canonical Book of the Buddha's Lengthy Discourses, Volume I*, Berkeley: Bukkyo Dendo Kyokai America.

Jayatilleke, K.N. 1948: "Some Problems of Translation and Interpretation I", *University of Ceylon Review*, 7: 208–224.

Johnson, Will 2012: *Breathing Through the Whole Body, The Buddha's Instructions on Integrating Mind, Body, and Breath*, Rochester: Inner Tradition.

Jones, J.J. 1952/1976 (vol. 2): *The Mahāvastu, Translated from the Buddhist Sanskrit*, London: Pali Text Society.

Kuan Tse-Fu 2008: *Mindfulness in Early Buddhism, New Approaches Through Psychology and Textual Analysis of Pali, Chinese and Sanskrit Sources*, London: Routledge.

— 2017: [Review of Palumbo 2013], *Journal of the American Oriental Society*, 137.2: 444–448.

Ledi Sayādaw Mahāthera 1999/2011: *Manual of Mindfulness of Breathing, Ānāpāna Dīpani*, U Sein Nyo Tun (trsl.), Kandy: Buddhist Publication Society (online version).

Levine, Stephen 1991: *Guided Meditations, Explorations, and Healings*, New York: Anchor Books.

Liu Zhen 2010: *Dhyānāni tapaś ca*, 禅定与苦修, Shanghai: 古籍出版社.

Mayeda Egaku 1985: "Japanese Studies on the Schools of the Chinese Āgamas", in *Zur Schulzugehörigkeit von Werken der Hīnayāna-Literatur, Erster Teil*, H. Bechert (ed.), 94–103, Göttingen: Vandenhoeck & Ruprecht.

Namgyal Rinpoche 1992: *The Breath of Awakening, A Guide to Liberation Through Ānāpānasati, Mindfulness of Breathing*, Kinmount: Bodhi Publishing.

Ñāṇamoli, Bhikkhu 1952/1982: *Mindfulness of Breathing (Ānāpānasati), Buddhist Texts from the Pāli Canon and Extracts from the Pāli Commentaries*, Kandy: Buddhist Publication Society.

— 1982: *The Path of Discrimination (Paṭisambhidāmagga)*, London: Pali Text Society.

— 1991: *The Path of Purification (Visuddhimagga) by Bhadantācariya Buddhaghosa*, Kandy: Buddhist Publication Society.

— 1995/2005: *The Middle Length Discourses of the Buddha, A Translation of the Majjhima Nikāya*, Bhikkhu Bodhi (ed.), Somerville: Wisdom Publications.

Nhat Hanh, Thich 1988: *The Sutra on the Full Awareness of Breathing, With Commentary by Thich Nhat Hanh*, A. Laity (trsl.), Berkeley: Parallax Press.

— 1990: *Transformation & Healing, The Sutra on the Four Establishments of Mindfulness*, A. Laity (trsl.), Berkeley: Parallax Press.

Pa-Auk Tawya Sayadaw (no date): *Mindfulness of Breathing (Ānāpānassati)*, Singapore: Pa-Auk Meditation Centre.

Palumbo, Antonello 2013: *An Early Chinese Commentary on the Ekottarika-āgama, The Fenbie gongde lun* 分別功德論 *and the History of the Translation of the Zengyi ahan jing* 增一阿含經, Taipei: Dharma Drum Publishing Corporation.

Pradhan, Ayodhya Prasad 1986: *The Buddha's System of Meditation*, New Delhi: Sterling Publishers.

Radhakrishnan, S. 1953/1992: *The Principal Upaniṣads, Edited with Introduction, Text, Translation and Notes*, New York: Humanity Books.

Rosenberg, Larry 1998: *Breath by Breath, The Liberating Practice of Insight Meditation*, Boston: Shambala Publications.

Samtani, N.H. 1971: *The Arthaviniścaya-Sūtra & Its Commentary (Nibandhana) (Written by Bhikṣu Vīryaśrīdatta of Śrī-Nālandāvihāra), Critically Edited and Annotated for the First Time with Introduction and Several Indices*, Patna: K.P. Jayaswal Research Institute.

— 2002: *Gathering the Meaning, The Compendium of Categories, The Arthaviniścaya Sūtra and Its Commentary Nibandhana*, Berkeley: Dharma Publishing.

Schlingloff, Dieter 1962: *Dogmatische Begriffsreihen im älteren Buddhismus, Ia, Daśottarasūtra IX–X*, Berlin: Akademie Verlag.

Senart, Émile 1890 (vol. 2): *Le Mahāvastu, texte sanscrit publié pour la première fois et accompagné d'introductions et d'un commentaire*, Paris: Imprimerie Nationale.

Shaw, Sarah 2018: "Tradition and Experimentation: The Development of the Samatha Trust", *Contemporary Buddhism* (online version: DOI: 10.1080/14639947.2018.1521606).

Shukla, Karunesha 1973: *Śrāvakabhūmi of Ācārya Asaṅga*, Patna: K.P. Jayaswal Research Institute.

Shwe Zan Aung and C.A.F. Rhys Davids 1915/1979: *Points of Controversy or Subjects of Discourse, Being a Translation of the Kathā-vatthu from the Abhidhamma-Piṭaka*, London: Pali Text Society.

Solé-Leris, Amadeo 1986/1992: *Tranquillity & Insight, An Introduction to the Oldest Form of Buddhist Meditation*, Kandy: Buddhist Publication Society.

Sucitto, Ajahn 2011: *Meditation, A Way of Awakening*, Malaysia: Sukhi Hotu.

Ṭhānissaro, Bhikkhu 2012: *Right Mindfulness, Memory & Ardency on the Buddhist Path*, Valley Center: Metta Forest Monastery.

Thiṭṭila, P.A. 1969: *The Book of Analysis (Vibhaṅga), The Second Book of the Abhidhammapiṭaka, Translated from the Pāḷi of the Burmese Chaṭṭhasaṅgīti Edition*, London: Pali Text Society.

Vajirañāṇa Mahāthera, Paravahera 1962/1975: *Buddhist Meditation in Theory and Praxis, A General Exposition According to the Pāli Canon of the Theravāda School*, Kuala Lumpur: Buddhist Missionary Society.

Vimalaramsi, U 1995/2006: *The Ānāpānasati Sutta, A Practical Guide to Mindfulness of Breathing and Tranquil Wisdom Meditation*, Carmel: The Buddhist Association of the United States.

Virtbauer, Gerald 2016: "Presencing Process: Embodiment and Healing in the Buddhist Practice of Mindfulness of Breathing", *Mental Health, Religion & Culture*, 19.1: 68–81.

Waldschmidt, Ernst 1950: *Das Mahāparinirvāṇasūtra, Text in Sanskrit und Tibetisch, verglichen mit dem Pāli nebst einer Übersetzung der chinesischen Entsprechung im Vinaya der Mūlasarvāstivādins, auf Grund von Turfan-Handschriften herausgegeben und bearbeitet*, Berlin: Akademie Verlag.

— 1956: *Das Mahāvadānasūtra, ein kanonischer Text über die sieben letzten Buddhas, Sanskrit, verglichen mit dem Pāli nebst einer Analyse der in chinesischer Übersetzung überlieferten Parallelversion, auf Grund von Turfan-Handschriften herausgegeben*, Berlin: Akademie Verlag.

Walshe, Maurice 1987: *Thus Have I Heard; The Long Discourses of the Buddha*, London: Wisdom Publications.

Woodward, F.L. 1930/1979 (vol. 5): *The Book of the Kindred Sayings (Saṃyutta-Nikāya) or Grouped Suttas*, London: Pali Text Society.

Yamabe Nobuyoshi and F. Sueki 2009: *The Sutra on the Concentration of Sitting Meditation (Taishō Volume 15, Number 614) Translated from the Chinese of Kumārajīva*, Berkeley: Numata Center for Buddhist Translation and Research.

INDEX OF SUBJECTS

INTRODUCTORY NOTE

References such as '178–9' indicate (not necessarily continuous) discussion of a topic across a range of pages. Wherever possible in the case of topics with many references, these have either been divided into sub-topics or only the most significant discussions of the topic are listed. Because the entire work is about 'mindfulness of breathing', the use of this term (and certain others which occur constantly throughout the book) as an entry point has been minimized. Information will be found under the corresponding detailed topics.

INDEX LOCORUM

WINDHORSE PUBLICATIONS

Windhorse Publications is a Buddhist charitable company based in the UK. We place great emphasis on producing books of high quality that are accessible and relevant to those interested in Buddhism at whatever level. We are the main publisher of the works of Sangharakshita, the founder of the Triratna Buddhist Order and Community. Our books draw on the whole range of the Buddhist tradition, including translations of traditional texts, commentaries, books that make links with contemporary culture and ways of life, biographies of Buddhists, and works on meditation.

As a not-for-profit enterprise, we ensure that all surplus income is invested in new books and improved production methods, to better communicate Buddhism in the 21st century. We welcome donations to help us continue our work – to find out more, go to windhorsepublications.com.

The Windhorse is a mythical animal that flies over the earth carrying on its back three precious jewels, bringing these invaluable gifts to all humanity: the Buddha (the 'awakened one'), his teaching, and the community of all his followers.

Windhorse Publications
17e Sturton Street
Cambridge CB1 2SN
UK
info@windhorsepublications.com

Perseus Distribution
210 American Drive
Jackson TN 38301
USA

Windhorse Books
PO Box 574
Newtown NSW 2042
Australia

THE TRIRATNA BUDDHIST COMMUNITY

Windhorse Publications is a part of the Triratna Buddhist Community, an international movement with centres in Europe, India, North and South America and Australasia. At these centres, members of the Triratna Buddhist Order offer classes in meditation and Buddhism. Activities of the Triratna Community also include retreat centres, residential spiritual communities, ethical Right Livelihood businesses, and the Karuna Trust, a UK fundraising charity that supports social welfare projects in the slums and villages of India.

Through these and other activities, Triratna is developing a unique approach to Buddhism, not simply as a philosophy and a set of techniques, but as a creatively directed way of life for all people living in the conditions of the modern world.

If you would like more information about Triratna please visit thebuddhistcentre.com or write to:

London Buddhist Centre
51 Roman Road
London E2 0HU
UK

Aryaloka
14 Heartwood Circle
Newmarket NH 03857
USA

Sydney Buddhist Centre
24 Enmore Road
Sydney NSW 2042
Australia

Also from Windhorse Publications

Satipaṭṭhāna: the direct path to realization

Bhikkhu Anālayo

This best-selling book offers a unique and detailed textual study of the Satipaṭṭhāna Sutta, a foundational Buddhist discourse on meditation practice.

This book should prove to be of value both to scholars of Early Buddhism and to serious meditators alike. – Bhikku Bodhi

. . . a gem . . . I learned a lot from this wonderful book and highly recommend it. – Joseph Goldstein

An indispensible guide . . . surely destined to become the classic commentary on the Satipaṭṭhāna. – Christopher Titmuss

Very impressive and useful, with its blend of strong scholarship and attunement to practice issues. – Prof. Peter Harvey, author of *An Introduction to Buddhist Ethics*

ISBN 9781 899579 54 9 | £17.99 / $28.95 / €19.95 | 336 pages

A Meditator's Life of the Buddha: based on the early discourses

Bhikkhu Anālayo

The author offers an inspiring biography of the Buddha based on the early discourses. By focusing on his meditative development and practice – on the Buddha as a meditator – Bhikkhu Anālayo seeks to provide inspiration and guidance to all meditators, of any tradition and any level of experience. Each of the twenty-four chapters concludes with suggestions to support meditative practice.

While offering a scholarly portrait of the Buddha, this book is also a testament to the overarching unity of the various early Buddhist schools in their conception of the Buddha's life, a unity that coexists along with a rich diversity in their detailed narrations about particular events in that life. – Bhikkhu Bodhi, scholar and translator

An inspiring guide that will accelerate the reader's own journey of awakening. Highly recommended, and sure to inspire dedicated meditators! – Shaila Catherine, author of *Focused and Fearless: A Meditator's Guide to States of Deep Joy, Calm, and Clarity*

ISBN 978 1 909314 99 3 | £14.99 / $19.95 / €17.95 | 280 pages

Compassion and Emptiness in Early Buddhist Meditation

Bhikkhu Anālayo

Exploring the meditative practices of compassion and emptiness, Bhikkhu Anālayo casts fresh light on their earliest sources in the Buddhist tradition.

This book is the result of rigorous textual scholarship that can be valued not only by the academic community, but also by Buddhist practitioners. This book serves as an important bridge between those who wish to learn about Buddhist thought and practice and those who wish to learn from it. As a monk engaging himself in Buddhist meditation as well as a professor applying a historical-critical methodology, Bhikkhu Anālayo is well positioned to bridge these two communities. – 17th Karmapa Ogyen Trinley Dorje

In this study, Venerable Anālayo brings a meticulous textual analysis of Pali texts, the Chinese Āgamas and related material from Sanskrit and Tibetan to the foundational topics of compassion and emptiness. While his analysis is grounded in a scholarly approach, he has written this study as a helpful guide for meditation practice. – Jetsunma Tenzin Palmo

This is an intriguing and delightful book that presents these topics from the viewpoint of the early suttas as well as from other perspectives, and grounds them in both theory and meditative practice. – Bhikshuni Thubten Chodron

Anālayo holds a lamp to illuminate how the earliest teachings wed the great heart of compassion and the liberating heart of emptiness and invites us to join in this profound training. – Jack Kornfield

This scholarly book is more than timely with its demonstrations that teachings on emptiness and compassion that are helpful to practitioners of any form of Buddhism are abundant in early Buddhist texts.
– Rita M. Gross

Arising from the author's long-term, dedicated practice and study, this book provides a window into the depth and beauty of the Buddha's liberating teachings. Serious meditation students will benefit tremendously from the clarity of understanding that Venerable Anālayo's efforts have achieved. – Sharon Salzberg

ISBN 978 1 909314 55 9 | £11.99 / $17.95 / €16.95 | 232 pages

Mindfully Facing Disease and Death: compassionate advice from early Buddhist texts

Bhikkhu Anālayo

This unique anthology from the Buddha's early discourses focuses on guidance for facing disease and death, and has the overarching theme of *anukampā*: compassion as the underlying motivation in altruistic action.

The author draws on his own translations from the Chinese *Āgama* collection, presented here for the first time, alongside their counterparts from the Pāli texts, enabling readers to compare the parallel versions in English translation. Taken together with Bhikkhu Anālayo's practical commentary we gain a first-hand impression of what early Buddhism had to say about disease and death.

These teachings invite us to integrate their guidance directly into the laboratory of our own meditation practice and life, in the spirit of deep investigation and inquiry. As committed meditation practitioners know first hand, there is no more worthy or meaningful introspective undertaking in the world, nor a more difficult challenge for human beings to adopt and sustain throughout life. – From the Foreword, Jon Kabat-Zinn

An invaluable and extraordinary resource on the profound teachings by the Buddha on dying, death, and grieving. Bhikkhu Anālayo has given a great gift to all of us by bringing together in this book the compassionate wisdom of the Buddha on our mortality. – Roshi Joan Halifax

This is an indispensable book for serious students of Buddhism. It has the potential to transform the lives of everyone who reads it. – Toni Bernhard

I believe the Buddha would rejoice in this book and exhort all of us to read it and apply the medicine within. This will help to bring about the deepest healing of all – the healing of the mind and the heart – even if we are slipping over the final frontier of death itself. – Vidyamala Burch

ISBN 978 1 909314 72 6 | £13.99 / $19.95 / €16.95 | 320 pages

Satipaṭṭhāna Meditation: a practice guide

Bhikkhu Anālayo

Buddhist meditator and scholar Bhikkhu Anālayo presents this thorough-going guide to the early Buddhist teachings on *Satipaṭṭhāna*, the foundations of mindfulness, following on from his two best-selling books, *Satipaṭṭhāna* and *Perspectives on Satipaṭṭhāna*. With mindfulness being so widely taught, there is a need for a clear-sighted and experience-based guide.

Anālayo provides inspiration and guidance to all meditators, of any tradition and any level of experience. Each of the twenty-four chapters concludes with suggestions to support meditative practice.

This is a pearl of a book. The wise and experienced teacher is offering Dhamma reflections, illuminating the practice of Satipaṭṭhāna *with a fertile and colourful lucidity. It is a treasure-house of practical teachings, rendered accessible with a clear and simple eloquence, and with praiseworthy skill and grace.* – Ajahn Amaro

This breathtaking Practice Guide *is brief, and profound! It offers a detailed, engaging, and flexible approach to* Satipaṭṭhāna *meditation that can be easily applied both in meditation and day to day activities.* – Shaila Catherine, author of *Focused and Fearless: A Meditator's Guide to States of Deep Joy, Calm, and Clarity*

Once more Bhikkhu Anālayo has written a masterpiece that holds within it an accessible and clear guide to developing and applying the teachings held within the Satipaṭṭhāna-sutta. – Christina Feldman, author of *The Boundless Heart*

Anālayo has developed a simple and straightforward map of practice instructions encompassing all four satipaṭṭhānas *– the body, feelings, mind and* dharmas *– that build upon one another in a coherent and comprehensive path leading to the final goal.* – Joseph Goldstein, co-founder of the Insight Meditation Society, from the Foreword

Bhikkhu Anālayo presents the Buddha's practical teaching of the path to nirvana in one comprehensive whole: the wheel of satipaṭṭhāna. *He writes for people who practise, and his own shines through like a beacon. This makes it a very exciting guide for practitioners – the truth of it leaps out at you.* – Kamalashila, author of *Buddhist Meditation: Tranquillity, Imagination and Insight*

ISBN 978 1 911407 10 2 | £14.99 / $19.95 / €17.95 | 256 pages